Aspects of World History in Modern Times

Aspects of World History in Modern Times

(Revised Third Edition)

S.N. SEN
Formerly Professor of History
University of Calcutta
Kolkata

PUBLISHING FOR ONE WORLD

NEW AGE INTERNATIONAL (P) LIMITED, PUBLISHERS
(formerly Wiley Eastern Limited)
New Delhi • Bangalore • Chennai • Cochin • Guwahati • Hyderabad
Jalandhar • Kolkata • Lucknow • Mumbai • Ranchi
Visit us at www.newagepublishers.com

Published by New Age International (P) Ltd., Publishers
Revised Third Edition: 2007

ISBN : 978-81-224-2125-5

Rs. 100.00

C-07-04-1490

Printed in India at Mohan lal Printers, Delhi.
Typeset at River Edge, Delhi.

PUBLISHING FOR ONE WORLD

NEW AGE INTERNATIONAL (P) LIMITED, PUBLISHERS
(formerly Wiley Eastern Limited)
4835/24, Ansari Road, Daryaganj New Delhi - 110002
Visit us at **www.newagepublishers.com**

Preface to the Revised Edition

'Aspects of World History in Modern Times' prescribed for the Higher Secondary Education of West Bengal council include a brief review of the momentous period from the outbreak of the American War of Independence in 1776 to the emergence of the new world order in the last decade of the twentieth century. The book is intended primarily for younger generation who have had no opportunity of following tortuous course of World History interspersed in different books. I have tried to use the best secondary historical works and to bring it into harmony with the most recent investigations. I have incorporated the results of modern writings on the French Revolution, Industrial Revolution, Russian Revolution, the two World Wars, the genesis of the Cold War and its aftermath, as well as the challenge of Communism and the importance of the Middle East in the global politics. It is a difficult task to describe in a bare outline the amazing intricacies of international events that shaped the destiny of nations in the nineteenth and twentieth centuries. But an attempt has been made to stimulate the curiosities of students to the ever fascinating drama of modern Europe and the World.

S.N. Sen

Syllabus

Paper-II Aspects of World History in Modern Times

Unit—I : Age of Revolutions

1. A brief outline of
   (a) The American War of Independence (1776) : causes and results
   (b) The french Revolution (1789) : circumstances leading to the Revolution–the achievements of the Constituent Assembly, the Reign of Terror and the period of the Republic; Napoleon Bonaparte and the legacy of the Revolution.
   (c) The Industrial Revolution in England and Europe : the emergence of England as the 'first Workshop of the world'–the second phase of Industrial Revolution in France, Germany and Russia.

Unit—II : The Impact of Nationalism

2. The Vienna Settlement of 1815 : nationalism and dissolution of the Metternich system; the 1830 July Revolution and the 1848 February Revolution in France and their impact on Europe; the Second Empire; the Second Empire of Louis Napoleon in France.
3. The importance of 1870 in world history–Unification of Germany and Italy– 19th century nationalism, the emergence of nation-states and the new balance of power in Europe, economic nationalism in Europe.

Unit—III : From Empire to World War

4. European imperialism and the background to the First World War-reasons for the victory of Allied powers–the Versailles Settlement of 1919.
5. Attempts for collective security in the inter-war period : the League of Nations, Locrno Treaty–Dawes and Young Plans, Washington Treaties-Kellog-Briand Pact.

Unit—IV : The World Between two Wars

6. Background to the Bolshevik Revolution of 1917-impact of the establishment of the first socialist state on international relations-Lenin and the reconstruction of the Soviet Union.

7. The USA in the inter-war period : the Republican era (1921-33) : the economics boom; the 1929 economic crash; Roosevelt's New Deal.
8. Western Europe between the two Wars : Rise of Nazism in Germany and Fascism in Italy; the experience of the Third Republic in France; the experiment of National Government in England.

Unit— V : The Second World War

9. The approach to the Second World War: Aggressive nationalism of Germany, Italy and Japan; Failure of the Policy of Appeasement: Breakdown of the system of Collective Security and the League of Nations.
10. The outbreak of the Second World War : American entry in the war; Hitler's invasion of the Soviet Union and its implications for the course of the War: Causes of the defeat of Axis powers.

Unit—VI : The Cold War

11. Background to the Cold War; Manifestations of Cold War in international relation; especially the Berlin Crisis; the Korean War and the Cuban Missile Crisis; the emergence of the Third World.

Unit—VII : The Challenge of Communism

12. The Communist challenge of world politics: Rise of Communist China and its impact on international relations; Vietnam War and the Defeat of the USA.

Unit—VIII : The Muddle of the Middle East

13. The Middle East in World Politics : Establishment of Israel; Palestine question and Arab nationalsim; Egypt under Nasser and the Suez Crisis; Arab-Israeli war of 1956, 1967 and 1973.

Unit—IX : The New World Order

14. Post Stalin era in Soviet Union and its impact on World politics: the politics of disintegration of the Soviet Union and the end of the Cold War, remergence of a new World order.

Unit—X : The United Nation

15. The United Nations Organisation : the UN charter and organs of UNO, extent of success of the UNO in international relation.

Contents

UNIT - I

AGE OF REVOLUTIONS

The American war of Independence (1976) : causes and results

Background

The British established 13 colonies on the east coast of America during the 17th century. The most impelling motive was the desire for greater economic opportunity. The first three quarters of the 17th century saw the overwhelming number of English settlers in America. But after 1680, England ceased to be the principal source of immigration, as great numbers came from Germany, Ireland, Scotland, Switzerland and France.

Though the 13 colonies were regarded as part of the British empire, they were free to develop their self-governing institutions. The first step in this direction was a decision in 1619 on the part of the London (Virginia) Company to permit Virginia colonists representation in .the government. From that time onward, it became an accepted principle that the colonists had a right to participate in their own government. In Massachusetts, control of the government passed to elected representatives.

Down to 1763, Great Britain had formulated no consistent policy of empire for her colonial possessions. The guiding principle was that colonies should supply the mother country with raw materials and not compete in manufacturing. But this was not rigidly enforced and the colonists considered themselves as commonwealths or states having loose association with Britain. The distance of a 3000 mile sea between the new world and the mother country encouraged the colonies to defy authority of the British Parliament.

The Seven Year's War brought about the final expulsion of the French from the North American continent. Canada became British and British territories had been more than doubled in North American alone. Britain required huge sums of money for defence and administration of the new territories. But the situation in America was anything but favourable. The British government decided to tighten up the enforcement of its trade regulations and to make the colonies pay a share of the costs of imperial defence.

The principal parliamentary enactments down to the close of the Seven Year's War had been the various Navigation Acts. These enacted that colonial produce was to be exported only in British ships; some commodities were to be sent to no country but Great Britain; and some were to be shipped to Britain first and thence to other parts of the world. There were also laws restricting the manufacture of certain articles in the colonies.

After the Seven Years' War, Britain attempted to tighten her control over the colonies. While reorganising the empire, British statesmen declared the supremacy of Parliament. They insisted in the words of the Declaratory Act of 1766 that the Colonies "have been, are, and of right ought to be, subordinate unto and dependent upon the imperial crown and Parliament of Great Britain" and that Parliament had "full power and authority to make laws and statutes of sufficient force and validity to bind the colonies and people of America...in all cases whatsoever".

Causes of War

The economic causes of the American War of Independence were most important. To support the colonies required money and this could be achieved only at the expense of colonial self-government. Thus, the Sugar Act of 1764 imposed a tariff on all sugar or molasses imported by the colonists from foreign countries. Amended two years later, this act had the raising of revenue as its sole purpose. The Sugar Act of 1764 was virtually a re-enactment of the Old Molasses Act of 1733. The amended Sugar Act put a modest duty on molasses from all sources. The Act also levied duties on wines, silk, coffee and a number of other luxury articles. To enforce the Act, British warships were stationed along the coast to prevent illegal trading. British tax collectors were empowered to search private houses for smuggled goods.

Another cause of discontent lay in the fact that the export tax on continental goods shipped to the colonies from Great Britain was raised in 1764 from 2.5 per cent to 5 per cent. Most of the colonists incurred heavy debts to British merchants. At the beginning of the revolution, it was computed that Virginia owed to the British merchants over two million pounds. To repay the debts most provinces issued a good deal of paper money after 1750 and made it legal tender. But the British Parliament stoutly opposed the measure and in 1764 forbade the colonies to make paper money legal tender for debts.

Among the economic causes were involved land speculation and the settlement of the West. Needing new land, various colonies claimed the right to an extension as far west as the Mississippi river. By the close of the Seven Years' War there was a great scramble for land in the West. Many of the war veterans had been granted western lands and bounties. One land company after another was being organised. Many great men-Benjamin Franklin, George Washington, Sir William Johnson were keenly interested in westward expansion. But fearing that this land hunger would provoke a war with the Indians and to prevent the colonists from spreading too far west, the British government proclaimed in 1763 that all western territory be reserved for the use of the Indians. Thus, at one stroke the British government swept away every western land claim of the 13 colonies.

Another ground for dispute lay in the question of imperial defence. Believing that the colonies were incapable of defending themselves it was proposed that they should maintain a force of ten thousand men, part of the cost to be borne by the colonists themselves. In 1765, Lord Grenville passed the famous Stamp Act in the Parliament with little opposition. The Act required that revenue stamps be affixed to all newspapers and legal and other documents. But the Act raised a storm of protest. Organisation like 'Sons of Liberty' came into existence and mob violence broke out in several places. From Massachusetts to South Carolina, the mobs forced the tax collectors to resign their offices and destroyed stamps and other property. Business came to a temporary standstill. Delegates from nine of the colonies met together at New York in October 1765 and denied the right of the British Parliament to tax America. Opposing the Stamp Act, Benjamin Franklin declared that the

Thirteen British Colonies Before American War of Independence (*dotted section*)

colonists would not submit to the tax unless compelled by force of arms Grenville resigned and the new Prime Minister, Marquess of Rockingham, repealed the Stamp Act in 1766.

But it was only a respite for a year. The British King George III and his minister obstinately persisted in their attempts to tax the colonies. In 1767, Charles Townshend, British Chancellor of the Exchequer, passed an Act (Townshend Act) which imposed duties on tea, paper, glass, lead and painters' colours. The revenue from the new taxes was to be used to support colonial governors, judges, customs officers and the British army in America. Again the colonies protested boycotting the articles on which British taxes had been levied. In 1770, the enforcement of the new tax provoked violence at Boston. This came to be called the Boston Massacre. Once again Parliament yielded to pressure. Under the auspices of the new Prime Minister, Lord North, the Parliament repealed all the Townshend duties save that on tea. The tea tax was retained because as George III said, there must be one tax to keep up the right of Parliament.

The next step was the formation of a system of Committee of Correspondence throughout the colonies. Sam Adams of Massachusetts, a born propagandist and organiser, was the prime mover in this task. The object of the Committee was to state the rights and grievance of the colonists and to communicate with other towns on these matters. These committees soon transformed themselves into revolutionary organisations. A Tory writer later testified: 'This was the source of the rebellion. I saw the small seed when it was planted. It was as a grain of mustard I have watched the plant until it has become as a great tree' .

Due to the Townshend Tea tax the colonists had boycotted the tea and the powerful East India Company fell into financial difficulties. To help it, the British government allowed it to send tea to America at a price which made smuggling unprofitable. Great indignation was aroused in the colonies. At every port the people were determined to resist it. On the night of December 16, 1773, a group of Boston citizens led by Sam Adams himself boarded a British ship and dumped 342 chests of tea into the harbour. "Thus", said John Adams rapturously, "is the most magnificent movement of all. This destruction of the tea is so bold, so daring so firm, intrepid and flexible, and it must have so important consequences, and so lasting, that I cannot but consider it as an epoch in History".

The Boston incident precipitated the crisis. Ignoring the plea of Burke and Chatham, George III and the majority in Parliament adopted a series of drastic acts. One destroyed some of the most liberal features of the much-cherished charter of Massachusetts.

Instead of subduing the colonies, these harsh acts of Parliament galvanised them to a course of action. At the suggestion of the Virginia legislators, colonial representatives were summoned to discuss the united interest of America. On September 5, 1774 the first Continental Congress met at Philadelphia with every colony except Georgia. Its 51 delegates included Washington, Benjamin Franklin, John Adams, John Dickinson and other able men. They addressed to the King and people of Great Britain a Declaration of Rights and Grievances, in which they asserted that the provinces had the power to legislate on their own affairs while conceding Parliamentary regulation of external commerce and imperial affairs.

But above all, the Continental Congress adopted two measures which widened the breach between the colonies and the mother country. One was the preparation of an agreement which bound the colonies to stop all imports of English goods and exports to British ports. The other step was the drafting of a resolution by which Congress declared that if force were used against the people of Massachusetts, all America ought to support them in resistance.

George III and Lord North had no intention of making concessions. George III wrote: "The die is now cast, the colonies must either submit or triumph".

Parliament declared that Massachusetts was in rebellion and decided to suppress the revolt. On April 18, 1775 skirmishes broke out at Lexington and Concord. The Revolution had begun.

The Second Continental Congress met in Philadelphia on May 10, 1775. Vainly did Benjamin Franklin plead for conciliation. The Congress made a stirring declaration of the cause and necessity of taking up arms.

> Our cause is just. Our union is perfect. Our internal resources are great... The arms we have been compelled by our enemies to assume, we will... employ for the preservation of our liberties, being with one mind resolved to die free men rather than live slaves.

The Congress appointed Colonel George Washington, Commander-in-Chief of the American forces.

On August 23, 1775, King George issued a proclamation declaring the colonies to be in a state of rebellion. In January 1771, was published Thomas Paine's 50 page pamphlet, *Common Sense*. In vigorous style, he emphasised the necessity of independence. Kings were 'crowned ruffians' and there was no necessity of remaining loyal to the King. On May 10, 1776 the Continental Congress adopted a resolution of separation from the mother country. A committee of five, headed by Thomas Jefferson, drew up a formal Declaration of Independence and proclaimed it on July 4, 1776. It set forth a philosophy of human freedom which became a dynamic force for the succeeding generation:

> That all men are created equal, that they are endowed by their creator with certain inalienable rights, that among these are life, liberty and the pursuit of happiness–that to sacure these rights, governments are instituted among men, deriving their just powers from the consent of the governed. That whenever any form of government becomes destructive of these ends, it is the right of the people to alter or to abolish it, and to institute new government, laying its foundation on such principles and organising its powers in such form, as to them shall seem most likely to effect their safety and happiness.

Thomas Jefferson went so far as to argue that frequent revolutions were a good 'medicine' for democracy. 'The tree of liberty' he said 'must-be refreshed from time to time with the blood of patriots and tyrants'.

Results of the War of Independence

The revolt of 13 colonies against England afforded France an opportunity of recovering her lost territories—Canada and Mississippi Valley. Between the years 1688 and 1763 England fought against France four wars the result of which was the elimination of France as a serious commercial rival of England. Naturally France allied herself with the United States and declared war on Great Britain. Spain and Holland soon joined France. Thus, the 13 colonies had valuable allies while the rest of Europe was unsympathetic to England. They disliked England's practice of searching and seizing neutral vessels in wartime and led a league of armed neutrality to defend their commercial rights against England.

After prolonged deliberations involving England, the Colonists, France, Spain and Holland, the Treaty of Versailles was signed in September 1783. The most important clause was the recognition of a new independent power—the United States of America. By this treaty, France acquired St. Lucia and Tobago in the West Indies and Senegal on the West African coast. In India, Surat, Pondicherry and Calicut were restored to France and in return, England recovered Grenada, Dominica and St. Vincent. Spain received the island of Minorca and the American territory of Florida. Holland concluded a separate peace in 1784 by which she received back her conquests with the exception of Negapatam.

But the effects of the war were profound in Europe. Spain lost Gibraltar. In the south-east of Europe Catherine, free from interference by the west, was able to infiltrate into the Turkish empire. In Britain, there was a demand for radical reform of the constitution. On the outbreak of the war, Wilkes had declared that the American War was one of the strongest arguments for regulation of the franchise.

The American Revolution marked a significant step in the development of republican and democratic ideas. The ringing phrases of the Declaration of Independence on Liberty, Equality and the Rights of Man found echoes in France and elsewhere. Many French officers like Lafayette had served in America while Franklin in France had been an eloquent champion of the new principles. When in 1787 America developed new constitutions, these documents served as models to France and elsewhere. The success of the American Revolution struck a decisive blow both at divine-right monarchy and at aristocratic privilege.

French Revolution (1789-1814)

The French Revolution was an uprising of the French people against privilege and autocracy. Of all the countries of Europe, France was deeply affected by social inequalities and arbitrary rule of Bourbon Kings. But it cannot be said that the French Revolution was inevitable. "The Revolution was not a Niagra in the stream of national life, its incidence and situation determined by the presence of a single great fault in the social strata: it was rather the result of the confluence of a host of contributory currents, small and great, flowing together to swell suddenly into a mighty flood."[1] The revolution underwent a process of dramatic change during a period of 20 years. Though the much cherished dreams of liberty were not immediately realised, the impact of the French Revolution was profound. While the English Revolution of 1688 and the American Revolution of 1776 were chiefly political, the French Revolution of 1789 was social, political, economic and religious.

Social Causes

Though France was the most advanced of all the continental countries in the second half of the 18th century, yet socially it had some glaring defects. French society was divided into three hostile groups—the clergy, nobles and the third estate—each with its own privileges.

The first estate or clergy constituted less than 2 per cent of the French population. The clergy was itself divided in two classes: higher clergy and lower clergy. The higher clergy—archbishops, bishops and lower abbots—often enjoyed great wealth. They had large estates and indulged in luxury and vices without caring for their ecclesiastical duties. But the lower clergy, recruited from the ranks of the commoners, profited little by the privileged position of the order. Constituting about two-third of the order, this group furnished spiritual guidance to the mass of the people.

The second estate-the nobles—was divided into three sections—country nobles, official nobility and the nobles of the court (courtiers). The country nobles had small incomes and exacted the

[1] Cobban Alfred: *A History of Modern France,* I, p. 137.

utmost farthing from their tenants. The official nobility-some four thousand in all—chiefly centred in the Parlement of Paris. They were opposed to the freedom of the press and to all reform. Much more conspicuous were the great nobles, courtiers. Enjoying immense privilege, they did nothing but consumed the resources of the bankrupt government. The third estate was a comprehensive category. At the top were financiers, merchants, office holders and professionals who had vested interest and some privilege. But many of them suffered from the numerous restrictions on them. The King monopolised salt and other necessary commodities; and manufacturing and trade were minutely regulated by the decree. But the great bulk of the third estate—more than 20 million—was peasants. The peasants had to pay rent to their feudal lords, tithes to the church and taxes to the king. It has been estimated that a French peasant could count on less than one-fifth of his income for use of himself and his family.

Political Causes

The government of France in the 18th century was a highly centralised despotism. The French monarchs—Louis XV (1715-74) and Louis XVI—were weak and lacked the essential qualities which could make them great and enlightened rulers. Believing in the Divine Right, the kings imposed taxes and made laws by royal edicts. The king could *issue letters de cachet*, a warrant and could keep any body in prison for any length of time. Justice was administered by close corporation of lawyers known as *Parlements*. Of these, the Parlement of Paris was the most important.

The ambitious foreign policy of the Bourbon monarchs in the 18th century had brought France on the verge of bankruptcy. The Seven Year War had resulted in the loss of the French colonies. The French intervention in the American War of Independence had brought prestige but it was purchased at the supreme sacrifice of immense treasury.

Economic Causes

The evil which was immediately obvious was financial. France was threatened by an appalling bankruptcy. The privileged few would not pay while the overtaxed middle classes and peasants could not pay. Two bad harvests in a row, cattle disease, had all helped to push up the price of food. The unemployment in Paris caused by industrial depression coupled with the uncertainties of 1789, led to the worsening of the situation. Real wages in rural France declined before 1789 and price inflation had been felt for about the same time. "Thus peasants and urban craftsmen and workers were drawn together in common hostility to the government, landlords, merchants, and speculators; and these classes entered the Revolution in a context of increasing poverty and hardship rather than of prosperity".[2]

INTELLECTUAL REVOLT

There had been growing in Europe throughout 18th century, a revolutionary spirit. This spirit, was fostered particularly by the writings of French thinkers and literary men, the philosophers. French held the foremost place in the world of thought. But this Enlightenment was heralded by the work of such men as Locke, Hume, Gibbon, Robertson in England; Lessing and Kant, Goethe and Schiller in Germany, Benjamin Franklin in America. By 1780s the philosophic tide had reached European intellectuals, but the concrete achievements were not substantial. As Kant declared in 1784, it was the age of Enlightenment, but not an Enlightened Age.

[2] Rude George: *Revolutionary europe*, p, 74

The French Revolution has frequently been ascribed to the influence of the philosophers or writers of the eighteenth century. The books which issued in great numbers from the facile pens of Montesquieu, Voltaire, Rousseau, Diderot, Quesnay and many others, stirred the intellectual world to its depth. Voltaire (1694-1778) was of all of them the most conspicuous and the most brilliant. His chief attack was directed against the Church. 'Annihilate the infamous thing', he wrote. In his *Letters on the English* he pointed out that the Church and nobility in England were not exempt from direct taxation. His wit and satire and his bitter attack on the Church and other pillars of the Old Regime made him popular than any others. As a reformer he was far in advance of Montesquieu, for he did not hesitate to attack 'privilege'. Thanks to his brilliant pen, he enjoyed a celebrity far greater than any of his contemporary philosophers. He was courted by Frederick the Great and Catherine II, and his home was a Mecca for hundreds of persons. Though he was the prince of rationalists, Voltaire believed in absolute monarchy. As he said that he preferred to be ruled by one fine lion than by two hundred rats.

Montesquieu (1689-1755), a French lawyer and nobleman, was an admirer of the British Constitution. It was a monarchy, which was limited in power and controlled by an elected assembly. He emphasised the necessity of separating the three powers of government, the legislative, executive and judiciary. His famous book, *The Spirt of the Laws* which appeared in 1748, had a tremendous success. In his satire, *The Persian Letters*, Montesquieu attacked the privileged aristocracy, the corruption of the court and the folly of religious intolerance.

The most revolutionary among the philosophers was Jean Jacques Rousseau (1712-1778). Napoleon once declared that if Rousseau had never lived there would have been no revolution. The influence of his books *The Social Contract* (1762) and *Discourse*, was profound. His principal theory was that man was essentially good, but corrupted by civilisation. 'Man is born free, but everywhere he is in chains'. All government was the outcome of an agreement of contract framed by the people for the promotion of their welfare. Hence, all government rests upon the consent of the governed and no ruler can deprive the individual citizen of his natural rights to life, liberty and property. It was Rousseau who made famous the doctrine of "popular sovereignty". Above all, he inspired men to believe in democracy and equality and seemed to open to the individual a new world.

A group of writers known as Physiocrats or the Economists strongly criticised the economic system of France. They were much influenced by the writings of Adam Smith, the English economist who is usually regarded as the greatest protagonist of free trade. Protectionism benefited nobody; therefore all restrictions were bad. Free trade would raise the price of goods, higher prices would stimulate productivity, and so in the long run there would be economic prosperity. Accordingly, Physiocrats advocated the abolition of control on the grain trade and of internal customs barrier. Their leader was Quesnay. His *Theory of Taxation*, Mirabeau's *Friend of Mankind* moulded their thought. They advocated complete free trade. They held that land was the chief source of wealth and so all taxation should be reduced to a single land-tax.

The most learned of all this series of philosophers was Denis Diderot, who with the aid of a multitude of collaborators, published an encyclopaedia. Originating in a project merely to translate Chamber's Cyclopaedia (1728) into French, this enterprise was an attempt to summarise the current state of knowledge and 'to transmit it to the men who shall come after us, so that the works of past centuries should not have been works useless for the centuries that shall follow, our descendants, becoming better informed, shall become at the same time more virtuous and happier, and so that we do not die without having deserved well of the human race?' The encyclopedia was an attempt to convince the people the value and importance of certain ideas. This work consisted of 35 large volumes. Many of the articles made critical attacks on the privileged and the clergy.

While the Intellectual Revolution gave the French people ideas of freedom and of fraternity, the American Revolution inspired and influenced the 1789 revolution. In 1776, the 13 English colonies in America issued their famous Declaration of Independence, proclaiming to the world that 'Man is endowed by his Creator with certain inalienable rights, among which are life, liberty, and the pursuits of happiness'.

Responsibility of the French Monarchy (1774-1789): Attempts at solving the financial difficulties of the monarchy: Aristocratic Revolt

The government of France in the 18th century was a highly centralised despotism. After Louis XIV (1648-1715), the monarchy had lost a great deal of vigour and its ability to maintain the loyalty of their subjects. This was due in part to the indolence and personal failings of Louis XV (1715-74), and in part, to the high-handedness of the bureaucracy. Louis XV was never a friend of the parlements; he wanted to silence them once and for all. Most of the Frenchmen protested against the policy of the King and the early 1770s saw the beginning of a crisis of confidence in French public life.

Louis XVI on ascending the throne in 1774 was eager to bring about substantial reforms in the administration. Unlike his predecessor, he had a high sense of personal responsibility. The old parlements were restored. Between 1774 and 1787, they never prevented the government from raising any tax . Louis XVI's government pursued two-fold policy. One was to support the American rebels in their conflict with Great Britain. But the war dealt a ruinous blow to the already overburdened finances of the state. The second policy was the avoidance of bankruptcy. Turgot made it a keystone of his programme when he took charge of the finance in 1774. But within two years, he had fallen having antagonised everybody by abolishing the corvee (a levy on the peasant) and removing restrictions on the wine and grain trades. Louis XVI dismissed him without the opportunity to attempt further reforms. Louis XVI next entrusted the finances to Necker, a vainglorious Swiss banker. He despised the parlements and advocated provincial assemblies. By his ability to raise loans he financed the American war without introducing new taxation. In 1781, he published the *Compte Rendu* the first public balance sheet of the financial situation of France. But when in the same year he tried to engross over-all control of policy, the king dismissed him from office.

Necker's two immediate successors were not capable and had to bear the odium of raising taxes. Finally, the King appointed Calonne. The new finance minister began by restoring confidence in the stability of royal finances. With confidence thus restored, Calonne was able to resume the policy of borrowing. But by August 1786 he found that he had exhausted the market and could borrow no more. Undismayed Calonne presented the King with a plan for a general land tax to be levied on all classes without distinction, and for the creation of Provincial Assemblies to supervise its collection. To boost production, Calonne proposed other measures—the abolition of internal customs barriers and the freeing of the grain trade from government regulations. Since there was no prospect of persuading the *parlements* to accept such a proposal, he hastily summoned an Assembly of Notables in February 1787. The members of the Assembly of Notables were all nominated by the King and the Assembly itself had not met for 160 years. From the start everything went wrong. The majority opposed the proposals. In vain, he appealed to the patriotism of the assemblage. But Lafayette, a Notable announced that there was only one body competent to undertake reforms and that was the Estates-General.

Calonne fell in 1787 and was succeeded by Cardinal de Brienne. To everyone's astonishment, Brienne took up his predecessor's plan almost unchanged. The notables resumed their oppositions and on May 25 the notables were dissolved. Brienne now adopted the normal procedure of presenting his edicts for registration by the *parlements*. In 1787, the popularity of the *parlements* or the sovereign courts, as they were called, were such that they seemed in a position to dictate their will to the king. But these bodies were determined not to sanction proposals that the Notables had felt unable to agree to. The only body with that right, declared the Paris *parlement* in August 1787, was the Estates-General. But Brienne was equally adamant. He invoked the King's authority which overrode the *parlement's* objections, promulgated the fiscal decrees and exiled the Paris magistrates. But it was the *parlement* that won the day. The provincial courts, to whom Brienne now turned, rallied to the support of their Paris colleagues. Brienne had no option but to yield and parlement was reinstated in September. Arthur Young reported that France was 'on the verge of some great revolution in the Government'.

Calling of the States General

During the years 1787 and 1788, France was undergoing a serious crisis. The harvests were bad and brought extreme social distress. But that this would develop rapidly into a revolution was anticipated by no one. Faced with this crisis, the king consented to summon the States General on 1 May, 1789, the national parliament of France which had not met since 1614. According to old custom, each Estate had voted as a unit, and two out of the three could carry any measure. The members of the third estate demanded that the three orders were to meet as a single chamber in which each individual should have a vote. Their deputies numbered 621 against 285 for the nobles and 308 for the clergy, giving the third estate a slight majority.

When the States General met at Versailles on 5 May, 1789, the deputies were uncertain how to proceed. No reform programme was offered to them. The king ordered the deputies to vote as three separate bodies, so that nobles and clergy together would be able to outvote the third estate. The third refused to yield. For five weeks they urged members of the nobility and the clergy to join them in one great assembly. The third estate led by Sieyes, had asked: 'what is the third estates? It is everything', he replied. The Commoners' determination soon split the clergy, some of whom crossed over to join the third estate on 15 June. Two days later, this already mixed group assumed the title of the National Assembly and invited the other orders to work together for the reform of France. With this step the constitutional history of France took a decisive turn. On 20 June 1789 when the members of the third estate went to the assembly hall, they found the entrance blocked by soldiers. Repairing to the indoor tennis court nearby they solemnly swore not to separate until they had drawn a new constitution. The 'Tennis Court Oath' was the actual beginning of the French Revolution as it marked a defiance of the king. On 23 June, the king announced many important reforms in finance and administration but insisted the three orders should meet separately. The nobility, triumphant, withdrew from the hall. But the third estate remained in gloomy silence. 'You have heard His Majesty's orders', said the master of ceremonies. Then Mirabeau thundered 'Sir, go tell your master that we are here by the will of the people and nothing but bayonet shall drive us out'. The king gave way. On 27 June, he directed the three orders to sit together in a single assembly. A contemporary English traveller noted in his diary 'the whole business now seems over and the revolution complete.' The third estate had won its first battle. That night Versailles was illuminated.

Constituent Assembly

The king speedily regretted its concessions and troops were massed at Versailles and Paris. On 11 July, Necker, the popular idol, was dismissed and ordered to leave the country immediately. The people of Paris, goaded by hunger, rioted for three days and on 14 July stormed Bastille, the royal prison fortress and a symbol of Bourbon autocracy. It was a great psychological and symbolic turning point : the old absolute monarchy in France was dead. Rioting was not confined to Paris. Outbreaks occurred in various parts of France. On 5 October, a hungry crowd of several thousand men came to Versailles and got hold of the king and the queen. 'We have got the baker (king), and the baker's wife (queen) and the baker's little boy (Dauphin)', so according to legend, the rabble shouted. They were brought to Paris and soon after the National Assembly followed. Despite royal misgivings, the revolution was moving swiftly.

The Constituent Assembly was in session until September 1791. The greatest and most permanent achievements of the Revolution were effected during these two years. During the August days of 1789 the Constituent Assembly abolished the old privileges. In the session of 4 August all vestiges of feudalism, all the ancient inequalities were swept away. The peasants were now free to till their farms and enjoy the fruits of there labour without paying tithes to the Church or feudal dues to the nobility.

The second achievement of the Constituent Assembly was the 'Declaration of the Rights of Man and of the Citizen' on 26 August 1789. The Declaration made private property a sacred and inviolable right along with freedom of conscience, freedom of press, and freedom of the citizen from arbitrary arrest. It announced that 'Men are born and remain free and equal in rights', and it defined these rights as 'liberty, property, security and resistance to oppression.' According to a French historian the Declaration was a 'death certificate of the Old Regime'. There were marked similarities to the American Declaration of Independence (1776). Although the Declaration tried to be universal, it did not set out to be comprehensive. Economic equality and state obligation to the poor were not mentioned. Although citizens were invited to take part in law making, no specific rights of suffrage were granted. It deliberately omitted any declaration of duties, an omission not remedied until 1795.

A third and more practical achievement of the Constituent Assembly was its reorganisation of the country's administration. It abolished special privileges of guilds, towns and provinces. The old 32 provinces were abolished and France was divided into 83 departments. Each department was subdivided into districts, cantons and communes. Local officials were to be elected by the people and a new system of courts with elected judges was established.

The assembly could not ignore the financial difficulties. It could not collect direct taxes at once. In November 1789, it decreed the confiscation of landed estate held by the Church and against this property as security it issued paper money (called assignats). But paper money was issued in excessive quantities and it became practically valueless.

Another act of the Constituent Assembly changed the relations between the French State and the Catholic Church. In February 1790, the monasteries and other religious communities were suppressed. In July 1790, the state enacted the so-called Civil Constitution of the Clergy which regulated relations of Church and State. By this new law, the bishops and priests were reduced in number. They were to be elected by the people and paid by the state. The Catholic Church was, in effect, made it department of the State. All bishops and priests were required to swear allegiance to the Civil Constitution of the Clergy. About half the priests refused to take the oath. In April 1791 the Pope Pius VI condemned the Civil Constitution.

By September 1791, the Constituent Assembly drafted written constitution and compelled the king to accept it. It provided for a separation of power among executive, legislative and judicial branches of the government. There was to be only one chamber—the Legislative Assembly. The king's power very much reduced; laws were to be made and taxes levied only by the Assembly. Along with liberty and equality the Constituent Assembly proclaimed the sanctity of property. All internal restrictions of the free passage of goods were abolished. On other hand, the protective system of tariffs on goods coming into France was strictly preserved.

Estimate of the Work of the Assembly

Although the Declaration tried to be universal, it did not appear to be comprehensive. Economic equality and state obligation to the poor were not mentioned. Though the Declaration of Rights had proclaimed the right of all citizens to take part in the making of laws, it had not granted the specific right of suffrage to all citizens. The Declaration moreover omitted any Declaration of Duties, an omission not remedied until 1795. In June 1797, the Assembly passed the famous La Chapelier Law, by which, combination of workers were declared illegal, and the law was not finally repealed until 1884.

In economic policy the Assembly's bourgeois character was evident. Although service dues were abolished, peasant was obliged to pay an indemnity in order to extinguish certain rights of the manorial lords to their property. A majority of the peasants simply refused to pay any compensation.

The Civil constitution of the clergy alienated the clergy from the Revolution and caused a schism in the Church which profoundly disturbed the religious life of the nation. The new constitutional church itself lost credit and was separated from the State, until the Old Church was reestablished on new foundations by Bonaparte's Concordat of 1801.

Nevertheless, with all these shortcomings, a solid core of constructive legislation survived the revolutionary period and was to influence the monarchies and republic of the nineteenth century. Though the immediate gain of the wage-earner was little, tax-exemption and privileges of the nobles had received cruel blow; equality before the law and 'career open to talents' remained. France retained her administrative and economic unity and the peasants became proprietors of the soil and were freed from tithe and feudal obligations. "In fact a great deal of what was permanent in the legislation of the revolutionary years was that contemplated or begun by the Constituent Assembly; and it is no exaggeration to maintain that the legacy that the Revolution left was, in substance, that conceived in the decidedly bourgeois image of the men of 1789"[3]

Before the acceptance of the constitution in September 1791, the king and the queen had tried to escape (June 1791) from Paris. But they were detected at Varennes near the border and brought back to Paris.

Clubs, Association, Moderate and Radical Opinions till 1799

The French Revolution gave rise to many clubs and associations and led to the growth of moderate and radical opinions. The radicals, not content with the reforms introduced by the Constituent Assembly, believed in the further extension of the Revolution so that its fruits could benefit the common people.

---

[3] Rude George: *Revolutionary Europe,* 1783-1815, p.120

The Jacobin Club was the most important organisation which capitalised popular unrest and acted as an agency in moulding public opinion. This society with its seven thousand branches in the provincial towns, carried on through newspapers a ceaseless propaganda against the monarchy. Out of this famous club was to emerge an important grouping, known as the Jacobins to distinguish them from the moderate elements. Socially the Jacobins were bourgeois, but politically they tended to become proletarian. The importance of the Jacobin Club lay in the fact that in alliance with the Paris Commune, the former played a dominant role in the Revolution.

The King's attempted flight confirmed the suspicion that he was a counter-revolutionary. The political clubs of Paris demanded the King's deposition and the declaration of a republic. A massive demonstration at Paris on July 17,1791 was dispersed by Lafayette and the National Guard. In the aftermath of the massacre, hundreds of deputies seceded from the Jacobin Club and formed a rival association of conservative views, the Feuillant Club. From that time emerged a group, known as the Cordeliers and led by such men as Danton, favouring the dethronement of the King. Jacobins, Cordeliers and sans-culottes (the small shop-keepers and wage-earners) were united in common opposition to the Constituent Assembly.

Legislative Assembly (1 October 1791-20 September 1792)

When the Constituent Assembly completed its work, the Legislative Assembly took charge. The new representatives–745 in number—were divided into several parties. The constitutionalists, called the Feuillants, was perhaps the largest party. They wanted to retain the monarchy with the limitations imposed on the power of the King. The Girondists, so called because many of their leaders came from the department of the Gironde, were radical as they favoured a republic. But the Girondins, being well-to-do men of property, did not like interference in propertied interests. It is obvious that the Girondists represented the bourgeoisie and that the Jacobins were the champions of the proletariat. The Jacobins were the extreme section who relied for the success of their cause on brute force. The Jacobins exercised nationwide influence by organising branch clubs of middle class radicals all over the country. Their leaders were Robespierre, Danton and Marat.

In internal affairs, the Legislative Assembly accomplished little, since foreign problems overshadowed all others. The French Revolution was a menace to the existing order. Many of the nobles and clergy had fled abroad (emigres) and tried to invoke the sympathies of the foreign powers for reestablishing the King's authority.

Friction soon developed between the king and the Legislative Assembly. The king refused to accept a law condemning to death all emigrant nobles who did not return before January 1792. The result was that on 20 June 1792 the mob of Paris broke into the royal palace of Tuileries and threatened the king.

Pretext for war was not lacking. The Girondists were in favour of it. The extreme radicals like Marat and Robespierre opposed war on the ground that it would call forth a military dictator. 'Crush our internal enemies first,' Robespierre said, 'and then march against foreign ones'. Leopold II of Austria, brother of Queen Marie Antoinette, wife of Louis XVI, had a deep personal interest in the fate of the French monarchy. He complained of French encouragement given to a revolution in Belgium and of German princes dispossessed of feudal rights in Alsace. In August 1791 the rulers of Austria and Prussia (Frederick William II of Prussia) issued the Declaration of Pillnitz announcing that the cause of Louis XVI was an object of common interest to all sovereigns of Europe. Though the declaration had no direct importance, it angered patriotic Frenchmen and weakened the position of Louis XVI. In January 1792, the Girondists demanded that the Emperor Leopold II withdraw his troops from the French frontier and expel the emigres from his territories. When Francis II, the successor of Leopold II rejected the ultimatum, the Legislative Assembly on 20 April 1792 declared war—a war which was to be European and which was to last 23 years.

After war had begun, the Duke of Brunswick, commander of allied armies of Austria and Prussia, issued his famous manifesto (25 July 1792), declaring his intention to restore the king and punish the rebels. The reply of Paris to the Duke of Brunswick was a bloody insurrection on 9-10 August 1792. On 10 August, the king was suspended from his functions. It was the end of constitutional monarchy in France until 1814. For the next few weeks, France was in a state of practical anarchy. Riots, murders and attacks on property were daily occurrences. Early in September, the frantic mob broke in to the prisons of Paris and cruelly massacred hundreds of royalist prisoners. It was perhaps a darkest chapter in the history of the Revolution. On 6 September, the Commune of Paris issued a proclamation calling for a cessation the massacres. On 20 September, the French army checked the allied advance at Valmy. Meanwhile, the Legislative Assembly was dissolved and was replaced by the Convention. On 21 September, the king was deposed and a republic established.

The Convention (September 1792-October 1795)

During the next three years, the Convention performed the two-fold task of consolidating the revolution within France and of waging successful foreign war. In the next six weeks after Valmy the French armies liberated Savoy, crossed the Rhine to take Frankfurt and overran Belgium after a brilliant victory at Jemappes. The new Republic gained in self-confidence and decided upon the trial of the king. Louis XVI was condemned to death by a vote of 387 to 334. On 21 January 1793, he was beheaded. The Girondists did not really wish for the king's death. The real victors were the Jacobins.

Meanwhile, the war assumed a new dimension. France had been at war with Austria and Prussia. Now England, Russia, Spain, Holland, and the states of Germany and Italy entered the war against her. The allied armies reoccupied Belgium and the Rhineland and again invaded France. Against this danger, the Convention acted with utmost energy. A new national army was organised under the direction of Lazare Carnot By the end of 1793 Carnot was able to raise a militia of 7,70,000 men.

In this way, France met a coalition and won victories which would have surprised the most orthodox critics. By the spring of 1794, the revolt in the Vendee had been broken; the British had been repelled at sea; the Prussian and Austrian forces had been pushed back out of Alsace and by June Belgium was again in French occupation. But the victories of the Republic were won at a terrible cost.

In the midst of foreign war and civil strife, the National Convention accomplished some social reforms. It devised a plan for national education, began the task of compiling a national code of laws, abolished slavery in the colonies and protected women's property rights. It introduced the simple and convenient metric system of weights and measures. It established the fundamental principle of inheritance that has marked modern France-the principle that no person may bequeath his property to one direct heir to the exclusion of others but that all children must inherit equally. The grain price was fixed; large estates were broken up and offered for sale to poorer citizens in lots of two or three acres. In 1795 the Convention drew up a new constitution for France. The country was to be ruled by a Directory of five members, who were to hold office for five years, one director retiring each year. The constitution also provided for a two-chamber legislature elected by indirect and somewhat restricted suffrage.

Region of Terror (2 June 1793-July 1794)

With the monarchy overthrown and under the threat of foreign invasion, the National Convention entrusted supreme executive authority to a Committee of Public Safety, first created in April 1793. There was another committee—Committee of General Security—which was especially concerned with police functions. The immense powers of both committees were virtually at the disposal of Robespierre and his two colleagues-Saint-Just and Georges Couthon. There also existed in Paris a special court known as the Revolutionary Tribunal which was charged with trying and sentencing any person suspected of treachery. In a speech Saint-Just defined the principles of the Terror. Not only treachery but indifference would be punished.

Such were the principal organs of the terror. By September 1793 the Terror was supposed officially to begin. It was not, at all events, more terrible than the reign of anarchy that preceded it. It was organised terror in contrast to the terror of the mob. As Danton said 'Let us be terrible in order to dispense the people from being terrible.' It is an interesting fact that Danton, Marat had all judged that some sort of dictatorship was a necessary outcome of the Revolution. Even Edmund Burke, a bitter critic of the Revolution, had foretold the ultimate appearance of the dictator. Robespierre was the main brain behind the terror and he was determined to suppress all resistance by rigorous terrorism. In mid-October 1793 Marie Antoinette went to the guillotine. Two other well-known women followed her-Madame Du Barry and Madame Roland. The Revolutionary Tribunal of Paris condemned to death 2,639 people; revolutionary courts condemned in all about 17,000. The rest of the terror's 40,000 victims mostly died in summary mass executions in various places. Danton, who had been a prominent figure since its outbreak, was guillotined in April 1794 as he counselled moderation.

For a hundred days, Robespierre was virtual dictator of France. In July 1794 the emergency ended as French armies swept into Belgium again. In March 1795 (Treaty of Basel) the Prussians made peace, agreeing secretly to cede France the left bank of the Rhine in return for territory in Germany. In June 1795, Spain made peace. Only England and Austria remained in the field against France. The crisis that had sustained terror ceased to exist and there was widespread desire to end the terror and to return to normal conditions. Members of the Convention fearing that they would be victims of the next purge conspired against Robespierre. On 28 July 1794 Robespierre, Saint-Just and others were executed. The terror had come to an end in the blood of its own champion.

Though the leaders of the Terror governed ruthlessly, they were not blind to the social, economic and administrative problems that plagued the country. The Law of Maximum (September 1793) had given protection to the common man by controlling prices and wages. Social security was provided which granted aged, ill or disabled small income and free housing if needed. Granaries were established in each district. A national food committee was vested with arbitrary power to seize food and control distribution. Another committee controlled industrial production. Feudal rights were abolished without any indemnity in June 1793. Some land redistribution was effected by a law which confiscated the property of emigres. The economic programme of the Terror was capped by the famous Decrees of the Ventose (February-March 1794) which confiscated the property of suspects and its distribution to poor patriots of the communes.

The terrorists promoted science and technology. Carnot introduced balloons for observation. He also established a telegraph between Paris and Lille. The terrorists made elaborate plans for a complete system of elementary and secondary schools, both tuition free. Elementary education was to be compulsory for all. Some institutions of higher learning planned under the terror became permanent. The most important are the Ecole Polytechnique (Polytechnic School) and the Ecole Normale Superieure (Great Normal School or Teachers' College).

Much of the terror was senseless. It was not an ordered movement. But the Convention did marvellous things and achieved more than any earlier government. It changed the world indirectly by raising a new standard of administrative achievement. Apart from this, the lasting results of its efforts were more negative. It can hardly be doubted that the terror hardened attitudes both for and against the revolution.

Directory (October 1795-November 1799)

The Directory was ill-fated from birth. The men who became Directors were self-seeking politicians of little ability. The aims of the new ruling class were a constitutional parliamentary system on a narrow social basis so as to prevent personal dictatorship. 'They succeeded in preventing a repetition of Robespierre's revolutionary dictatorship only at the price of producing Napoleon's military dictatorship'.

But the domestic record of the Directory was not bad. Its success was aided by successive years of good harvest and a general recovery of the economy. The government's economic policy was one of the laissez-faire. Firm control was established over foreign exchange. The French industry was protected by the imposition of high tariff duties. The government reorganised poor relief, improved internal communications, and undertook comprehensive industrial planning.

There were drastic budgetary and fiscal reforms, initiated largely by Jacques Ramel, Minister of finances. He repudiated two-thirds of the national debt. Ramel also introduced a permanent system of direct taxes -on business licenses, land, personal property and servants. Additional money was acquired by revising the system of indirect taxes.

Despite its achievements, the Directory lacked public confidence from its inception. The executive grew weaker. In the end, what remained of the regime could be saved only by appeal to the military.

SIGNIFICANCE OF THE REVOLUTION

The French Revolution is one of the most important events in the history of Europe. It was a great triumph for the idea of democracy when it enshrined the principles of liberty, equality and fraternity. Liberty implied that government should function according to the sovereign will of the governed and not according to the dictates of an autocratic king. The individual should be guaranteed possession of personal liberties which no state might curtail. Such were freedom of opinion, worship and press. The French Revolution proclaimed the liberty of owning private property as an inherent right of man.

The greatest gift of the French Revolution was the idea of equality. The Declaration of 1789 asserts that all men have an equal right to well-being and the pursuit of happiness, an idea which the famous French scientist Lavoisier was probably the first to proclaim as a political doctrine. Kant went so far as to reject all hereditary privileges. Equality meant that all men were equal before the law. It also meant the abolition of privileges, the destruction of feudal system, the end of serfdom. Fraternity was the watchword of the new French nationalism. It was the most potent force in reshaping the boundaries of Europe. The whole of Western Europe between the Pyrennes and the Baltic became infused with the ideals of Revolution.

One of the greatest gifts of the Revolution to France was uniformity of institutions for all her people. France was at last a political and economic unit, with a common administrative system and a unified body of law. And finally, the emergence of a free, landowning peasantry was a permanent result of the Revolution. But the peasants in other countries did not experience French principles at first hand. In Russia, the years 1796-98 saw more peasant unrest with 278 outbreaks occurring in 32 provinces. 'All the peasants', wrote a landlord in 1797, 'have the thought that there should be no nobles ... This is the self-same ... spirit of insubordination and independence, which has spread through all Europe.'

Though the results of the French Revolution were not enduring in some countries, but in the Low countries, in some of the states along the Rhine, those of southern Germany, and the Kingdom of Naples, feudalism gave way to civic equality and religious equality. Even the regeneration of Prussia was un-doubtedly the result of the same forces. As an eminent writer puts it 'No country that had been touched by French influence became ever quite again what it had been before.'

Another great legacy of the French Revolution was the idea of nationalism. This new factor in European politics was destined to act as a potent force in reshaping the boundaries of Europe. The erection of a Kingdom of Italy and the revival of a part of Poland did much for Italian and Polish nationalism; and the German people were animated in their war of liberation. There was a nucleus of intellectuals in almost every country, ready to fight for the principles of democracy and nationalism -all inspired by that movement which had shaken the old regime. But the arrangement of 1815 put an end to all this force of nationalism.

Apart from these tangible results, the French Revolution also left the tradition of popular upsurge and violence which were reenacted throughout Europe in 1848 and in France in 1871. The Spanish liberals of 1830 and 1836, like the French, German and Italian liberals of 1847-48, drew their inspiration from the Declaration of the Rights of Man and the Constitution of 1791. In England, the great popular ferment of 1830 and 1831 was attributed to the French Revolution. Many of the later revolutionaries -Lamartine, Kossuth , Mazzini, Garibaldi-derived their inspiration from the Girondists and Mountain in 1792; and everywhere insurgent nationalists inherited the tricolour of revolutionary France.

The French Revolution was hailed by the contemporaries as something unique in the annals of history. Kant predicted in 1798 that the memory of this phenomenon would ever remain in the history of mankind. Some twenty-five years later, Stendhal declared: 'In the two thousand years of recorded world history so sharp a revolution in customs, ideas and beliefs has perhaps never occurred ever before.' Hegel compared the Revolution to a marvellous sunrise. Other leading thinkers of his generation such as Fichte and Schelling, the aged Kant and the historian Herder, all welcomed the Revolution in no uncertain terms. Arthur O'Connor was not vainglorious when he declared in a speech to the Irish Parliament in May 1796 that 'the whole European mind had undergone a revolution neither confined to this or that country.'

The French Revolution did not bring about the complete enfranchisement of the people. The history of the nineteenth century is one of gradual but definite step towards the sovereignty of the people much of which can be traced to the influence of the French Revolution. In England radical leaders like Tom Paine, Home Tooke, Thomas Hardy welcomed the Revolution as the greatest event since American Independence. In November 1793 there met, in Edinburgh, a British Convention demanding universal suffrage and annual elections. Thus the Revolution 'brought on the stage of human affairs forces which have moulded the thoughts and actions of men ever since and have taken a permanent place among the formative influences of modem civilisation'.

Rise of Napoleon

Napoleon Bonaparte was born at Ajaccio in Corsica on 15 August 1769 shortly after the island was purchased by France from Genoa. In his youth his great ambition was to free Corsica from French control. He was educated at the military schools of Brienne and Paris. At sixteen he became a sub-lieutenant of artillery. By 1793 he was a Colonel. In the struggle between the Girondists and the Jacobins, Napoleon sided with the latter. In 1793 he distinguished himself by driving the English from Toulon. It was his first victory, the presage of his future greatness. He was given the rank of Brigadier-General. He further made his mark in 1795 by defending the Convention against the royalist insurrection. Napoleon impressed the Directory with his military skill and in 1796 he was appointed commander-in-chief of Italy where he laid the foundation of his imperishable military fame. His Italian campaign lasted a year from April 1796 to April 1797. He was a military genius. His policy was to see that his enemies did not unite and then to beat each in turn. With amazing speed and brilliant tactics, Napoleon led his forces across the Alps, humbled the Sardinians and occupied every fort in Northern Italy. Sardinia was compelled to cede Nice and Savoy to France. When Bonaparte's army approached Vienna, Austria sued for peace. By the Treaty of Campo Formio (October 1797) Austria gave up Belgium to France and abandoned to her the left bank of the Rhine. In return, Venice was handed over to Austria.

On his return to France, Napoleon was received with wild enthusiasm. But the time was not ripe for him to impose his authority upon the people. Napoleon, therefore, persuaded the Directory that it was in the best interest of France that England should be ruined. She was the soul and purse of the continental opposition. He took his army to Egypt and thence across the desert of Sinai towards the East. But he never reached India. He actually lost most of his fleet, failed to conquer Syria and barely got back to France (October 1799) through Nelson's fleet after abandoning his army. He arrived Paris at the most opportune moment.

Consulate to Empire

The Directory had proved itself highly incompetent. Almost none of its members had any ability. National finances were again in chaos. The Directory maintained itself with the active assistance of the army. To the autocratic monarchs of Europe it was apparent that the Revolution was more dangerous to their security than it had been in 1792. Consequently England found no difficulty in persuading Austria and Russia to join her in a Second Coalition against the French Republic. But the Directory proved itself highly incompetent in conducting the campaign of 1799 against the Second Coalition. The French army lost many battles in that year. The French army was driven from Italy. Napoleon was the man of the hour. At this moment-Napoleon arrived from Egypt. By *a coup d' etat* in November 1799 he overthrew the Directory. He then promulgated a new constitution which in theory continued the Republic but in fact established a military dictatorship. The executive power was vested in the three consuls who were to be elected by the Senate for ten years. All the powers were vested in the First Consul, who was Bonaparte himself. The new constitution was approved by a large majority. Though the age of divine-right monarchy had ended in 1789, the age of dictatorship began in 1799.

Under the existing constitution Napoleon enjoyed but a 10-year term as First Consul, and he had besides to share the power with two colleagues. Such a position could hardly fulfil his ambition. Bonaparte was a masterful opportunist guided by intuition into forces at work. After he had achieved new glories for France by crushing the Second Coalition, he was awarded in 1802 with the position of Consul for life. Two years later in 1804, by another popular vote, he was proclaimed "Emperor of the French", his rule being made hereditary. On 2 December 1804, in the presence of Pope Pius VII, Napoleon placed a crown upon his head. "I found the crown of France lying on the ground", Napoleon once said, "and I picked it up with my sword".

Reforms and Conquests of Napoleon-His Fall

Between 1800 and 1803 Napoleon could devote himself to the internal reorganisation of France. Some of the reforms had been carried out during the Revolution. But it was Napoleon, who using the ablest men regardless of their past loyalties, provided the driving spirit behind all these reforms.

Administration: Realising the danger of too much decentralilsation, Napoleon centralised everything. He controlled the law-making process through his Council of State. It was divided into sections for war, marine, finance and legislation. The local government divisions were retained, but they became subject to prefects and mayors, the nominees of the First Consul. Paris was divided into 12 districts, each under a mayor, while the city was under the authority of a prefect of police. Thus Bonaparte completed the work of centralisation begun by Richelieu.

A reorganisation of the judiciary was also effected. All judges were appointed. Supervising the system were the Chancellor and Council of State. At the top stood the Court of Cassation. It had civil and criminal jurisdiction but did not decide cases. There were civil courts of first instance, civil appeal courts, and criminal courts. At the lowest level there were the justices of peace in the canton.

Financial Reforms: Napoleon put the financial administration in proper order. He reduced the public expenditure by rigid economy. He increased the national income by centralising the system of collecting taxes. The Bank of France was founded in 1800 and in 1803 it was given the monopoly of issuing bank-notes. Thus, France enjoyed a degree of stability she had never known before.

Napoleon imitated the better features of the age of Louis XIV. He inaugurated a series of public works. Napoleon continued the protectionist tariff policies of the Directory which were directed primarily at Britain. Everything possible was done to promote industry. There was a growth of 25 per cent in French industry. It may be said that the groundwork for the Industrial Revolution in France was laid during the Napoleonic period. Nepoleon's engineers built or repaired about 50,000 miles of roads. Even remote village was benefited.

Religion: Napoleon regarded religion as a useful political instrument, a social cement and a safety valve. 'The people must have a religion and the religion must be in the .hands of the government'. He wanted to come to an understanding with the Church, for he believed that religion was essential to strengthen his political career. 'A State without a religion is like a vessel without a compass', he said. He made a treaty of Concordat with the Pope Pius VII in July 1801 whereby he set aside the Civil Constitution of the Clergy. He guaranteed freedom of worship and recognised Catholicism as the religion of the majority of the French people. By the Concordat the higher clergy, though appointed by the state, must receive the confirmation of the Pope; the lower clergy were to be appointed by the bishops. In return the State undertook to pay the salaries of all. In April 1802

Bonaparte embodied the Concordat in a general Law of Public Worship which subjected the clergy to minute state regulation. Napoleon's ecclesiastical settlement was a compromise. It left both extremes dissatisfied as it did not restore to the Church its property which had been confiscated during the Revolution. Nevertheless, the settlement continued in force till 1905.

Legal Reform: The Code Napoleon: "My real glory", said Napoleon at St. Helena, "is not having won forty battles. What will never be effaced, what will endure for ever, is my Civil Code." One of the greatest evils of the ancient regime was the lack of a uniform code of law. With the help of a commission of jurists, Napoleon in 1804 evolved the Code consisting of 2,287 articles. The Code laid emphasis of the principles of Roman law, which made it more acceptable to other European countries in later times. There were five codes in all: the Civil Code, the Code of Civil Procedure, the Code of Criminal Procedure and Penal Law, the Penal Code and the Commercial Code. Of the five codes, the civil code was the most important. These codes granted religions toleration, civil equality, equality of inheritance, enjoined civil marriage and permitted divorce. On the other hand it upheld strongly the bond of family life, the paternal authority, the sanctity of private property and subjection of women. 'The Codes preserve the essential conquests of the revolutionary spirit-civil equality, religions toleration, the emancipation of land, public trial, the jury of judgement'. Napoleon was rightly regarded as a Second Justinian. In Holland, Germany and Italy, wherever the French armies marched, the Code exercised enduring influence. As a matter of fact, the Codes presented to Europe the main rules which should govern a civilised society.

Legion of Honour: Napoleon created a new aristocracy of merit by introducing the Legion of Honour in 1802. This he distributed primarily to soldiers but also to civilians of high merit.

Education: Napoleon ensured free social and educational opportunity and made possible 'career open to talents.' In his attitude towards culture, Napoleon could hardly be called liberal. The purpose of the schools, according to him, was to rear up faithful citizens, taught by men with fixed principles. He established four types of schools: primary, secondary, semi-military boarding schools, and schools for technical training. At the head of all was the Imperial University created in 1808. He reorganised the Institute de France which had been established in 1795 for higher study and research. He prohibited the study of moral and political sciences. Napoleon preserved and expanded the Bibliotheque Nationale (National Library) and provided the Archives Nationale a new home in 1804. The whole structure formed a rigid hierarchy with an imposing bureaucratic apparatus centred in Paris and charged with regulating the educational life of France down to the smallest detail. He was equally opposed to freedom of the press.

Other achievements: Napoleon inaugurated a series of public works. He laid roads, cut canals, fostered agriculture and commerce. He improved Paris and converted the palace of Louvre into a museum. The general condition of France showed visible sign of improvement. People from Britain and elsewhere flocked to Paris to witness the new scientific system of government inaugurated by Napoleon. It must be remembered that Napoleon's domestic policy was throughout subordinated to military necessities. There was little original in his social and political schemes. The great merit about his statesmanship is not its originality, but the boundless energy and the strength of will with which he carried it out. Though Napoleon was a child of the Revolution, he showed no appreciation of the value of political liberty.

Thus by his work of reorganisation, Napoleon purged the Revolution of the features which seemed to make for chaos and retained those which might be calculated to render the State a more efficient machine. In that sense, he harnessed the Revolution to the chariot of autocracy. 'I am so much identified with our monuments, or institutions, all our national acts, that one would not know how to separate me from them,' said Napoleon in 1815. It is true that the Napoleonic genius still pervades France through the Code Napoleon, the judiciary and administration. His immediate successors might repudiate his work, they could not undo it, and the Napoleonic state was long to outlive its author and the ends to which he had directed it.[4]

Conquests of Napoleon

War with England being temporarily suspended in 1801 by the Peace of Amiens, was again renewed in May 1803. Napoleon planned a great invasion of England which never materialised. Moreover, in the battle of Trafalgar (near the Strait of Gibraltar) in October 1805, the British naval commander Nelson annihilated the main body of the combined French and Spanish fleets.

Napoleon had to fight against a grand coalition of England, Austria, Russia and Sweden in 1805. Abandoning his projected invasion of England, Napoleon marched his armies into Germany and defeated the Austrians at Ulm (20 October, 1805). Then he entered Vienna and defeated the combined Austro-Russian armies on the field of Austerlitz, in Moravia on 2 December 1805. By the Peace of Pressburg, Austria gave up Venetia and Tyrol and recognised the Kingdoms of Bavaria, Wurtemburg and the Grand Duchy of Baden as independent states. "Roll up the map of Europe", Pitt, the English Prime Minister is reported to have remarked after Austerlitz, "it will not be wanted these ten years". In 1806 the Holy Roman Empire came to an end and Napoleon reorganised further German territory in the Confederation of the Rhine.

In October 1806 in two swift battles-Jena and Auerstadt-Napoleon defeated the Prussians and entered Berlin on 25 October. In the spring of 1807 Napoleon's army advanced towards the Baltic and won a complete victory at Friedland over Tsar Alexander I of Russia. By the Treaty of Tilsit July 1807) the two Emperors agreed to divide Europe into two spheres of influence. At Tilsit Napoleon reached the height of his power. Central Europe lay at his feet. Moreover Tilsit led Napoleon into further adventures which ended in disaster.

His fall : The three blunders which combined to ruin Napoleon were the continental system, the Spanish expedition and the invasion of Russia.

After Tilsit, England remained as the arch enemy of France. In 1805 Napoleon had defeated Austria, in 1806 Prussia, in 1807 Russia. After Trafalgar, Napoleon found British sea power invincible. He, therefore, tried to ruin Britain by indirect means. He sought to cripple Britain by closing its markets and thus reducing its exports. By a series of decrees, he prohibited the importation of British goods, not only into France, but into oher parts of Europe as well. This method of trying to ruin Britain was known as the "Continental System".

The use of economic wcapons in the struggle for power was not new. Immediately after the declaration of war in 1793, France annulled the hated commercial treaty of 1786. All British goods were excluded from France. As early as 1796 there was a proposal to exclude British trade from the continent. Napoleon did not have to invent the Continental System. He found an idea already in existence and used it for his own purpose. Before the inception of this policy, the Pope had been forced as early as 1797 to close his ports to British trade. Since 1799 Napoleon had followed the

[4] Cobban Alfred: *A Hisdtory of Modern France,* Vol II, 1799-1871, p.38

mercantilist policy of his predecessors in excluding British goods from France and her 'natural frontiers'.

Britain replied by issuing a series of royal 'Orders in Council'. Thus, the ports of France were declared to be in a state of blockade. Neutral ships were forbidden to go to the Continent. Britain had the advantage of sea power and strictly enforced their orders. Napoleon replied, in turn, by extending the operation of the continental system: his further Decrees at Fontainebleau and Milan (October-December 1807) threatened all neutral shipping with forfeiture that had touched a British port or had submitted to search by the British navy. Neutral vessels became objects of prey for both the British and the French.

Britain suffered severely from this so-called 'Continental System'. The restrictions on the export of British goods to the continent caused serious industrial depression. This also led to a rise in the price of gold which had to be exported to pay for imports. But on the whole the system 'increased rather than diminished the commercial prosperity of England.' Though the European markets were closed to Britain, the rest of the world was open to her. She also found new markets, particularly in Brazil, Spanish America, Near East and in the Baltic.

It was not possible to seal up the whole continent. The Ottoman Empire was outside the range of French activity and much merchandise was shipped into Turkish ports. Moreover, it was impossible to prevent smuggling. British goods were in great popular demand on the continent; even Napolean had to issue licenses for the importation of certain British goods. Restricted in Europe, British merchants rapidly expanded their trade in distant areas such as Spanish America. Everywhere the continental system came to be hated. When Pope Pius VII refused to enforce the continental blockade Napolean imprisoned him and seized the Papal State (1809). The Italians resented the debasement of the Papacy, 'one of the historical glories of their country.' 'Among Napolean's grave errors there was none destined to shake so profoundly the fabric of his power, not in Italy alone, but all over the Catholic world, as this gratuitous affront, to the Papal See and to the Roman tradition'. In 1810, he deposed his brother, Louis, King of Holland, for not enforcing the blockade and annexed Holland.

When the economic crisis of 1811-13 burst on Europe, it was attributed to the continental system. In France, itself, there was widespread unemployment. Napolean modified his economic legislation and this was the virtual end of the real enforcement of the Continental System. French ships were allowed to trade with England under a neutral flag.

The Spanish War: In order to enforce the Continental System on Portugal, an ally of England, Napoleon concluded a secret treaty with Spain for the partition of Portugal. The royal family of Portugal fled to Brazil in South America. Then Napolean forced the Bourbon King of Spain to resign all claims to the Spanish Throne. In May 1808, Napoleon placed his elder brother Joseph on the throne.

Thus, Spain was in possession of France. 'The Pyreness existed no longer'. But Napoleon's Spanish policy was his great blunder. Decres, a contemporary said: "The Emperor is mad, absolutely mad; he will destroy himself and all of us with him". He could not realise how difficult it was to subdue proud Spanish people amidst its mountains and arid plains. Spanish peasantry made common cause with nobles and priests. Guerilla force drove Joseph from Madrid and defeated two French divisions in the field at Baylen in July 1808. Thus, began the Peninsular War which lasted until 1813 and which baffled him at every stage and ultimately brought disaster to him. 'If I thought it would cost me 80,000 men I would not attempt it, but it will not cost more than 12,000,' Napoleon said. It cost him half a million men and perhaps his throne. Backed by British naval power and British forces under Sir Arthur Wellesley, (later Duke of Wellington) the Spaniards cleared the Peninsula in 1813. Napoleon remarked later, "It was the Spanish ulcer that ruined me." The significance of the Spanish war lay in the fact that it was the beginning of a nationalist movement of resistance in other parts of Europe.

Napoleon underestimated the strength of the Spanish national resistance. Religon and national pride were the chief passions of the Spanish people which goaded them to an obstinate resistance to the French. 'It is a country', said King Joseph, 'like no other; we can find in it neither a spy nor a courier to carry messages,' Spain never succumbed, even in its hour of crisis, to Napoleon. The French Emperor had to learn that 'a whole people is more powerful than a disciplined troops.' Moreover, instead of harnessing all his re-sources into the enterprise, Napoleon hurried away in 1809 before he himself had completed the conquest of Spain. He did not support Massena in 1810; he withdrew Soult in 1812; and in 1813 made futile efforts "to hold Spain with armies which, if transferred to Central Europe, might have saved the Empire." Moreover, the physical features affording great facilities for guerilla warfare harassed the French armies and ultimately enfeeble them. In addition, the help of the British was of utmost importance to the Spaniards. 'The British armies had rarely enjoyed upon the Continent a more convenient theatre of war than the territory of Spain and Portugal'

Invasion of Russia : The Franco-Russian alliance rested on temporary convenience. The ambitions of Napoleon and Alexander were in direct conflict as both wanted to dominate the Near East. Napoleon's reconstitution of Poland as the Grand Duchy of Warsaw was intolerable to Alexander. Moreover Napoleon's efforts to enforce the Continental System on Russia alienated Alexander. Russia needed British manufactured goods and gradually Alexander relaxed restriction of trade with Britain.

In 1811, Napoleon assembled in Poland a Grand Army of 4,50,000 men. In June 1812, the Grand Army crossed the Niemen river and proceeded to capture Moscow. The Russians avoided battle and retreated. Only once at Borodino (7 September 1812) a battle was engaged which cost both sides heavy losses. A week later, Napoleon entered Moscow only to find it deserted and in flames. It was clear that this was no war against armies; it was the nation against which he had to fight. Winter approached with no sign of Russian surrender. Disease and famine made his further stay at Moscow untenable. On 22 October Napoleon evacuated Moscow and began his retreat through devastation and closely followed by Russian forces. Meanwhile Russian winter came in which perished thousands of solders. He lost some 2,50,000 killed and 1,00,000 taken prisoner. It was his costly defeat. It was a tragedy almost without parallel in history.

Napolean pronounced that he had been defeated by the Russian winter. But his own bad decisions made his army the victim of the weather. He advanced too far in Russia; he overstretched his supply lines; he delayed too long in Moscow. In broader context, Napoleon's major mistake was probably in not finishing the Peninsular war first before undertaking the Russian campaign. As it was, he committed himself to a two-front war in 1812. While he marched into Russia, Wellington won startling victories over King Joseph.

In January 1813, Prussia made alliance with Russia and agreed not to make a separate peace. Ever in the hour of crisis, Napoleon won important victories, at Lutzen and at Bautzen, against the Russians and Prussians. Metternich, the Austrian Chancellor, proposed an armistice which Napoleon signed in June 1813. But negotiations broke down and Austria declared war. In August Napoleon won a victory at Dresden. But less than two months later in October 1813, Napoleon was decisively beaten at the battle of Leipzig in which he lost 50,000 men.

France had now to face the horrors of invasion. Early in 1814 three large foreign armies moved into France from the north and east, while Wellington entered France from the south, from Spain. Paris fell by the end of March and a week later (7 April) Napoleon abdicated the throne. He was exiled to the small island of Elba in the Mediterranean, where he was granted sovereign rights. The French monarchy was restored in the person of Louis XVIII, the brother of Louis XVI.

Hardly had Louis XVIII begun to establish a stable new government, when Napoleon escaped from Elba and entered Paris on 20 March 1815. The masses of the French men welcomed him. He raised a new army and marched into Belgium. There on 18 June at Waterloo, he met Wellington and Blucher and was defeated. Even had Napoleon won the day, he could not have hoped to triumph over the determined armies of Britain, Russia. Prussia and Austria. Napoleon abdicated a second time and was again exiled to the remote island of St. Helena in the South Atlantic. There he lived for five and a half years where he died in 1821 at the age of 52. In his last will, Napoleon gave vent to his feeling against England he had been unable to subdue. 'I die before my time, killed by the English oligarchy and its hired assassins', he had said. His constant wars left France crippled and destitute of resources. France was unable to fight a major war until 1870 and then only to be defeated. Some Frenchmen called him the 'Corsican ogre', and Thomas Jefferson compared him with the' Attila of the age'.

The great legacy which Napoleon bequeathed was that he gave an impetus to Nationalism in Europe. Napoleonic conquests roused a fierce national patriotism in opposition to French nationalism. In Germany and Italy, French rule fanned a fierce patriotism. In Poland, Napoleon intensified national patriotism by the creation of a Polish national state in the Grand Duchy of Warsaw. Napoleon's invasion of Egypt brought western ideas to Ottoman territory. Napoleon's occupation of the Dalmation Coast promoted nationalist ideas among the Yugoslavs. A new wave of patriotism surged through the Russians who considered war against Napoleon as a 'fatherland war'. The Napoleonic wars also stimulated patriotism among the Austrian peoples. An increased nationalist sentiment among the several peoples-German, Hungarian, Italian, Yugoslav and Czech-dealt a grave blow to Empire's future unity. The people's war in Spain strained Napoleon's resources to a breaking point. Last but not the least, Britain's national patriotism was the chief instrument in breaking the power of the Corsican.

Causes of Napoleon's Downfall

Napoleon asserted that he was the Child of the Revolution. But in important points he was opposed to the ideas of the Revolution. In his desire to extend his dominions, he showed himself strongly anti-national, especially in Prussia and Spain. The absolute government which Napoleon established was the negation of the idea of the 'sovereign people'.

By establishing a strong efficient central government, Napoleon saved France from anarchy. His foreign policy in the beginning was national and served the best interests of France. But later on after the Treaty of Tilsit, his foreign policy caused incalculable harm to France. In his determination to humble Britain and his ambitious desire to dominate Europe, he led France to grandiose scheme of conquest which drained the country's resources and paved his ultimate downfall. After Austerlitz none of his wars had the approval of France.

Unlike Richelieu and Louis XIV, Napoleon was not content with the natural frontiers of France. In his desire to dominate other countries, he ruled despotically over the conquered territories. 'War and despotism were inseparable and ingrained parts of his nature.' He dreaded the naval power and commerce of Great Britain. His obsession against England led him to declare in November 1797: 'Our Government must destroy the English monarchy or it must expect itself to be destroyed by these active islanders.' The Continental System was an attempt to unite Europe against Great Britain to ruin the latter's commerce. However, it proved a failure.

His success emboldened him to further acts of aggression and united Europe against him. He transgressed the limits of practical statesmanship and regarded himself as a modem Charlemagne. Apart from his ambition of making himself masters of Europe, he cast his eyes towards the East. 'We are going to make an end of Europe...and become masters of India.'

He was blind to the strength of national feeling. The example of the successful national resistance which Spain offered to his aggression was emulated by Russia and Prussia. He lost more than 500,000 men in the Russian campaign, his greatest folly, which gravely impaired his prestige.

Despite the gift of strategic imagination with which he was endowed and his inspiring leadership which led him to repeated victories, he failed to secure effective co-operation among his generals. In his last two campaigns, Napoleon was faced with overwhelming numbers. Almost all Europe was in arms against him. This meant that he has a long line to defend and that he had often to depend upon his generals for important manoeures. It is also worthy of note that owing to the Russian campaign, Napoleon lacked sufficient cavalry to follow up a victory. To cap all, there was the drain of the Peninsular War. A large force had to be deployed on the line of the Pyrennes and thanks partly to the superior generalship of Wellington, the French were gradually being pushed back into their own territory.

THE INDUSTRIAL REVOLUTION IN ENGLAND

The term 'Industrial Revolution' was first used by the French in the 18th century. But the term was specifically used to 18th century England which underwent a great transformation from predominantly agricultural and commercial pursuits owing to the invention and introduction of machines.

By the 18th century Britain emerged as the unchallenged ruler of the seas, arbiter of the world's most lucrative trade and principal centre of finance. Capital accumulated in large quantities. The British had a sound monetary system. The use of capital was expedited by the Bank of England, by efficient handling of governmental finances and by the rise of a London money market where bills could be discounted and shares bought and sold. Moreover, Joint stock banks which were legalised in 1826 also stepped in to finance industry.

There was also the human factor. In Britain population was growing rapidly. There existed an abundant supply of cheap, servile labour including female and child labour. There was some immigration into Britain which also provided the labour force. The Huguenots who had come to England, in the later years of the seventeenth century brought with them their skills, particularly in silk weaving.

Britain provided many of the best sailors in Europe. The artisans were distinguished for their high standard of workmanship; British inventors were noted for their daring originality. There was no scarcity of capital After 1714, the maximum legal rate of interest was 5 per cent. Thrift, integrity and hard work were characteristic of many elements of the English population which could not be found together in any other nation.

England outstripped all other nations in developing techniques and machines necessary for large-scale industry. The story of the cotton textile inventions, associated with the names of Kay, Hargreaves, Arkwright, Crompton, Cartwright, is familiar. Large-scale production followed when the textile mills were operated by water or even steam power. By 1835, there were nearly 1,06,000 power looms in the British Isles. The story of the metal industries is familiar. The age of iron and coal was ushered in by a long series of inventions which made it possible to produce and use coal, iron and steel on a large scale.

England was endowed with ample resources needed for industrialisation. Rich in iron and coal, and its ample water resources enabled England to become the industrialised nation of the world. The coalfields of Britain were larger and situated very near to important harbours. On the basis of iron, coal and textiles Britain built up a civilisation which generated new hopes to other countries.

The existence of a considerable degree of political freedom in England provided an atmosphere peculiarly favourable to industrial invention. The ruling aristocracy of England was interested in commerce and they offered help for private enterprises. The English Parliament of the eighteenth century too fostered trade and commerce. Apart from being the leading maritime and colonial power England had been less disturbed than other European countries by political disturbances and wars in the eighteenth century.

Industrial Revolution would have been impossible but for the inventions. A handful of enterprising Englishmen succeeded by their ingenuity in transforming the economic life of the country. They were inspired by the idea that knowledge was a growing thing and that by observation and experience new truths could be brought to light.

Thus by the beginning of the 19th century, England had all the essential elements for the rapid growth of large-scale factory production. Having undergone a certain degree of industrialisation in cotton textiles and the metal trades she was to become the workshop of the world.

SCIENTIFIC INVENTIONS

With few exceptions England prior to the late 18th century imitated rather than initiated new technology. But then for a time she took world leadership in inventiveness. She produced a series of inventions that transformed England's methods of production beginning with the cotton textile industry. In 1733 by his invention of the flying shuttle, John Kay doubled the work which the weaver could perform, besides improving its quality. He was followed by James Hargreaves, whose spinning jenny in 1754 multiplied eight-fold and more the productive power of the weaver. In 1769, Richard Arkwright, invented the water-frame which produced a fine, strong thread. He was the founder of the English cotton industry. He made a series of inventions for spinning cotton which rendered large-scale production possible. In 1799 Samuel Crompton built a spinning mule. With this machine stronger and finer thread could be spun than by hand. An English clergyman named Edmund Cartwright invented an improved loom—an automatic weaving machine. Hargreave's Jenny, Arkwright's water-frame, Crompton's mule and Cartwright's automatic loom brought about an enormous expansion in the cotton trade.

Steam engine: The advent of steam engine in industry opened up a limitless range of opportunity. Thomas Newcomer was the first to invent a steam engine which was used for pumping water from the coalmines. But at deep levels it was useless. James Watt perfected the system. It was James Watt, who brought the steam engine directly into the service of the textile industries.

Iron and steel: The increased use of coal and iron was another determining factor of the industrial revolution. In the beginning charcoal was used for smelting iron ore. In 1809, coke was used in the place of charcoal which led to much greater use of iron. The process of making steel from iron also underwent great improvement. Herry Bessemer announced in 1859 the process by which cast iron could be converted into steel.

COMMUNICATIONS

The use of steam engine in locomotives began in 1800. In the next year Richard Trevithick made a pioneering venture for running a steam locomotive for a distance of 90 miles. The steam locomotive was first made practical use by a colliery worker, George Stephenson. His Rocket locomotive, tested in 1829, was able to pull a train of cars at the sensational speed of 20 miles per hour. By 1838, Britain had 500 miles of track and by 1848, 5,000 miles and 16,000 miles by 1886.

Meanwhile, steam engine was used for maritime communication. Robert Fulton (1765-1815) launched his first steamboat on the Seine river in France in 1803. But it was in 1838 that the first oceanic voyage was made by the steamships—Sirius and the Great Western.

Studies of electricity by Faraday and others led to the perfection of telegraphic communication. In 1844, the first telegraph line was established in America. Within a generation the continents were linked together by lines and underwater cables.

Consolidation in Britain

The Industrial Revolution gathered great momentum in England after 1820. One of the reasons for the unprecedented expansion of the British economy was the cheap supply of labour. The population growth was about 16 to 17% per decade after 1820. In the 1840s the influx of Irish refugees after the potato famines swelled the labour force in England.

In the first quarter of the 19th century Britain had all the prerequisites for the rapid growth of large-scale factory production. She had undergone a certain degree of industrialization in cotton textiles and metallurgical industries. In the coming decades, she was to become the workshop of the world.

English exports of cotton goods rose in value from 19 million pounds sterling in 1830 to 56 million in 1870. Similarly, coal and iron production increased at a tremendous pace. The biggest advance took place in the methods of large-scale conversion of iron into steel. Between 1856 and 1870, the price of steel was considerably reduced in Britain.

New industries came into existence. Gas was first used for cooking in 1832. Electricity, telegraph, photography, rubber industry made amazing progress. In the 1850s James Young discovered how to make naptha, lubricating oils and kerosene by distilling crude oil.

The most striking feature of the Britain's industrial growth was the decisive revolution in communication. In 1830, men still went on foot and in that year Liverpool and Manchester railway line was opened. By 1867 more than 12,000 railway lines were opened in Great Britain. The significance of the railways lay in the fact that they not only stimulated industrial growth but also provided the economy with a network of communication which enlarged its productive horizon. It has been said "it was the sheer scale of the railway investment boom of the 1840s that makes it so significant a feature of the industrial revolution in Britain."

Along with the introduction of railways, improvement in ocean transportation took place. The opening of the Suez Canal in 1869 gave great impetus to sea-borne transport. Though it was built with French capital, more than half the shipping that passed through it was the British.

The second phase of the Industrial Revolution in England was marked by the accumulation of capital in the hands of the British industrialists. They now invested in factories and shared the profits. As joint-stock companies grew in number, it became easy for the rich man to invest in industry and reap the profits. Industrialization increased the amount of capital in England; from 2,500 million in 1833, it rose to 6000 million in 1865.

Thus the English industrial revolution had brought a capitalist industry state. By 1880 the population of Britain had grown by leaps and bounds and four out of every five persons lived in towns; agriculture accounted for only about a tenth of the gross national product and more than a third of the nation's expenditure went on imports. The British economy became less open as the spread of the industrial revolution in the rest of the world forced Britain to adopt more defensive commercial policies.

Industrialization in the Continent of Europe with special Reference to France, Germany and Russia.

The first countries to industrialize rapidly after Britain were Belgium and France. After the French Revolution, British goods flooded the continental markets delaying economic growth of the continent. But Belgium and France had a history of technical skills and shared the rich mineral resources. Because they lacked credit and transport, their economic development proceeded slowly, but eventually they overcame this difficulties.

Belgium was the first to introduce railways, machine tools, mechanized textiles and new banking institutions. These innovations made her preeminent in continental industrialization. By mid-century Belgium was keeping pace with England and its self-sustaining economy was much admired. But toward the end of the 19th century, population increased tremendously and its mines failed to produce sufficient coal and iron for domestic use. Belgium then began to import more of both materials than it exported.

Compared to other countries, industrialization in France was slow in the beginning of the 19th century. This was due to war, disorder and inflation. The only sector to have made progress was cotton-spinning. France lacked adequate suppliers of coking coal and good quality iron-ore.

After the French Revolution, with the direct participation of the government of Louis Philippe and later subsidies from Napoleon III, French industries developed behind a wall of tariffs. The construction of railways begun in 1842 helped the process of industrialization. In 1848, 1800 kilometers were opened to traffic as against 10,000 kilometres in England, Germany and even Belgium. The most active period of construction were between 1852 and 1860. About 9,000 kilometres were in use in 1860 and their length had doubled in 1870.

Along with the introduction of railways, power-driven machinery revolutionised French textile industries. From the middle of the 19th century several factors were responsible for the growth of the French industries: unification of the home market by railways, use of new techniques in various sectors and the development of foreign competition.

The average annual rate of industrial growth in France between 1815 and 1913 was about 1.61 per cent. Although their achievements at home were not flattering, French capitalists and engineers prompted industrialization on the continent. By 1814 French foreign loans amounted to about 10 billion dollars. French capital and engineers also built the Suez Canal in 1869.

Despite vast resources of coal and iron, Germany was originally more backward than France. Most Germans were peasants. Capital was lacking and commercial banking was non-existent. There was scarcely a beginning of industrialization in the first quarter of the 19th century. The formation of a Customs Union (Zollverein) in 1834 which embraced most German States of 1842 removed many trade barriers. Apart from enlarging markets for agricultural goods, it also served to stimulate commerce and to create a desire for improved means of communication. In 1839 with aid from British capital, the first important German railway was built and by 1848 there were some 4000 miles of railway connecting Berlin with Hamburg, Prague and Vienna. The political unification of Germany created the largest single market in Europe.

After 1874 industrial investment took the lead. It rose from 14 per cent in the early 1850s to more than 56 per cent at the end of the 19th century. By 1875 Germany was producing more iron and coal than France and Belgium. By 1910, she became the greatest industrial producer in Europe and the second trading nation in the world.

Till 1870, 64 per cent of the population of Germany was still rural and agricultural. But after 1870 changes became so rapid that defied description. The dazzling rate of growth was due to the adoption of latest technology as well as to the character and intelligence of the German people. Nineteenth century industry was founded on coal and iron, and the German Empire possessed much of these resources. As Keynes observed with some exaggeration: "The German Empire has been built more truely on coal and iron than blood and iron."

In sharp contrast, industrialization in Russia was slow and uneven. Russian resources were immense but its institutions were primitive. Emancipated but illiterate peasants constituted vast segment of the population, but a landed aristocracy dominated society. As late as 1900 about 80 per cent of the population derived its income from agriculture.

The Czarist government, defeated militarily by industrial powers in 1856 and 1878, took interest in the economic development of the country. The Crimean War led to a rapid growth of railroads. By 1870, there were about 11,000 kilometres of track. The railroads did not cross Siberia until 1905. The government laid special emphasis on heavy industry rather than on consumer goods. At the opening of the 20th century, Russia was fourth in pig iron production. The period from 1906 to 1914 witnessed spectacularly rapid investment and growth.

Elsewhere industrialization appeared slowly before 1870. Holland, Sweden, Spain and Poland took the lead. Bohemia including Prague and Austria especially Vienna became the centres of new mechanized industry. Cavour of Italy promoted industrialization by bringing a few steam engines into Northern Italy (Piedmont). But, by and large, Europe, with the exception of Britain, France, Belgium and Germany, was before 1870, more or less agricultural.

The United States was endowed with rich resources and her great potential attracted foreign capital. Immigrants and the enterprisers built the superb railroad network that linked east and west into one gigantic market. By 1870 that network was tied with steamship lines on both oceans allowing the commerce of the world to flow in. After 1861, the United States forged ahead with the support of the government which was aware to the needs of industry, agriculture and finance.

Japan emerged rapidly after 1860 from feudalism and set out to modernise the country. Borrowing from advanced nations, the government sponsored industry and commerce. Despite serious shortages of raw materials, industry grew rapidly after 1890.

Effects of the Industrial Revolution upon Contemporary Society and Politics

'The Industrial Revolution opened the way to a new world.' With the increase of production in land and industry population grew rapidly. Most of the population growth was centred in cities which assumed importance with the establishment of factories. By 1851, half of England's population had become urban. With the rise of the cities important changes occurred in the structure of the society. The familiar division of landowner and peasant, merchant and artisan continued. But new classes like industrial capitalist and wage-earning proletarians emerged. The Industrial Revolution made capitalists the supreme masters of industry. The wage-earning proletarian was wholly dependent. Along with the fear of unemployment, the new proletariat lived in abject poverty. Though in 1925 the workers were permitted to form unions by the Parliament, the latter forbade them to organise strikes.

The dismal condition of workers created by industrialisation produced sharp reaction among the thoughtful men. An humanitarian factory owner Robert Owen upheld the view that the capitalists should share a portion of his profits with his employees. The French aristocrat, St. Simon advocated that the State should assume control of production and distribution. Chales Fourier, another Frenchman pleaded for a new social organisation based on cooperative communities. But more practical socialist was the Frenchman, Louis Blanc who preached that everyone should be remunerated according to his needs. Another Frenchman, Proudhon wanted to abolish private ownership of property. But the greatest advocates of Socialism were Karl Marx (1818-1883) and Friedrich Engels (1820-95). For Marx and Engels history was a struggle between classes especially between the upper middle classes (bourgeoisie) and the proletariat. In the Communist Manifesto (1847), Marx made a fervent appeal to the workers of the world to unite.

In England, the State began to interfere for the better protection of the working class. Bismarck's State Socialism found general acceptance in Europe. Though new policy of the State hardly realised the ideals of the proletariat, it marked a step forward to meet the claims of that class.

The Industrial Revolution brought about a change in the political life of the England. The House of Commons were elected on a narrow franchise and undemocratic system. A movements for a reform in the House of Commons began. The First Reform Act of 1832 granted to the Industrial bour-geoisie a voice in the Parliament through it did not confer the franchise on the labourer. The Reform Act of 1867 nearly enfranchised all the working men in the towns. In 1884, the franchise was extended to agricultural labourers. In 1901 the British working men organised the Labour Party.

The influence of Industrial Revolution was felt in British foreign policy. She was anxious to find new markets for her ever-increasing volume of trade as well as to secure raw materials for industries. The Industrial Revolution was a revolution in consumption as well as in production. Larger production necessitated large consumption.

The Industrial Revolution gave a great impetus to nationalism. If nationalism was intensified, so was internationalism.. The vast international trade that grew up as a result of the Industrial Revolution led the various nations to unite into a common economic life.

The Industrial Revolution enabled the European power to establish economic control over Asia and Africa. Apart from providing raw materials to the European powers, these countries became the scene of international conflict. There were Anglo-French rivalry in Asia and Africa, Anglo-Russian rivalry in Central Asia, Franco-Italian and Franco-German rivalry in Africa. As major power rivalries became tense, military expenditure rose. These developments climaxed in the year 1914. The disciples of Adam Smith had not visualised industrial warfare.

The Industrial Revolution was a growing process; it did not stop abruptly in the middle of the 19th century. This the steam engine was followed by the turbine, the gasoline engine and the electric motor. Human endeavour and scientific discipline enabled men to establish the telegraph, the telephone, radio, television and space technology. The Industrial Revolution heralded the dawn of a new era—an era marked by the man's bold mastery over the forces of nature.

The Industrial Revolution bequeathed us many problems—problems which were many, formidable and pressing. As a recent writer has observed:

> The Industrial Revolution has invaded the world, turned our very existence upside down and overthrown the structure of all existing human societies in the course of only eight generations. And today it is beginning to press with great urgency new problems of such enormity that the human mind can hardly grasp them—the uncontrolled increase in population, the hydrogen bomb; the pollution of the atmosphere; the destruction of the natural surroundings by industrial waste... the breaking up of the traditional state; the scientific organisation of uncontrolled centres of power... Under the weight of these problems, the old structures crumble.... Everyone has been taken by surprise.'[5]

ESSAY TYPE QUESTIONS

1. What were the causes of the American War of Independence?
2. What were the immediate consequences of the War of American Independence? Discuss its far-reaching significance in the history of civilization.
3. Give a brief account of the social, political and economic condition of France before the outbreak of the French Revolution.
4. Discuss the causes of the French Revolution.
5. How far were the philosophers responsible for the French Revolution?
6. Assess the achievements of the Constituent Assembly.
7. Describe the causes of the Reign of Terror in France and estimate its success.
8. Indicate the different stages by which Napoleon rose to the supreme position.
9. Describe the reforms of Napoleon Bonaparte.
10. Analyse the cause of the downfall of Napoleon.
11. Mention the various factors that led to the emergence of British as an industrial state in the 18th century.
12. How and with what success did Britain become the leading industrialised nation in the 19th century?
13. Discuss the industrialisation of Europe with special reference to France, Germany and Russia.

[5] Cippola, Carlo M.(ed.); *Fontana Economic History of Europe: The Industrial Revolution* Vol.3, pp. 20-1

SHORT ANSWER TYPE QUESTIONS

1. Mention the economic grievances of the American colonies.
2. What were the various taxes imposed by England on the American Colonies?
3. Discuss the economic causes of the French Revolution.
4. Write a short note on the Physiocrats.
5. What was 'Aristocratic Revolt'?
6. What was the impact of Rousseau's ideas?
7. Discuss the importance of the fall of Bastille.
8. Why did war break out between France and the European powers in the initial stage of the Revolution?
9. What were the achievements of the Convention?
10. How would you justify the Reign of Terror?
11. Analyse the achievements of the Directory.
12. What was the significance of the French Revolution?
13. Write a short note on the Code Napoleon.
14. What was 'Continental System'? How far was it responsible for Napoleon's downfall?
15. What is Industrial Revolution?
16. Mention the various scientific inventions made in England in the 18th century.
17. Discuss the role played by the railways in Britain's second phase of industrialisation
18. What were the causes of industrialisation in Germany?
19. Discuss the characteristic features of industrialisation in France.
20. Who wrote *Common Sense*?
21. Who drafted the Declaration of Independence and when?
22. Name the treaty which put an end to American war of Independence. When was it signed?
23. Who was Rousseau?
24. What were the major divisions of the French society?
25. What were the major divisions of the French Revolution?
26. What is Code Napoleon?
27. Who was Robespierre?
28. Mention the name of important political clubs in France.
29. Name the instruments of the Reign of Terror.
30. When was Napoleon dethroned?
31. When and between whom was the Treaty of Tilsit signed?
32. Who was the paymistress of repeated coalition against France?
33. Name the final battle that sealed the fate of Napoleon.

34. Who invented the following:
    (*a*) Flying Shuttle (*b*) Water-frame (*c*) Spinning Jenny
    (*d*) Automatic Loom (*e*) Steam-engine
35. When was Gas used for cooking?
36. When was the Suez Canal opened?
37. What was Zollverein? When was it formed?
38. Who were the greatest advocates of Socialism?
39. Who wrote the *Communist Manifesto*?
40. When was the Labour Party in England formed?

IMPORTANT DATES

1.	July 4, 1776	:	Thomas Jefferson's Declaration of Independence
2.	September 1783	:	Treaty of Versailles
3.	July 14, 1789	:	Fall of Bastille
4.	1791-92	:	Constituent Assembly
5.	1792-95	:	Convention
6.	January 21, 1793	:	Execution of Louis XVI
7.	1793-94	:	The Terror
8.	1795-99	:	The Directory
9.	1796-97	:	Bonaparte's Italian Campaign
10.	October 1797	:	Treaty of Campo Formio (between France and Austria)
11.	1799	:	Consulate : Napoleon made First Consul
12.	1802	:	Napoleon made Consul for life
13.	1804	:	Napoleon: Emperor of the France
14.	July 1807	:	Treaty of Tilsit
15.	1808-14	:	Peninsular War
16.	1814	:	Invasion of France
17.	June 18, 1815	:	Battle of Waterloo
18.	1733	:	Invention of Flying Shuttle by John Kay
19.	1769	:	Richard Arkwright invented the water frame
20.	1800	:	Use of Steam Engine in locomotive
21.	1844	:	First telegraph line established in America
22.	1832	:	Gas used for cooking
23.	1834	:	Custom Union (*Zollverein*) formed in Germany
24.	1847	:	*The Communist Manifesto* by Karl Marx
25.	1901	:	Formation of Labour Party in Britain

UNIT - II

The Impact of Nationalism

After the fall of Napoleon in 1814, it was decided that a Congress should be held at Vienna to undertake the task of territorial reconstruction. The territorial settlement made at Vienna was signed in June 1815 before the battle of Waterloo. It was in effect made by the representatives of the five great powers. These were the Tsar Alexander I of Russia, Metternich, the Chancellor of Austria, King Frederick William ill of Prussia, Lord Castlereagh, the British Foreign Secretary and Talleyrand, the skillful representative of France. All the powers were represented in the Congress except Turkey. After much bargaining, the treaty was signed on 9 June 1815.

One great principle underlying the Vienna Settlement was the restoration, as far as possible, of the boundaries and reigning families of Europe, as they had been before 1789. It was this principle of legitimacy which Talleyrand urged in order to preserve France. In line with this principle, the Bourbons were reinstated in Spain and in the two Sici1ies, the House of Orange in Holland, the House of Savoy in Sardinia, the Pope in the Papal State and a number of German princes in their former possessions. The Swiss Confederation was restored. In the name of legitimacy, Austria recovered Tyrol and most of the territories she had lost.

The second principle involved compensations to those who had played major roles in defeating Napoleon. Prussia was strengthened. She was given a large slice of Saxony, Westphalia and more territory along the Rhine. The strengthening of Prussia on the Rhine made her ultimately the national champion of Germany against France.

Germany was reconstituted as a loose confederation of 39 states with a Diet consisting of delegates of the various rulers. Austria presided over the Diet and dominated the Confederation.

Austria recovered certain Polish lands and received Northern Italy, henceforth to be known as the Lombardo-Venetian Kingdom. She also recovered the lllyrian provinces along the eastern coast of the Adriatic which she had lost in 1809. She also got Tyrol and other valleys of the eastern Alps. Moreover, the restored rulers of Parma, Modena and Tuscany in north-central Italy belonged to the Habsburg family.

Britain, the most persistent enemy of Napoleon and the pay-mistress of the allies took her reward in the form of colonies and naval bases. She occupied Heligoland in the North Sea, Malta and Ionian Islands in the Mediterranean, Cape Colony in South Africa, Ceylon in the Indian Ocean.

The third principle which guided the Congress of Vienna was to provide guarantee for the future peace of Europe by weakening France. She was reduced to the boundaries which she possessed before the outbreak of the Revolution. Steps were taken to surround France with strong states as bulwarks against future aggressions. Thus, in the north Belgium, previously an Austrian province, was joined to Holland as one kingdom under the House of Orange. In the south-east, the kingdom of Sardinia-Piedmont was strengthened by the acquisition of Genoa.

Among other important changes Norway was taken from Denmark and joined with Sweden. Switzerland was strengthened by the addition of three Cantons which had previously been incorporated in France.

Criticism of the Settlement

The territorial adjustments made at the Congress of Vienna ignored the principles of liberalism and nationalism. It was in defiance of the principle of nationalism, Austria was given a commanding position in Italy, that Norway was handed from Denmark to Sweden and Belgium was united with Holland. Germany and Italy were left in fragments. In Germany, Metternich's policy was to 'divide and rule'. A loose German Confederation comprising the 39 states to which Germany was now reduced, was set up under the presidency of Austria. 'The German Confederation was a mockery of national unity'. In Italy Metternich's aim was to keep her weak and divided and he succeeded in his object. The Congress of Vienna supported Metternich's contention that Italy was a geographical expression. Gentz, the Secretary of the Congress wrote after reviewing the work of the Vienna Congress:

> Men had promised themselves an all-embracing reform of the political system of Europe; guarantees for peace; in one word, the return of the Golden Age. The Congress has resulted in nothing but resotration; agreements between the Great Powers, of little value for the future balance and preservation for the peace of Europe; quite arbitrary alterations in the possessions of less important states... The Protocol of the Congress bears the stamp rather of a temporary agreement than of work destined to last for centuries.

In ignoring the philosophy of the revolution, the makers of the Vienna Settlement weakened the whole structure they were so laboriously erecting. In 1830, the Belgians rose in revolt and destroyed the arrangement of 1815. The arrangements concerning Italy and Germany lasted for half century and underwent profound change thereafter. Among the disaffected were also the French who regarded their natural boundary taken from them. The break-up of Poland was in gross violation of the principle of nationality. Thus, the Congress of Vienna which sacrificed the principles of nationality could not endure long. In the next half century Europe was destined to witness many wars and revolutions. The Vienna settlement was framed by monarchs and as such it ignored the aspirations of the people. "The real charge that may be brought against the monarchs of Vienna is that they ignored the challenge of the French revolution; that they failed to see that the new forces of democracy and nationality were becoming determining political factors."

But the Congress of Vienna made some significant contributions. The Congress established the important doctrine of international rivers. The abolition of Slave trade which had been effected by Britain in 1807 was agreed to by France, Spain, Portugal and Holland.

Metternich System

The period from 1815 to 1848 has usually been called the 'Era of Metternich' for during these years he was the central figure in European politics. For the preservation of Habsburg dominion inhabited by Hungarians, Czechs, Slovaks, Croats, Rumanians, and Poles, Metternich devised his famous system. He was the apostle of conservatism. 'Govern and change nothing' was his watchward.

Believing that nationalism and liberalism and other revolutionary principles were responsible for disturbances in Europe since 1789, Metternich wanted that all Europe must be rid of these contagions. His ideal was a reactionary Europe propped up under the hegemony of Austria.

Metternich

In Germany, Metternich frustrated the fulfilment of nationalist hopes. At his initiative the German Diet in September 1819 passed the Carlsbad Decrees. These decrees dissolved the patriotic student societies and enforced a rigid censorship of the press. These decrees remained in force nearly 20 years. The following year Metternich persuaded the German states to restrict the subjects that might be discussed in parliamentary assemblies.

It was in Italy that Metternich made his influence felt through the Habsburg princes restored to power in 1815. Everywhere there was censorship, popular ignorance and poverty. The strength of Metternich's system in Italy lay in the division which prevented any concerted nationalist movement of independence.

To sustain Habsburg domination in Austria and elsewhere called for constant vigilance and fixed determination.. Both of these qualities Metternich had. In his vision internal and international affairs were inseparable. He wanted to crush the spirit of revolution everywhere and to maintain the balance of power in Europe, Metternich came to the conclusion that the restored monarchs must combine themselves and prepare a machinery for concerted action. It was Metternich who invented the periodic Congresses to resolve all disputes that might endanger the peace of Europe.

The fundamental weakness of Metternich system was that it only postponed the day of reckoning. It secured a false appearance of unity. The forces of revolution, driven under-ground, erupted with so violent force in 1848 that the system crumbled.

The Revolution of 1820

The chief European powers who made territorial settlement at Vienna were determined that they must keep Europe at peace. Two international organisations were ready to do this—the Holy Alliance and the Quadruple Alliance. The Holy Alliance met with failure. But the same could not be said of the Quadruple Alliance signed on November, 20, 1815 by the four great powers-Austria, Russia, Prussia, England. But the Quadruple Alliance was an opportunistic alliance of Great Powers. 'After 1820, the Congress System became in effect a trade-union of Kings for suppressing the liberties of peoples.'

In Spain, there was opposition to King Ferdinand VII, who on his restoration in 1814, had abolished the constitution of 1812 and brought back the old absolutism. A mutiny occurred in the army and rioting broke out in various parts of Spain. The King, out of fear, restored the constitution of 1812. Subsequently, however, with the help of the French armies, Ferdinand VII, suppressed the rebellion and annulled his promises. Events in Spain, likewise helped to put an end to a simultaneous liberal revolt in Portugal.

Revolt in the Spanish Colonies of Latin America

Influenced by the spirit of nationalism released by the French Revolution and encouraged by the success of the American colonists in their struggle against England, the Spanish colonies of Latin America revolted against the mother country. In 1811, Venezuela declared independence. Though Spain succeeded in quelling the revolt in the colonies by 1816, the revolution revived with double force. The revolution assumed a new direction under the direction of Simon Bolivar, who vowed to free his country from Spanish rule. In May 1819, after crossing the Andes he defeated the main Spanish army at Boyaca (August 7). A proclamation of the union of New Granada and Venezuela in the Republic of Colombia followed. Bolivar became the first President of the Republic. Equador was liberated in 1822. Meanwhile, Peru still remained to be freed. Bolivar defeated the Spanish army in August 1824 and on December 9, the last Spanish Viceroy laid down his arms. Peru was declared independent. The last to be freed was upper Peru and this was accomplished in 1825. In August 1825, the republic of Bolivia was born. In compliment to Bolivar, it took his name. "Liberator of Colombia, dictator of Peru, President of Bolivia, Bolivar, at the end of 1825, had reached the height of his power and fame. He was dreaming now of a Spanish American League of Nations, its seat at Panama."[1]

The Greek War of Independence (1827-29)

The Greeks were the first to achieve their emancipation. Though forming part of the Ottoman Empire, the Greeks enjoyed a practical independence subject only to their sending to Constantinople an annual tribute in money and in sailors to man the imperial navy. The memories of Hellenic culture also contributed to the independence of the Greeks. In Greece, a linguistic and literary revival associated with the name of Korais heralded a national uprising. Moreover ideas of liberty and nationality propagated by the French Revolution helped the awakening of the Greeks. Secret societies like Philike Hetaireia (Association of Friends) multiplied. Organised at Odessa in 1814 this society by 1820 enrolled 200,000 members. It aimed at the expulsion of the Turks from Europe and the re-establishment of the-Greek empire.

In 1821, Prince Alexander Ypsilanti revolted in the Romanian principalities of Wallachia and Moldavia. He had counted on Russian and Romanian support. In this expectation he was disappointed by both the powers. His force was defeated by the Turks in June 1821. Ypsilanti fled to Hungary where he remained a prisoner until his death in 1828.

Yet Ypsilanti's abortive rising had sparked revolt in Morea and in the Greek islands where it rapidly developed into a War of Independence. The Greek War of Independence forms an important chapter in the history of Europe in the 19th century. Begun in 1821 the war lasted till 1830 when the Greeks achieved their independence. From 1821 to 27, the Greeks fought alone against the Turks. This period was followed by foreign intervention. The war was fought with great ferocity on both sides. The Greeks attempted to make it a war of extermination. In revenge, the Turks hanged the Patriarch of Constantinople, the head of the Greek Church, in his robes in front of the Cathedral on Easter-day (22 April 1821). Russia was excited by the execution of the Patriarch and it was feared that she would at once attack Turkey. Austria and England at once took measures to prevent this danger. For the moment the struggle was localised.

In 1822, Turks slaughtered over 20,000 Greeks in Chios and almost recaptured control of the peninsula. But the Greeks had command of the sea and the Turks had other troubles to contend with in Syria and in Persia. In January 1822, the Greeks declared their independence and promulgated a constitution. The Sultan of Turkey appealed for aid to Mehmet Ali, Pasha of Egypt who was promised the principalities of Syria, Damascus and Morea as the price of his assistance. Mehmet Ali sent his son Ibrahim and a disciplined army to Morea. The Greek cause appeared to be hopeless

[1] *The New Cambridge Modern History,* Vol. IX (1975), p. 627.

when Russia intervened. In 1825, Tsar Alexander, reluctant to intervene, was succeeded by Nicholas I, more interested in Balkan possibilities. Everywhere-in France, Germany, England and Switzerland-Philhellenic Societies were formed.

Canning, the British Foreign Minister, decided to act lest Russia might gain dominance in the Balkans. In April 1826, an agreement between Britain and Russia was reached in the Protocol of Petersburg. According to the Protocol Greece was to remain tributary to the Sultan though she was to become virtually independent. Turkey rejected the Protocol. The French government indicated its approval of Anglo-Russian policy. In July 1827 by the Treaty of London, the three powers-Britain, Russia and France-agreed to compel the Sultan to accept their mediation and to recognise the autonomy of the Greeks. The Sultan again refused. The consequence was a naval battle at Navarino on 20 October, 1827 a battle which arose accidentally but which ended in the destruction of the Turko-Egyptian fleet.

Meanwhile the new English ministry under Wellington, Canning having recently died, described the Battle of Navarino as untoward incident. The result was the British withdrawal from the Greek question and allowing Russia a free hand. In 1828 Russia declared war against Turkey. After preliminary reverses, the Russian army reached Adrianople (September 1829). In 1830, Greek independence was ensured, its independence being guaranteed by Russia, France and Britain. In 1833, the new state became a monarchy in the person of Otto I, Prince of Bavaria. The Greek War of Independence was a heroic and epic struggle which fired the Balkan peoples with the nationalist sentiment. This also gave a new turn in the foreign policy of Russia and the latter came to regard Balkan question as more worthwhile than an occupation of the Turkish capital.

July Revolution of 1830: Causes

After the fall of Napoleon, the Bourbon line of King was restored in the person of Louis XVIII, brother of Louis XVI. The new monarch was determined to act constitutionally. He issued the famous Constitutional Charter which established a legislature of two houses-the Chamber of Peers, appointed for life and the Chamber of Deputies, elected for a period of five years by a restricted body of voters. The Charter also proclaimed that all were equal before the law and to be equally eligible for all public positions. Yet equality of the people did not exist. France was still in a political sense the land of privilege, only privilege was no longer based on birth but on fortune.

Louis XVIII was confronted by two hostile parties. On the one hand, there existed the Ultra Royalists who were more loyalist than the king. On the other hand; there were the moderates who based their policy on the maintenance of the Charter. There was also a party of the Left-Republicans, Bonapartists and others.

From 1816 to 1820, the government of France with the assistance of two successive ministers-Richelieu and Decazes, was able to proceed on liberal lines. But in 1820, Duke of Berry, the intended heir to the throne, was murdered. This caused much indignation and strengthened the Ultra-Royalist. Richelieu returned for a short time, but he could do nothing against the forces of reaction which had set in. The successor of Richelieu was Villele who remained in office from 1821 to 1827. By his reactionary measures, he imposed the censorship of the press and drastically revised the electoral law to the advantage of the wealthy class. The elections of 1824 returned an overwhelming majority of the Ultras of which only 15 were liberals. In 1824, the aged Louis XVIII died, leaving the throne to his younger brother, Charles X.

The new king, Charles X was a man of little common sense. He was ultra-reactionary and was regarded as the head of the emigres. He strengthened the power of the Church and permitted the Jesuits to return to France. The election of 1827 returned a majority adverse to the ministry and Villele resigned office.

Villele's successor was Martignac. He pursued a policy of compromise which, however, met with no support either from the Liberals of from the Ultra-royalists. Charles X dismissed Martignac and appointed in 1829 a most unpopular minister, Prince Polignac. The new minister announced his determination to reorganise society, to give the clergy their weight in State affairs, 'to create a powerful aristocracy and to surround it with privileges'. The French people protested. They began to talk of the Revolution of 1688, of William of Orange, and of Parliamentary Monarchy. Societies to resist illegal taxation were formed. Agitators, like Lafayette, toured the country.

Charles X fell back upon the schemes of spirited foreign policy which, he thought, would reconcile France to the loss of liberties. The French army moved to Algiers and its conquests laid the foundation of the French dominion in North Africa. But Paris, however, was not interested in Algiers, but in the crucial controversy between Crown and people. The Chamber of Deputies petitioned the King to dismiss Polignac. In 1830, Charles dissolved the Chamber. In the elections which ensued, the government was in a hopeless minority. This was the occasion for the coup d' etat. The king's mind was fixed. 'Concessions ruined Louis XVI', said he, 'I have either got to mount a horse or a death-cart'. On 25 July 1830, Charles X signed four fateful ordinances which abolished the freedom of the press, dissolved the newly-elected chamber, changed the electoral law in favour of the wealthy class and called for new elections.

These ordinances were unconstitutional, unpopular and intolerable. The moment these ordinances were published, the Paris journalists met and Thiers drew up the protest: "The regime of law is interrupted; that of force has begun. The government has violated the laws; we are dispensed from obeying it'. On 27 July barricades were erected in the streets of Paris. On the next day, the insurgents captured Hotel de Ville and hoisted the tricolour flag. The royal troops were without guidance and lost control of the city. On 31 July, Charles X abdicated in favour of his grandson, the Count of Chambord (who was also known as Duke of Bordeaux) and fled to England with his family.

The revolutionaries were undecided. Some of them advocated a republic. But others felt that it might invite the intervention of the Great Powers. The liberals, headed by Thiers and Lafayette, finally decided in favour of Louis Philippe, Duke of Orleans, a member of the Bourbon family. Louis Philippe was the son of that Duke of Orleans called Philippe Egalite who had conspired against Louis XVI and had died in guillotine in 1793. He himself had fought for his country at Valmy and Jemappes and had then gone into exile. Fifty-seven years at the time of his accession to the throne, Louis Philippe adopted republic and revolutionary ideas. He took the title of 'King of the French' instead of 'King of France' and announced 'The Charter shall henceforth be a reality.'

Consequences of the July Revolution

The July Revolution was an unexpected affair. It had brought about the end of Charles X and had inaugurated the reign of Louis Phillippe. It resulted mainly in the transfer of administration from one set of politicians to another. The changes introduced into the constitution were of minor importance. The king was deprived of the power to issue ordinances in emergencies and the right of legislation was given to the Chamber. Press restrictions were abolished. Catholicism ceased to be the established religion. But franchise was not adequately extended.

But the real merit of the revolution lay in the fact that its significance was negative rather than positive. There could be no question that in any struggle between the king and the nation, the latter was bound to prevail. The revolution struck a balance between liberty and order, parliamentarism and authority. The Revolution of 1830 was the complement to the Revolution of 1789. For the future, the principles of secularism, equality and constitutional liberty, rested on firm foundation.

It was an old saying that when France caught cold all Europe sneezed. The effects of the July revolution were felt in other countries as well. In 1830, Belgium rose in revolt against Holland to which country they had been annexed by the Peace of Vienna. Not only were the two countries separated by history and tradition but the Belgians were industrial while the Dutch were agricultural. Thanks to Britain and France an international conference of 1831 recognised the independence of Belgium. But it was only in 1838 that the Dutch accepted the Treaty of 1831 and recognised Belgian independence. The independence and neutrality of Belgium was guaranteed in 1839 by the great powers.

In Germany especially in Hanover, Saxony, Hesse-Cassel, Bavaria, Baden and Wurttemberg, riots and demonstrations frightened the rulers into granting liberal constitutional. But in Germany liberalism gained a temporary triumph. By 1835 reaction was again triumphant.

In Italy the liberals raised a tricolour flag in the Papal States while outbreaks in Parma and Modena forced their Habsburg rulers to flee to Vienna. But Metternich was quick to suppress the outbreaks by rushing troops into Italy. Despite their immediate failure, the revolutions of 1830 gave birth to Italian movement for national regeneration.

In November 1830, Poland rose in revolt against Russian rule. By the autumn of 1831, the Russians were able to crush the rebellion.

Although Britain did not experience any revolution in 1830, the demand for liberal reform was growing. In 1832, the first Reform Act was passed which increased the number of voters by giving the urban middle class the right to vote. Thus, political power was henceforth shared between the landed and the business classes.

February Revolution of 1848: Causes

Louis Philippe's legal title to the throne of France was very weak. He was invited to ascend the throne by only 219 members of the Chamber of Deputies out of 430, a bare majority. Though the franchise was slightly extended, it was still open only to the wealthy. Louis Philippe's government rested, therefore, on the support of the bourgeois, the well-to-do trading and manufacturing classes.

As Louis Philippe's rule lacked any popular sanction, it had many enemies from the start-Legitimists, Bonapartists and Republicans. The Legitimists defended the rights of Charles X and his descendants. The Bonapartists recalled the glorious days of Napoleon and looked with contempt upon a king whose foreign policy was timid. The Republicans were opposed to any form of monarchy.

In June 1832, an insurrection broke out in Paris. It was important as being the first republican outbreak since 1815. The government passed a law restricting the right of association. Hardly had the new law been passed than new insurrections broke out in several cities. The most important was that in Lyons in April 1834 which grew out of labour troubles. Determined to strike hard at all opponents, the government secured the passage in 1835 of new laws—September Laws—concerning the special (assize) courts, the jury system and the press. Special courts were established to judge summarily all those attacking the security of the state. Press censorship was re-established. These laws greatly weakened the July Monarchy.

The parliamentary history of France during the 10 years from 1830 to 1840 was marked by instability. There were 10 ministers within 10 years. Yet there was a fairly continuous policy. The main work was to consolidate the July Monarchy, to put down its enemies and to keep peace with the foreign countries. In 1840 Guizot, the reactionary became the Prime Minister who remained in power till the monarchy collapsed in 1848.

The three things which combined to overthrow the Orleans monarchy were timid foreign policy, the growing tide of socialism and Guizot's reactionary measures.

In the 30s, Louis Philippe was determined at all costs to avoid war. In spite of the sympathy of the French people, he gave no support to the insurrection in Poland and Italy. In the crisis of the East in which Mehmet Ali, Pasha of Egypt, declared war against Turkey, France, alone, sided with the former. The diplomatic isolation of France was clear when the Powers–Russia, Prussia, Austria and Britain—met in London in 1840. They made a treaty with Turkey, pledging themselves to force Mehmet Ali to terms. Finally, Louis Philippe estranged England by a diplomatic conflict over the affairs of the Spanish marriage. In that country the Queen Isabella and her sister Louisa, were both unmarried. It was arranged that they should marry the two sons of Louis Philippe. Because of opposition, Isabella married her cousin, the Duke of Cadiz and Louisa married the Duke of Montpensier, son of Louis Philippe. The two marriages were celebrated on 10 October, 1846 though the French government had promised the British that Louisa should not many a French prince until Isabella was married and had children. The result was that Louis Philippe had lost the friendship of Britain, his best in Europe.

The July Monarchy was a government of the bourgeoisie, of the capitalists. Under Louis Philippe, France was passing from the old industrial system to the new factory system. This transition was in every country painful. The number of paupers doubled during the July Monarchy. The doctrines of socialism, advocated by Saint-Simon, Fourier and Louis Blanc spread far and wide among the workers. Saint-Simon preached the gospel of work—'man must work'. He believed that the State should own the means of production and should organise industry on the principle of 'Labour according to capacity and reward according to services'. Fourier advocated that each worker must share in its produce and be guaranteed a sufficient minimum to free him from anxiety. But the eloquent champion of Socialism was Louis Blanc, who in 1839 published the Organisation of Labour. The State must acknowledge and implement the 'right to work' and must protect the poor and the weak. 'The time for purely political movements in France is past', wrote Stein in 1842, 'the coming revolution cannot but be a social revolution'.

Guizot refused to recognise that France needed any change in her political institutions. He opposed any extension of the suffrage and any legislation for the labouring classes. 'What have they done for the past seven years', exclaimed a deputy in 1847: "Nothing, nothing, nothing" , "France is becoming bored", said Lamartine.

The amount of discontent with the government of France was steadily growing. Yet it could do nothing because the ministry was steadily supported by the Chamber of Deputies. Deputies were bribed directly or indirectly to support the government. About 200 of the 430 deputies were at the same time office-holders. The revolutionary movement began in 1847 when the opposition organised the 'reform banquet'.

On 28 December 1847, in a speech from the throne, Louis Philippe denounced agitations. The opposition arranged a great banquet in Paris on 22 February 1848. Eighty-seven prominent deputies promised to attend. In alarm the government prohibited the banquet. This prohibition led to the French Revolution of 1848. On 22 February, the populace crowded the streets shouting for reform. Students and workers clashed with the police. The National Guard was called out but refused to fire. The King dismissed Guizot and prepared to grant reforms. Now the republicans entered the scene. On 23 February, a Paris mob attacked Guizot's residence. On 24th morning the streets of Paris were barricaded by workmen. Louis Philippe, after vainly trying to win over the populace, abdicated in favour of his 10-year old grand-son, the Count of Paris and fled to England. Thus, in 1848, France became a Republic for the second time.

Causes of the failure of the July Monarchy

The Revolution of 1848 was the first in Europe to have a socialist tinge. But all was not well with the Revolution. The advanced programme of the new government-freedom of the press, universal manhood suffrage, a 10-hour work day, a guaranteed right to work, and an employer-worker council-aroused bitter hostility. Moreover, the elections for the National Assembly in May 1848, showed that the rest of the France was much less revolutionary than Paris. Republicans, monarchists and clericals who gained a majority in the elections were conservative as to social and economic matters. When the Assembly met at Paris in June 1848, it abolished the so-called 'National Workshops'.

The result was an outbreak of rebellion of the working class of Paris. The Assembly, in alarm, entrusted dictatorial power to General Cavignac to put down the rioting. The three days (June 24-26) there was fierce fighting in the streets of Paris. In the end, order was restored. Some of the rebels were shot. Louis Blanc fled to England and Proudhon was jailed.

The 'June Days' of 1848 sealed the doom of the Second French Republic. The Assembly prepared a Republican constitution providing for a President with a term of four years and for a one-house Legislature, both to be elected by universal manhood suffrage. But the working class would no longer support a Government which destroyed the 'National Workshops' while the peasantry and bourgeoisie grew more suspicious of Republican radicalism. In the general election for President of the French Republic, the successful candidate was Prince Louis Napoleon Bonaparte.

Consequences of the Revolution of 1848

The Revolution of 1848 was a momentous event in the history of Europe. The revolutionary cry 'All Change' sounded across Europe. "Hope lit the dawn of a new Europe; and mankind clambered into the trains of political and social upheaval"[2]. 'The right to work' became the battle cry of the revolutionaries. The startling novelty of 1848 was the announcement of an economic programme.

Social effects of the Revolution were considerable. The emancipation of the Austrian peasants from feudal dues and services was one of the few lasting achievements of the Revolution. Napoleon III was to give special attention to the condition of the workers. By challenging the economic privilege of the owners of property, the events of 1848 heralded the arrival of a new revolutionary

[2] AJP Taylor: *Europe: Grandeur and Decline,* p. 77.

class, 'the proletariat'. The appearance of the 'Communist Manifesto' frightened the bourgeois who feared the loss of their property. 1848 had inaugurated the age of the masses. Governments in future had to accept the fact that the masses held the master key of politics.

The effect of the Revolution on agrarian problem was much clear. This affected half Europe. The feudal system was abolished and the forces of reaction dared not to oppose it. '1848 did for Europe what 1789 had done for France. The abolition of serfdom and of all checks on individual freedom enabled both worker and peasant to move about at will'. This marked the emigration of Europeans which was to change the face of the earth.

The legacy of the Revolution of 1848 was the assertion of the principle of sovereignty of the people against the sovereignty of Kings. Though this had already served as inspiration to the French Revolution of 1789, its operations had been restricted. But the just act of the Revolution of 1848 in France was to abolish the property qualification and to proclaim universal suffrage. Only Hungary held out against universal suffrage until the 20th century.

Impact on Europe: Fall of the Metternich System

The year 1848 was distinguished by revolutionary outbreaks in several countries of Europe. In Austria, Hungary, Italy, Germany and elsewhere popular risings took place against foreign rule and repressive policy of Metternich

Despite the varied character of the Revolution of 1848, its general feature was protests against the settlement of 1815. In Italy and Germany, the revolutions were directed against the Vienna Settlement and the supremacy of the Habsburgs. In Austria and Prussia, people struggled for liberal self-government and greater constitutional liberties apart from struggles for national unification.

The events of 1848 demonstrated that nationalism was the most general force in European politics. It introduced great confusion in Italy, Germany, Hungary, and the Romans or various Slav races such as Croats, Serbs and Slovaks. German patriots denied Czech autonomy; Hungarian resisted Croatian and Serbian independence.

The revolutions of 1848 were the work of towns. Industrial development in most countries could not keep pace with the rapid growth of population. The result was that the towns experienced a low standard of life, acute hardship and unemployment. The conditions bred the revolutionary spirit. In France and Belgium, and to a certain extent in Germany and Italy, socialism had found roots in the industrial working classes.

The great merit of the Revolution of 1848 was that it marked the flight of Metternich from Vienna (March 13,1848). The flight of Metternich was of immense significance. It marked the fall of reaction and heralded the dawn of liberalism. Thus, "a man, who for 30 years had gagged the press, cowed or destroyed the parliaments, and imprisoned the revolutionaries of Central Europe, was hunted from his capital". Governments of Europe now became more accountable to the people they governed. Even at the height of his imperial power, Napoleon III based his empire on a popular parliamentary foundation.

The revolutionary movement brought notable gains to democracy and nationalism. Feudalism was abolished in the Habsburg dominions. Although it failed of its purpose, the Frankfurt Assembly was the first attempt to unite Germany. The year 1848 marked the emergence of the revolutionary proletariat. The appearance of the 'Communist Manifesto' frightened the bourgeosis who feared the loss of their property. "The age which began in 1848 was the age of the masses: the age of mass production, of mass migration and of mass war. In the pursuit of universal happiness, everything became universal: universal suffrage, universal education, universal military service, finally universal destruction. The historic task of the intellectuals was to sever mankind from its roots and to launch it on its career of movement. This was the task which was accomplished in 1848."[3]

Rise of the Second Empire in France-Louis Napoleon

Born in 1808, Louis Napoleon, was the son of Louis Bonaparte, younger brother of the great Napoleon. He had been educated in Switzerland and Germany and had gone to Italy in 1831. Louis Napoleon was a man of energy and was determined to win his uncle's throne. He tried to utilise the Bonapartist sentiment which was being revived. Twice-at Strasbourg in 1836 and at Boulogne in 1840-he had tried to seize government of Louis Philippe. Both attempts had ended in fiasco. After the second attempt he had been imprisoned for life in a fortress near the Belgian border. After six years imprisonment, he escaped in disguise to England, where he remained until the outbreak of the revolution of 1848 in France.

The fall of Louis Philippe allowed him to return to Paris and he was elected President of the Second French Republic in December 1848. Apart from glory, Louis Napoleon seemed to offer security and stability under a strong government.

He was a political adventurer, bent on securing power. He had no faith in the republicanism. In the elections, held in May 1849, for the Legislative Assembly a majority voted for the monarchists. Hereafter the Assembly arrested 33 republican deputies, and passed a new law restricting the freedom of the press. In the months that followed, the assembly passed a law restricting the franchise, thus depriving three million workingmen of the right to vote. To strike out republican influence in the schools, the Assembly passed the so-called Falloux Law, which largely subjected the educational system of the country to church control, while reserving supervisory rights to the state.

While the monarchists in the Assembly were thus de-stroying the republican movement, Louis Napoleon tried to strengthen his position. In October 1949, he dismissed his first cabinet of ministers. As for the policy of the new cabinet, he said boldly:

> The name of Napoleon is in itself a whole programme. It means order, authority, religion, popular welfare at home, national dignity abroad.

Meanwhile, he began to appeal directly to the people ignoring the protests of the Assembly. A conflict between Louis Napoleon and the Assembly became inevitable. The President was forbidden by Article 145 of the Constitution for re-election after the expiration of his four-year term. While Louis Napoleon had no desire to retire in 1852, the Assembly refused to consider changing the constitution.

During the night of December 1-2, 1851, Napoleon executed a coup and arrested most of the leaders of the Assembly. Riots took place but it was put down with severity. The critics of the President-Thiers and Victor Hugo-were compelled to leave the country. On December 21,1851, the French people in a plebiscite voted to empower President Louis Napoleon to prepare a new Constitution of the Republic. The new Constitution extended the President's tenure of power to ten years and vested him with unlimited power. The constitution kept a show of bicameral legislature, composed of a Senate of life members appointed by the President and a Legislative Body of 250 members

[3] Taylor, A.J.P. :*Europe, Grandeur and Decline* (1977), pp. 58-9.

elected for terms of six years by universal manhood suffrage. This was the system of government which was allowed to function in France till 1860. Louis Napoleon frequently appealed to the people and organised demonstrations to receive their greetings. For a year, he hesitated. Then on December 2, 1852, he became, through a national plebiscite, Napoleon III, Emperor of the French. The Second Republican was thus changed to the Second Empire.

'Like murmuring brooks that trickle down from the hill-sides to join in larger, stronger streams, were the beginnings of democracy and national patriotism'. By the 19th century the forces of democracy and patriotism had become too strong to be resisted. The Revolution of 1848 swept away Metternich, the arch-priest of reaction. But the two states—Italy and Germany—existed in 1848 as mere geographical and cultural entities.

The unification of both states required breaking the Austrian predominance in Central Europe, which had been established by the Congress of Vienna. When the revolution of 1848 failed to effect any change in the political situation of Italy and Germany. Cavour of Piedment and Bismarck of Prussia turned to foreign powers to bring about unification of their countries. In March 1861, the movement for Italian unification culminated in the proclamation of the Kingdom of Italy. After three major wars, Bismarck succeeded in unifying Germany and the King of Prussia was crowned as German Emperor in January 1871. Despite the success of nationalism in Italy and Germany, Poland which had been partitioned thrice in the late 18th century, failed to overcome the forces of reaction unleashed by Russia .md Austria.

Unification of Italy

Metternich once referred to Italy as and 'geographical expression'. There was, in truth, no Italian people. In the 19th century Italy lay under foreign domination. Austria was entrenched in the north. Lombardy and Venetia was under Austrian domination while in Central Italy-Parma, Modena and Tuscany-princes of Austrian birth ruled. In the south, a Bourbon dynasty governed the two Sicilies (Naples and Sicily). In the centre lay the Papal States which included Romagna, Bologna and Rome. It was only the Kingdom of Sardinia, which embraced the north-western corner of the mainland, Genoa and Piedmont—that remained independent of foreign control.

Napoleon's conquest of Italy was significant in more than one ways. He had brought together northern half of the peninsula into a Kingdom of Italy and established a uniform system of law and administration. The years following the Congress of Vienna were years of an uphill struggle of the Italians to achieve unity. But the obstacles to Italian unity seemed insurmountable. Austria was immensely strong and people were ignorant.

Secret Society—carbonari (Charcoalburners)—sprang up in the Kingdom of Naples and spread throughout Italy. Its object was to secure constitutional government, national independence and personal liberty for all peoples. In 1820, revolutionary movements occurred in Naples and Piedmont. But in both the states the movements were crushed by the Austrians. In 1830, also occurred equally unsuccessful risings in Modena, Parma and Bologna. Once more Metternich was supreme.

Mazzini: Young Italy

The failure of these risings demonstrated the weakness of the Carbonari. Its loose regional organisation and its failure to define its aims found little support among Italians generally. In 1831, a young Genoan, Giuseppe Mazzini (1805-1872) founded a new society 'Young Italy'. As a student,

Mazzini loved the works of the romantic writers of Italy, France, Britain and Germany. He declared 'place youth at the head of the insurgent multitude, you know not the secret of the power hidden in these youthful hearts, nor the magic influence exercised on the masses by the voice of youth'. Young Italy was to be a people's movement dedicated to the establishment of a free, independent, and republican Italian nation.

Mazzini's methods differed from those of the Carbonari in two main respects. First, he placed less emphasis on plots and secrecy, and more on propaganda. Secondly, he addressed himself not to the educated classes only, but to the people as a whole. Mazzini had a religious, almost a mystic enthusiasm for his work, for he loved Italy above everything else. Italy had a third life to lead. Once she had dominated the world through Rome; then through the Papacy; and now the third Italy, the 'Rome of the People', 'radiant, purified by suffering, would move as an angel of light among the nations'.

This noble dream was bound to have a limited appeal. The rural masses were generally unmoved by it and the middle classes were not attracted towards revolution that threatened the social as well as political structure. Nevertheless, Mazzini must be regarded as one of the pioneers in forging national unity. His ceaseless propaganda created a vigorous public opinion in favour of national independence, without which the great plans of unification could not have succeeded. He had all the faith of a prophet and the courage of a crusader. It was the kind of spirit that produced a Garibaldi. Even after his influence had begun to wane, it was strong enough to act as a spur to Cavour. His faith in liberation by popular insurrection had its greatest triumph in southern Italy in 1860. Among the makers of modern Italy, Mazzini holds an imperishable place as he laid the moral foundations of Italian unification. "Mazzini's impact outside Italy was no doubt greatest after his country had been unified... Not only in England, but in other European countries and also outside Europe, he was regarded as a hero and a prophet... In his lifetime, he was incomparably more effective than Marx".[3]

The next step in the movement of revolution was taken by the Neo-Guelfs whose leader Gioberti wanted to evolve a federation of Italian states under the Pope. But the great drawback of Gioberti was that he did not offer any programme for freeing Italy from the Austrians.

In 1846 with the election of Piux IX as Pope, Italian question entered upon a new phase. He championed the cause of nationality and introduced reforms in the government of the Papal States. In 1847 occurred the Milanese 'tobacco riots'. Then in January 1848, a revolution broke out in Sicily followed by that of Sardinia. Finally came the news of the March Revolution in Vienna, and all Italy took fire. The leadership was grasped by Charles Albert, King of Sardinia, who declared war against Austria. But in 1849, the Austrians won a decisive victory at Novara over the King of Sardinia. The threatening intervention of Louis Napoleon saved the Kingdom of Sardinia from total extinction. It has been said "Had he (Louis Napoleon) not been Piedmont's shield in 1849, he could not in 1859, have been her sword".

Thus ended in failure the first attempt of Italy to win unity and liberty. Charles Albert had declared that Italy could save herself without foreign ally. Now the Italians had learnt that with all their zeal they could not hope to contend against Austria unaided. There must be one Italian state around which the others might rally. Sardinia was the obvious choice which had now a new King, Victor Emmanuel II and a minister of exceptional talent in the person of Cavour.

[3] Beales Derek: *The Risorgimento and Unification of Italy* (1971), pp.56-57

Cavour and the Unification of Italy

An extraordinary farsighted statement, and a daring opportunist, Cavour was the man whom the *Risorgimento* needed. As a young man, he had travelled widely in England, France and Switzerland and became an enthusiastic admirer of parliamentary system of government and western methods of agriculture and industry. Early in life, he was instrumental in founding the *Risorgimento*, a newspaper devoted to the cause of national unity. After 1848, Cavour was convinced that popular insurrection would be of little help in achieving Italian unity. Mazzini he regarded as a fanatic. Italy could achieve unity only by expelling the Austrians from northern Italy and absorbing Lombardy and Venetia. This was a difficult task and could not be achieved by Italian alone. The aid of a foreign power was considered essential.

In October 1850, Cavour joined the ministry of Piedmont as minister of agriculture, commerce and marine. Being a convinced free trader, he negotiated commercial treaties with England, France and Austria. As minister of finance, which he also became, he raised capital by an internal loan, and an external loan from England. When Cavour became Prime Minister in November 1852, his just task was to improve railways, roads and ports, expand her commerce and strengthen her finances. One of his first tasks had been the dissolution of the monasteries. To carry out these reforms in his eight years as Prime Minister, Cavour had to overcome opposition from the King and from the Senate sometimes by devious means. Often he overrode his cabinet and set the tradition of taking action first and then asking parliament in ratification. To him a liberal end justified illiberal means. And yet he never tried to abolish Parliament.

With the vision of a true statesman, Cavour set himself to secure for Piedmont the active sympathy and cooperation of great European powers and finally to take up arms against Australia. The diplomatic web which he wove round Austria and finally outwitted her, was a master-stroke of statecraft. The real turning point came in 1855 when he entered the Crimean war as an ally of Britain and France and gained a place in the Congress of Paris (1856). He focussed the misrule of Austria and gained the sympathies of England and France for the cause of Italian unification.

Cavour had to proceed warily. He was advised by Britain and France not to force the pace in Italy by any irresponsible action. To maintain Piedmont's ascendancy in the national movement, Cavour followed a deliberately anti-Austrian policy. For foreign support Cavour turned back to Paris where Napoleon III had sympathy for the doctrine of nationality. In July 1858, Cavour met the French Emperor, Napoleon III, secretly at Plombiers in the Vosges. 'The drama', Cavour wrote to a friend, 'approaches its crisis'. The French Emperor agreed to assist Sardinia in a war with Austria on condition that Cavour provided a justifiable pretext. In the event of victory, Piedmont would be allowed to annex Lombardy and Venetia, Parma and Modena, and part of the Papal States. But Italy as a whole should be formed into a confederation under the presidency of the Pope. As reward for her services, France was to get Savoy and Nice which would give her natural boundaries in the south-east. Though the pact was only oral, Cavour was confident that Napoleon would keep it. In January 1859, the pact was embodied in a formal treaty between the two governments.

At the end of 1858, Austria had imposed military conscriptions upon Lombardy and Venetia which proved to be so unpopular that hundreds of persons fled to Piedmont. Austrian demands for their extradition and Piedmontese refusals to comply led to mounting tension. This gave Cavour an excuse for military preparations. In March 1859, it appeared that Napoleon III might have to withdraw from the Plombieres engagement owing to international pressure exerted upon him. Things looked so ominous for Cavour that he said in anguish, 'nothing remains for me but to put a bullet through my head'. But events played into his hands when Austria despatched to Turin an ultimatum demanding disarmament within three days. Austria provided the *casus belli* and the French troops marched again under a Bonaparte into the plains of Italy.

The War of Independence began in April 1859 and lasted less than three months. Aided by the French troops, the Sardinian forces defeated the Austrians at Magenta and Solferino and drove them out of Italy. But in the midst of success, Napoleon III drew back and concluded peace with Austria at Villafranca (July 1859). It was agreed that Lombardy should be ceded to Sardinia, Austria should retain Venetia and the rulers of Central Italy (Parma, Modena and Tuscany) would be reinstated in their duchies. An Italian Confederation would be formed under the presidency of the Pope.

The treaty of Villafranca came as a bolt out of the blue to Cavour. He resigned his office in disgust. But Victor Emmanuel had no alternative but accept the terms of the truce which were ratified in November by the Treaty of Zurich. But Central Italian duchies-Parma, Modena. Tuscany and Romagna ignored the treaty. A formal declaration by England in favour of permitting the duchies to decide their own destiny, did much to settle the issue. Cavour returned to office in January 1860. He negotiated with Napoleon III who agreed to abide by the result of a plebiscite on condition that Nice and Savoy should be ceded to him. By overwhelming majorities the Central Italian duchies voted in favour of union with the Sardinian monarchy. Nice and Savoy were restored to France. Thus, had closed a great phase in the work of unification.

Garibaldi and Italian Unification

While Northern Italy became united, much more remained to be done in southern Italy. Once again, Sicily proved to be the focal point. Crispi, a republican conspirator, was stirring Sicily to rebel against its Bourbon King. But he needed a soldier who could fan conspiracy into rebellion and he found it in the person of Garibaldi. After being expelled from Piedmont, Garibaldi had become a brilliant guerilla leader in his South American exile. He had returned in the hour of crisis, but in 1848 and 1859 he had been given a poor share in the war of independence. He had not anticipated the triumph of Italian unity in a form that Cavour had wrought. Though a temperamental, Garibaldi was a honest and a dauntless warrior. Garibaldi was a superb general for the sort of warfare involved. He was brilliant at sizing up the local situation, and his personality cast an extraordinary spell over his troops. When he was invited by the insurgents at Sicily to come to their aid, Garibaldi readily assumed the leadership. In May 1860, with a tiny force of 1000 Red-shirted volunteers, Garibaldi sailed to Sicily and made himself master of the island. Cavour was not at all sympathetic to Garibaldi's precipitate tactics.

Having taken Sicily, Garibaldi crossed the Strait of Messina on August 18, 1860, and in a few days became master of Naples. The Bourbon King Francis II did not even defend the capital, but fled to Gaeta. To have conquered a country of 11 million people in less than 5 months was a remarkable achievement. But it was Garibaldi's dream to free Italy. Cavour was aware of Garibaldi's military preparations and the latter's intention to march on to Rome. This would mean war with France and with the whole of Catholic Europe; this might entail a further conflict with Austria. Cavour also feared that the nationalist movement in the south might abandon Piedmontese leadership and turn republican. "Cavour was blinded by his rigid hostility towards the radicals. His primary object was that Garibaldi should fail; only in the second placed did he want Italy to be united".[4]

[4] Taylor A.J.P.: Cavour and Garibaldi in *Europe: Grandeur and Decline* (1977), p.84

It was a serious crisis and would only be surmounted by Victor Emmanuel's taking an open part in the drama. Cavour turned to his old ally, Napoleon III and after assuring him that the position of Rome itself would remain unaffected, sent the Piedmontese army to invade the Marches. On September 18, 1860, they defeated the Papal army at Castelfidardo, conquered Umbria and Marches from the Pope to 'save them from the revolution'. The victorious forces then crossed into the state of Naples and defeated the Neapolitans at Capua. Meanwhile, Garibaldi had also been involved in a series of dogged engagements with a large Neapolitan force. With his Red Shirts, he could carry the open country; but he was helpless against an army in prepared position. Even before the military issue had been decided, plebiscites were held in October in Naples, Sicily, the Marches, and Umbria which voted overwhelmingly in favour of union with Piedmont. In the face of this, Garibaldi surrendered his conquests to Victor Emmanuel and then passed into honourable retirement.

On February 18, 1861 the first all Italian Parliament met at Turin, representing the whole of the peninsula except Rome and Venetia and Victor Emmanuel II was declared King of Italy. Cavour did not live long to see the completion of his dream. On June 6, 1861, he died at the age of fifty-one after displaying uncommon political gift. It was an extraordinary achievement on his part to achieve Italian unification but his contribution to the territorial and administrative cohesion of Italy seems some-what less impressive. He showed scant respect for the wishes or the traditional usages of the southern provinces. He treated the Kingdom of Naples almost as if it were an African colony. He had done little to mitigate the sufferings of the land-hungry peasants or the poor. "Cavour always suspected Garibaldi; Garibaldi never suspected Cavour. Of course, Garibaldi disliked Cavour and resented his cession of Nice to Napoleon III. Garibaldi put Italy first. Cavour put himself first. Therefore, Cavour was bound to win in the end, despite the great advantages which Garibaldi accumulated in Sicily and Naples".[5]

Venice and Rome still remained to be won. Venice was acquired in 1866 when the outbreak of the Austro-Prussian War gave Italy an opportunity to strike a blow at her traditional enemy. Rome was taken when the French withdrew their garrison in 1870 as a result of the Franco-Prussian War. Thus, the unification of Italy was completed. Rome became the capital of the new Italian Kingdom, while the Pope, withdrawing behind the walls of the Vatican, continued his sullen opposition to the new regime.

Unification of Germany

The Congress of Vienna established a German Confederation of 38 states. It had a representative assembly known as the Federal Diet. The Diet could not be called a Parliament, as it represented sovereigns and not peoples. Each state was at liberty to make war or peace and to legislate without reference to the Diet. The presidency of the Diet was entrusted to the Austrian delegate. And Austria was dominated by its reactionary Prime Minister, Metternich.

In August 1819, Metternich called a meeting of the leading German states at Carlsbad. There he secured a series of decrees, called Carlsbad Decrees, for the suppression of liberalism throughout the Confederation. The whole educational system of Germany was placed under police supervision; press was subjected to rigid censorship. Finally a commission was set up at Mainz for the investigation of Secret Societies. The Carlsbad Decrees were the high water-mark of Austrian influence in Germany.

[5] Taylor A.J.P.: Cavour and Garibaldi in *Europe: Granndeur and Decline (1977), p. 85*

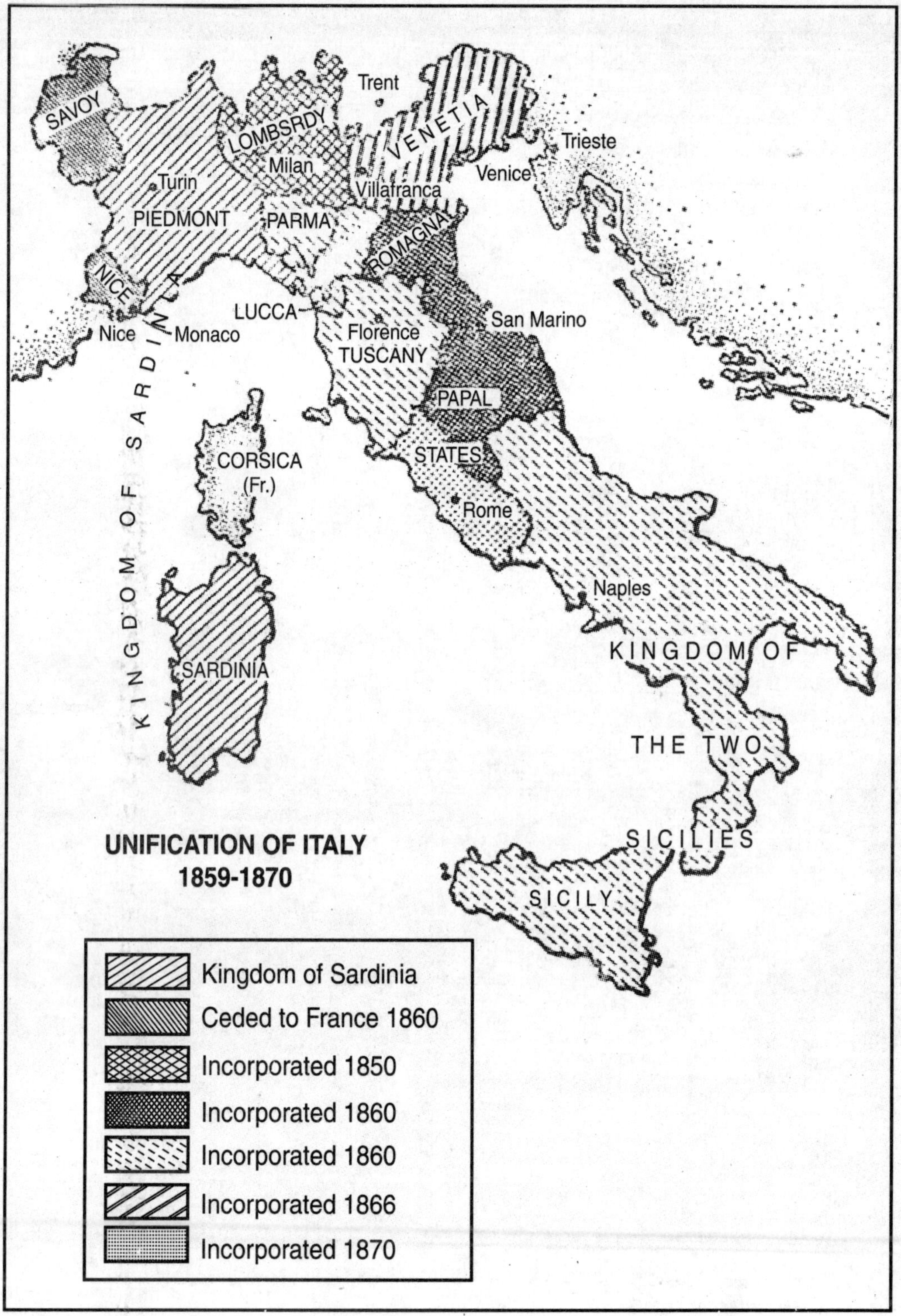
SAVOY
Trent
LOMBSRDY
VENETIA
Trieste
Milan
Venice
Turin
Villafranca
PIEDMONT
PARMA
ROMAGNA
NICE
LUCCA
San Marino
Nice
Monaco
Florence
TUSCANY
KINGDOM OF SARDINIA
PAPAL
STATES
CORSICA
(Fr.)
Rome
Naples
SARDINIA
KINGDOM OF
THE TWO
SICILIES
SICILY
UNIFICATION OF ITALY
1859-1870
Kingdom of Sardinia
Ceded to France 1860
Incorporated 1850
Incorporated 1860
Incorporated 1860
Incorporated 1866
Incorporated 1870

Two movement arose which greatly helped the transformation of German States. One was Zollverein and the other was Pan-Germanism. Until the beginning of the 19th century different tariff systems were in operations in Germany. Under these circumstances commerce could not flourish and industries could not expand. In 1818 Prussia abolished all internal customs and established free trade. She also established, little by little, a customs union or Zollverein in 1834 which by 1842 included all the German states except Austria. It created a real national unity in economic matters when Germany was politically disunited.

In Germany as in Italy, nationalism had made considerable progress in the realm of ideas. A great literary outburst had followed in the wake of the French Revolution and poets, philosophers and historians extolled the German idea. Fichte gave his *Address to the German people*; Hegel exalted the conception of the State and the historical role of the Teutonic race.

The February Revolution of 1848 brought about the downfall of arch-reactionary, Prince Metternich. German Austria became liberal and constitutional. The King of Prussia yielded to popular demand so far as to grant a constitution. The Diet called together a National. Assembly to meet at Frankfurt, in May 1848. The Assembly adopted in December 1848 a Declaration of the Fundamental Rights of the German people. A German Empire was to be founded, headed by King of Prussia as Emperor and controlled by a Parliament of two chambers. But the Assembly failed as the Prussian King could never bring himself to accept a crown as a gift of the people. The Prussian arms easily suppressed popular risings in Saxony, the Bavarian Palatinate and Baden. In May 1849, 65 members quitted the Frankfurt Assembly in a body, leaving the national cause to develop of itself. Thus, the Germans lost their chance to become united on a democratic basis.

Nevertheless on the question of German unity, King Frederick William of Prussia had some sympathy. He proposed a confederation of governments united under the hegemony of Prussia. To this, of course, Austria would not submit. Austria forced him to give it up in an agreement signed at Olmutz (November 1850) and the old German Confederation with its Diet, as established in 1815, was restored.

The Convention of, Olmutz left behind it bitter memories. Prussia had learnt the lesson that in her bid for power she must make her army formidable. It was not, however, until William I succeeded his brother, first-as Regent (1857) and then as King (1861) that the military reform was seriously undertaken. But in this project he was opposed by the Prussian Diet. In this crisis, he found a person in Otto Von Bismarck (1815-98) who could carry out the reforms against the Diet.

Bismarck's accession to power in 1862 was, therefore, a turning-point in the history of 19th century Germany. His strategic mastery and firm grasp of political reality, brought into play a new approach to the problem of German unity. His methods were new and the foundations on which he built were utterly different. Bismarck's aim was to achieve German unity without revolution. For this task, a firm grasp of the realities of power-politics was essential both in internal and foreign relations. He was well aware that not only France and Austria but Russia also had a direct interest in maintaining German disunity. Hence, there was a small prospect of establishing German unity unless the friendship or neutrality of big powers in Europe had previously been secured.

The new Prime Minister stated his point of view at once. "The great questions of our time will not be decided by speeches and majorities—that was the error of 1848—but by blood and iron". As Prussia's representative to the Diet of the German Confederation at Frankfurt he had treated Austria as the chief enemy. His policy was the unification of Germany under the auspices of Prussia. It was to entail three wars. Bismarck gained Russian friendship by supporting her against the Polish rebels in 1863. He lured Napoleon III by hinting that France might obtain compensation if Prussia were given a free hand in Germany.

(1) War with Denmark (1864)

In 1864, Bismarck came into conflict with Denmark over the duchies of Schleswig and Holstein. These duchies were peopled mainly by Germans but governed by the King of Denmark. Bismarck persuaded Austria to join with him in a war against Denmark. The combined forces were successful and by the treaty of Vienna (October 1864) Denmark gave Schleswig and Holstein to Austria and Prussia. Bismarck was keen on annexing the duchies, but he was more anxious to bring about a war with Austria in the future. He, therefore, came to a compromise in the Convention of Gastein (1865), which he said was like 'papering over the cracks' of his disagreements with Austria. Holstein was to go to Austria and Schleswig to Prussia.

(2) War with Austria

Bismarck was determined to bring about a war with Austria. Already having secured Russian friendship, he secured French neutrality by giving vague hints of compensation. He also negotiated a secret alliance with Italy (April 1866) for immediate war with Austria. As a reward Italy would get Venetia from Austria.

Bismarck complained about the Austrian government of Holstein which was stirring up trouble in Schleswig. At the same time he proposed a reform of the German Confederation in which Austria would be excluded. When Austria objected to the whole scheme, Bismarck made war. Austria was supported by South-German states. The war was of surprisingly short duration and is usually called the Seven Weeks' War. Austria was successful against Italy, but she suffered a crushing defeat at the hand of Prussia in the battle of Sadowa or Konnniggratz on 3 July 1866. By the final Treaty of Prague (August 1866) Austria was obliged to cede Venetia to Italy and Holstein to Prussia and to pay a small indemnity. Austria also agreed to the break-up of the German Confederation which was to be replaced by a new organisation, the North German Confederation under Prussian leadership. But Bismarck was careful not to make Austria bitter enemy and was anxious to be allied with her. Bismarck made no attempt to unite the whole of Germany; the South-German states were, for the present, left to themselves. 'We must be careful not to swallow more than we can digest', he said.

Franco-Prussian War

The victory of Prussia over Austria was a cruel blow to the French Emperor, Napoleon III. Public opinion in France was deeply roused by the rise of Prussia as a strong power in Central Europe. It has been said that 'it is France that was beaten at Sadowa'. Napoleon III demanded of Bismarck certain territories as compensation. But he seemed very uncertain as to what he really wanted. He demanded Mainz and the whole left bank of the Rhine. But Bismarck not only refused the proposal but he made it known to all by publishing it. The South-German states were taught to see in Napoleon a false friend. The French Emperor made a further bid for compensation by demanding Luxemburg. Bismarck was not unwilling to give up Luxemburg to France. But the King of Holland refused to sell it without the consent of the powers. The Treaty of London (May 1867) declared Luxemburg as a neutral territory under the guarantee of the Powers.

Such was the condition of France when Bismarck intended to provoke. He needed a war with France to complete the fabric of the German Empire. As Bismarck remarked afterwards; 'That A war with France would succeed that with Austria lay in the logic of history'. He found a pretext in the Spanish succession question. Spain, having a vacant throne to fill, offered it to Prince Leopold of Hohenzollern, who was related to the King of Prussia. Prince Leopold at first declined the offer. But Bismarck had seen his chance, because it would place a Hohenzollern on France's southern frontier.

Bismarck found it difficult to win over the Prussian King, William I, head of the house of Hohenzollern but he finally succeeded. He procured a renewal of the invitation and this time Prince Leopold accepted. Napoleon III was furious and sent strong protests to the Prussian and Spanish governments. Britain supported France. On 12 July 1870, Prince Leopold, under diplomatic pressure, withdrew his candidature. All seemed happily ended. But the French government decided immediately to push the matter further and sent Benedetti, the French ambassador, to King William at Ems, asking him to promise that Prince Leopold should never renew his candidature. The King courteously refused to give any such guarantee. When Benedetti asked for another interview, he replied that the incident was now closed. William then telegraphed to Bismarck the substance of the affair and authorised him to publish the message if he chose. This was Bismarck's opportunity and he used it cleverly to provoke the French to war. Without changing the actual meaning of the telegram, he published it in such a form that the Prussians thought that their ambassador had been insulted by the French King. On 19 July, France declared war. Once again Bismarck got what he wanted.

Lacking allies, France fought alone. French war machine, lacking clear leadership and ill-equipped for action, went badly. The German army, commanded as one unit by Moltke and organised with scientific precision, at once moved swiftly. The German armies won the battles of Worth (6 August) and Gravelotte (17 August), shut up Bazaine with 170,000 men in Metz and defeated MacMohan's attempt to relieve him at Sedan (1 September). On the following day Napoleon surrendered with his forces to the Germans. In Paris, a republic was proclaimed and a provisional government took over power. Paris went into a siege which lasted until the end of January 1871. On 28 January 1871 an armistice was signed and terms of peace were arranged. By the Treaty of Frankfurt (May, 1871), France surrendered Alsace and Lorraine and agreed to pay a heavy war indemnity, pending which a German army was to occupy the country. On 18 January 1871, in the Hall of Mirrors in the palace of Versailles, William I was proclaimed German Emperor. Thus, Bismarck's dream of German unification was fulfilled.

There has been considerable disagreement among historians about whether the unification of Germany was due to one coherent plan conceived in the master mind of Bismarck and then carried out with uncanny insight and clock-like precision. There is one remarkable piece of evidence which supports this view. Shortly before he came to power, Bismarck told Disraeli at a dinner in London in 1862, about his whole scheme. Disraeli, was reported to have remarked: 'What an extraordinary man Bismarck is? He meets me for the first time and he tells me all, he is going to do. He will attack Denmark in order to get possession of Schleswig-Holstein; he will put Austria out of the German Confederation; and then he will attack France—an extraordinary man.' Be that as it may, Bismarck was a brilliant opportunist, whose course of action always remained undecided and flexible until the last moment. First and foremost a Prussian nationalist as he was, he brought about the unification of Germany to subserve the Prussian interest.

Many years before 1871, the Prussian militarist, Clausewitz had said that there remained 'only one way for Germany to attain political unity, and that is by the sword; one of the states must bring all others into subjection'. The wars of 1866 and 1870 seemed to prove him right. In many respects it is true that 'Germany was a Prussian conquest won at the expense of Austria and France'. And yet this is not the whole truth. Many factors were responsible for the unification of Germany and it has been said perhaps with some justification that Germany was practically united before Bismark began to work at all. First among these was the fact the Austria was on the defensive, seeking to check Prussia's ambitions, but unwilling herself to shoulder the burden of German affairs. Secondly, the advent of the Industrial Revolution in Germany gave a great fillip to unification. The Zollverein of 1834 and the German Industrial Revolution which began after 1850 were milestones along the road to the Bismarckian Empire of 1871. They enhanced the sense of German unity and greatly favoured Bismarck's policy. The establishment of German unity was inevitable. But for Bismarck the unification of Germany might have taken a radically different course. Hostility towards Prussia and fear of Prussian hegemony had been lively in 1848. But Bismarck, aided by social and economic development overcame this hostility after 1866.

It will be of interest to compare Bismarck, the maker of modern Germany, with Cavour, the maker of modern Italy. The comparison reveals striking points of resemblance and of dissimilarity. Both sought the unification of their respective countries. Both were confronted by the same foe-Austria. In each case, superior statecraft overcame difficulties and achieved surprising success. Here the resemblance ends. The differences between Cavour and Bismarck were two-fold. In the first place, Cavour was a liberal who believed in free institutions whereas Bismarck was a reactionary who believed in force. Although Cavour employed force to expel Austria from the Peninsula, the unification of Italy was essentially a popular movement. On the other hand, the German Empire which Bismarck established rested upon the sword. In the second place, Cavour was content to merge Piedmont in Italy, while Bismarck could never agree to merge Prussia in a German national state. In a sense, Italy absorbed Piedmont, whereas Prussia absorbed Germany. Moreover, German unification posed problems for posterity as Prussia's predominance aroused resentment among the other members of the union. When Cavour died, his work was substantially complete; Bismarck left behind him problems which seriously threatened the structure which he created.

19th Century Nationalism, the Emergence of nation-states and the new blance of power in Europe.

During the first half of the 19th century, nationalism had been an ideology of the left. It had sprung into prominence during the French Revolution. The monarchs of Europe viewed it as a dangerous doctrine as it was closely associated with democratic agitation. After 1848, however, supporters of royalty began to use nationalism as a weapon against revolution. The first Napoleon, had used nationalism to establish his own power. His nephew, Napoleon III, fought the Crimean War partly to win national glory. Bismarck, succeeded in winning the support of his opponents in the Prussian Diet, by appealing to their growing national pride.

During the French Revolution, nationalists in every country began to think that their own nations were superior to other nations. The most obvious evidence of superiority was military power and thus nationalism became wedded to militarism.

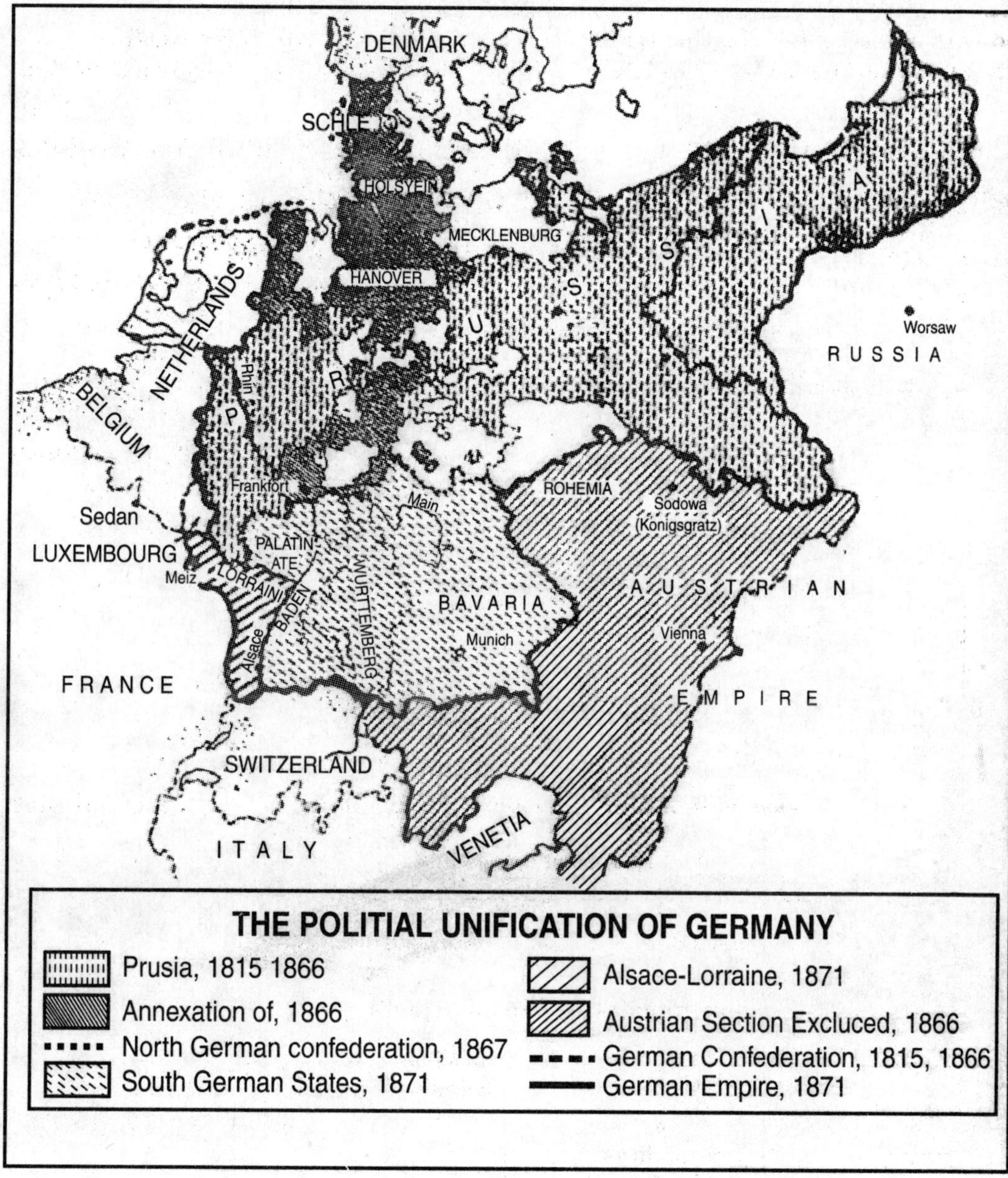

THE POLITIAL UNIFICATION OF GERMANY

In earlier times, civilization had been extolled and culture despised. Nationalism, now did the opposite. National cultures were extolled and the masses, who thought of themselves only as Frenchmen, Germans, English, or Russian, grew stronger. The passions of nationalism of ethnic minorities clashed with nationalism of the authorities. In the German Empire, conflicts emerged in the former Polish provinces, on the Danish border in Schleswig-Holstein, and in Alsace-Lorraine.

As the decades passed, nationalism-assumed a more menacing tone. It was in this sense that the term 'nationalism' entered general currency in the 19th century. Germany was to be for Germans alone, Romania for the Romanians. It was in imperial Germany, perhaps, that the ideas of 'blood and soil' took deepest root. In France, nationalism found its champion in the writing of Maurice Barres and of Charles Maurras. For them, France was for Frenchmen alone. In addition to Germany and France, it made a deep impact in Poland. In Italy, it was inherent in the activities of the irredentists, such as Gabriele D 'Annunzio, who were trying to seize Trieste and South Tyrol from Austria.

The Italian national liberation movement achieved its objective in 1871. It is known as it *Risorgimento*, 'The Resurgence' and its most effective leader was Court Camillo di Cavour (1801-1861). Mazzini created a national ideology and declared 'A nation is the universality of citizens speaking the same tongue.' The progress of the German national movement resembled that of its Italian courterpart in all essential respects. The Polish national movement had the longest history. It bred an armed rising in every generation between the partitions and the Second World War– in 1733, 1768, 1794, 1830, 1848, 1863, 1905, 1919, 1944. Within the Russian Empire, authorities were against the rising tide of nationalism. Byelorussians and Ukrainians were not permitted to possess a separate identity. Poles, until 1906, were not permitted any form of political expressions.

Balkan nationalism grew specially intense. The Ottoman Empire had always tolerated a large measure of religious and cultural autonomy, whilst stifling political aspiration. Assimilation into the ruling Muslim culture, in Bosnia, Albania and parts of Bulgaria, was low. As a result, Christian nations were waiting to emerge as soon as Ottoman power receded. Greece won its formal independence in 1832, the Romanian principalities (Wallachia and Moldavia) in 1856, Montenegro in 1860, Serbia and Bulgaria in 1878. The Albanians, the only predominantly Muslim in the region were kept waiting until 1913.

Some of the most prescient observers concluded that nationalism was no more than a phase. Speaking in 1882, Ernest Renan made the startling observation that no state of nation was eternal. Sooner or later something like a European Confederation would come into being. Metternich had once said 'For me, Europe has long held the essence of a fatherland.'

After 1871, the whole nature of the balance of power underwent a transformation. The relations of states towards one another had sharply deteriorated as a result of the cynical diplomacy of Cavour, Bismarck and Napoleon III. The idea of a general 'Concert of Europe' seemed to have been abandoned and instead there began a new era of popular hysteria in international relations.

The settlement of 1871 inaugurated a period of 43 years during which there was no war between the major powers. A new arrangement of European frontiers ensured which happened with dramatic rapidity. There now existed in Central Europe two large national states instead of the previous multitude of small non-national states. The territorial and political settlement rested on certain underlying principles. It rested primarily on the principle of nationality. The incorporation of all Italian-speaking people within the Italian Kingdom, and of Schleswig and Holstein, Alsace and Lorraine, into the new German Reich, exceplified this principle. But these rights were denied to the French inhabitants of Alsace-Lorraine and to the Danish inhabitants of Schleswig. Thus, the rights of national self-determination belonged only to those nations powerful enough to assert them.

The settlement of eastern Europe was at best only an interim arrangement. With continuing jealousy and tension between the great powers of the continent, Habsburg or Turkish disinegration, would inevitably bring furthers major wars. The disintegration of the Turkish Empire was to cause most of the great disputes until 1914. Meanwhile the overriding fact in Europe was the overwhelming superiority of Germany. The new colossus of Europe streching from the Vosges to the Vistula and from the Baltic to the Danube, became a menace to its neighbours. It included 41 million people which were fully utilised by the new Reich. The whole military forces were unified under the immediate control of Prussia.

Bismarck remained Chancellor till 1890 and applied his genius to secure the hegemony of Germany in Europe. 'He preserved and manipulated the settlement of 1871 in German interests, just as Metternich had used the settlement of 1815 in Austrian interests.' Britain, France and the Low countries despite their primacy in trade and industry, found Germany a formidable competitor in world markets. The eastern powers of Austria-Hungary, Russia and Turkey, because of their relative economic backwardness, lagged far behind German superiority in trade and commerce. "A great new dynamic generator of wealth and power had been built into the heartland of Europe; it soon made its impact felt throughout the whole continent.'

Economic Nationalism in Europe

Economic nationalism may appear as something more strictly defensive the desire of a nation to protect its economic life from foreign competition. A sense of solidarity was fostered when each nation tried to knit ties with other nations. In this manner, Industrial Revolution in a sense promoted nationalism. Improved means of communication, such as a network of railways accelerated the growth of a nation. As a complement to this development, the establishment of tariff walls led to the creation of each nation as an economic unit. Its ideal was that of national self-sufficiency. This in the long run, was one of the motives for the revival of imperialism. As a natural corollary, it was found imperative to protect home industries from foreign competition by means of tariffs. But the trend during the first half of the nineteenth century had been rather in the opposite direction. Under the influence of Adam Smith and the impelling necessity of securing food from outside, Great Britain adopted free-trade policy. Soon France under Napoleon III followed her example. Before long most of the continental nations were bound together by treaties which provided marginal duties on imports. It appeared as if Europe had been convinced of the necessity of economic interdependence. But the third quarter of the 19th century witnessed a return to economic nationalism. The rise of Germany, the competition of American wheat, and the rapid industrial development of the continent hastened the process. Bismarck, though by conviction a free trader, adopted protection in 1879 in response to the demand of the junkers. France followed suit and other nations also did the same. Only Britain still clung to free trade, but in the 90s, the conservative statesman, Joseph Chamberlain, raised the issue of tariff reform as a mild form of protection.

ESSAY TYPE QUESTIONS

1. Discuss the provisions of the Vienna Settlement. Critically examine the weakneses of the settlement.
2. What was 'Metternich System'?

3. Account for the revolution of 1820. What led the Spanish Colonies of Latin America to revolt?
4. How did Greece achieve her independence?
5. Analyse the causes of the July Revolution of 1830. What were its consequences?
6. Describe the causes and effects of the February Revolution of 1848.
7. Discuss the impact of the Revolution of 1848 on Europe.
8. Trace the rise of the Second Empire in France.
9. Trace the history of the Unification of Italy.
10. Assess the contribution of Cavour to the unification of Italy.
11. Examine Bismarck's contribution to the unification of Germany.
12. What were the chief characteristics of nineteenth century nationalism?
13. Trace the emergence of the new balance of power in Europe in the 19th century.

SHORT ANSWER TYPE QUESTIONS

14. What were the aims and objectives of the Vienna Congress?
15. Mention the basic principles that guided the makers of the Vienna Settlement.
16. What was the 'Metternich System'?
17. Write a note of the struggle of the Spanish Colonist of Latin America under the leadership of Simon Bolivar.
18. Discuss the significance of the Greek War of Independence.
19. What was the significance of the July Revolution of 1830?
20. Discuss the implications of the February Revolution of 1848 in Europe.
21. Why did 'Metternich System' collapse?
22. Analyse the stages by which Louis Napoleon became the Emperor of France.
23. Who was Mazzini? Discuss his role in the unification of Italy.
24. Who was Garibaldi? Assess his contribution to the unification of Italy.
25. Analyse critically the political condition of Germany till 1848.
26. Discuss the causes and results of the Austro-Prussian war of 1866.
27. What led to the Franco-Prussian War of 1870? What were its results?
28. How did the settlement of 1871 inaugurate a new arrangement of European politics?
29. Trace the emergence of economic nationalism in Europe in the 19th century.

OBJECTIVE-TYPE QUESTIONS

30. Who are the 'Big Four' in the Congress of Vienna?
31. Who was Metternich?
32. Who was Simon Bolivar?

33. Name the secret organisation of the Greeks.
34. Who was overthrown by the Revolution of 1830?
35. When did July Revolution in France take place?
36. Name the three socialists of France during the period 1830-48.
37. When did February Revolution take place?
38. Why and when Metternich fled from Vienna?
39. Who founded the Young Italy?
40. What was the name of the secret organisation in Italy?
41. When and between whom was the Treaty of Villafranca signed?
42. What was 'Seven Weeks' War?
43. When and between whom was the battle of Sadowa fought?
44. What Zolleverein? Why was it established?
45. Which country was compelled to cede Alsace and Lorraine to Germany in 1871?
46. When and between whom was the Treaty of Frankfurt signed?

IMPORTANT DATES

1.	June 9, 1815	:	The Vienna Settlement
2.	1815-48	:	Era of Metternich
3.	1824-30	:	Charles X, Emperor of France
4.	1830-48	:	Louis Philippe, Emperor of France
5.	1848-52	:	Second Republic of France
6.	1852-70	:	Napoleon III
7.	1831	:	Young Italy founded by Mazzini
8.	1848	:	February Revolution in France
9.	1852	:	Cavour became Prime Minister of Sardinia
10.	July 1858	:	Agreement of Cavour and Napoleon III at Plombieres
11.	July 1859	:	Armistice at Villafranca
12.	June 6, 1861	:	Death of Cavour
13.	1866	:	Austro-Prussian War
14.	1862	:	Bismarck as Prime Minister of Prussia
15.	1870-71	:	Franco-Prussian War
16.	May 1871	:	Treaty of Frankfurt

UNIT - III

From Empire to World War

Causes of War: Colonial Ambitions of the European Powers

The century between the Napoleonic wars and the First World War was for Europe, as a whole, the longest period of tranquillity ever experienced in the course of modern history. The wars for national unity in Germany and Italy, Greek War of Independence, the Crimean War, the Russo-Turkish War, the Boer War and the Russo-Japanese War were more or less restricted to few powers and did not lead into a general conflagration.

During the first three quarters of the 19th century, European powers did not show much interest in acquiring territories outside Europe. Most of the European powers were absorbed by domestic problems and friction with their immediate neighbours. But the last quarter of the 19th century witnessed an important feature in which empire-building became the accepted policy of all major powers. Economic factors played an important role in the growth of imperialist activity. The growth of European industry and the accumulation of excess capital created the necessity of finding new markets and new areas for capital investment.

It appears that the statesmen who directed the policies of the Great Powers were influenced by mutual suspicions They wanted to demonstrate their powers by increasing the overseas territory. It has been said of England by John Ruskin 'she must found colonies as fast and as far as she is able'. A similar argument had already been made in France by Leroy-Beaulieu, who stated that colonial expansion was for his country 'a matter of life and death'. The same thoughts were expressed in Germany. The basic cause of the First World War was provided by German imperialism with its *Weltpolitik* or world policy. According to a German historian the term *Weltpolitik* means that 'Germany has ceased to regard exclusively the continent of Europe in framing her policy'. The primary aim of German *Weltpolitik* was to dominate the Near and Middle East. Apart from imperialistic considerations, the exploitation of Asia Minor was advocated on economic grounds.

Anglo-German economic rivalry played a large part in bringing on the First World War. From 1898 to 1913, Germany made enormous export gains over England. For example, in this period England doubled its exports to the United States while Germany increased its own five times over. Thus, Germany by great efforts was gaining grounds and Britain was in danger of losing her economic prosperity. In a lesser degree, there were similar economic rivalries between Russia and Germany, between France and Germany and so on.

Political Alliances: Formation of the Triple Alliance and the Triple Entente

In 1872, Bismarck had formed the Three Emperor's League or Drei-Kaiserbund between the rulers of Germany, Austria-Hungary and Russia. But when in 1878 Russian interests clashed with Austria in the Balkans in consequence of the Russo-Turkish War, Russia withdrew from the League. In compensation, Bismarck in 1879 concluded with Austria-Hungary a treaty of reciprocal protection in case Russia should attack either power. In 1882, when Italy joined Germany and Austria, it came to be called Triple Alliance. Fearing that Russia might draw closer to France, Bismarck contracted Reinsurance Treaties of 1881 and 1887 with Russia and cultivated friendly relations with England. After 1890, when Germany failed to renew the treaty with Russia, the latter concluded an alliance with France in 1895. It bound both parties in the event of a German attack upon either to come to one another's assistance with a large army.

Towards the end of the 19th century, Britain had made vain attempts to form a rapprochement with Germany. In 1902, Britain's isolation was ended when she concluded an alliance with Japan. Thereafter in 1904 Britain concluded with France the *Entente Cardiale*, a cordial understanding. By this agreement, France recognised British control over Egypt while Britain promised not to oppose French claims in Morocco. Sir Edward Grey had declared as early as 1906 that this agreement would be morally as binding as a formal treaty of alliance: 'if there is war between France and Germany, it will be very difficult for us to keep out of it'. In 1907, Britain concluded a similar entente with Russia and settled their conflicting interests in Persia, Afghanistan and Tibet. Thus was born the Triple Entente between England, France and Russia. From 1907, Europe was grouped, somewhat artificially into two armed camps. Speaking of the years that preceded the Great War, Lord Oxford remarked:

> We were often conscious that we were skating on the thinnest of ice, and the peace of Europe was at the mercy of a chapter of unforeseen accidents.

Moroccan Crisis : The major powers of Europe clashed over territorial interests. Morocco, a backward country, bordering on the French empire in Africa, became the scene of international rivalry. The independence of Morocco had been guaranteed by an international congress at Madrid in 1880. But the French were anxious to gain control of Morocco. French control of Morocco would round off her large African empire stretching from Tunisia, Algeria, then to Morocco and through the Saharan desert hinterland to French West Africa. The French Foreign Minister Delcasse had obtained the assent of Italy in 1900 and Great Britain in 1904; and he had just reached an agreement with Spain giving the later a protectorate over the part not appropriated by France.

Germany, anxious to weaken the Entente between France and Britain, decided to exploit the Moroccan question for this purpose. Taking advantage of Russian's defeat by the Japanese when the former could give no support to France, the Kaiser (William II) landed at Tangier in Morocco at the end of March 1905. He dramatically declared the Sultan's independence in whose lands all foreign powers were to enjoy equal rights. Since Germany had no direct interest in Morocco, this was a provocative act. The French appeared to give way. The Germans demanded the removal of Delcasse, the French Foreign Minister and the architect of Entente. In June 1905, he was forced to resign. France also agreed to Germany's demand for an international conference to settle Morocco question. The conference met at Algeciras in Spain in January 1906. While France's special position in Morocco was recognised by the majority of powers, the French annexation of Morocco was forbidden and the 'open door' theoretically established.

The settlement of 1906 did not solve the Moroccan crisis. A second crisis arose in 1908 when three German deserters from the French Foreign Legion were sheltered by the German consul at Casablanca. The incident ended in arbitration at the Hague Tribunal which was unfavourable to Germany (November 1908). In February 1909, France and Germany signed a Declaration known as the 'Morocco Pact'. This recognised France's special political influence in Morocco, while giving to Germany equal economic opportunities.

Agadir Crisis : But the Franco-German agreement was not observed. The French discriminated against German trade and the Germans protested against the tightening of French control. The domestic situation of Morocco was also not stable. The Sultan was overthrown in 1908 and his brother usurped the throne. Though the new Sultan was recognised by the powers, he was not obeyed by many of his subjects. He appealed to France for aid. In April 1911 France sent troops to Fez, the Moroccan capital, to restore order. This action annoyed Germany. The Foreign Minister Alfred Yon Kiderlen Wachter, without warning, despatched the German gunboat Panther to the Moroccan port of Agadir in July 1911. Kiderlen's action was intended to be a 'bluff'. He demanded from France a large slice of the French Congo in return for her abandoning political designs in Morocco.

This menacing action puzzled Europe. To the western powers, German claim seemed as a mere pretext for military action. On July 21, 1911, Grey, the British Foreign Secretary, categorically told the German ambassador that Britain thought Germany's demands for the Congo excessive. The British Chancellor of the Exchequer, Lloyd George, in a public speech threatened to take action if Britain was disregarded in a matter affecting its interests. Encouraged by the British attitude, the French refused to make any concession. In the end, however, tension was relaxed when an accord was reached in the second week of October. Finally an agreement was signed on November 4, 1911. France was allowed to establish her protectorate over Morocco on condition that the 'open door' was maintained. In compensation Germany obtained two large strips of French Congolese territory. The Agadir crisis in 1911 served to quicken anti-German feeling in France and helped to consolidate the friendship between France and Britain. On the other hand it accentuated Anglo-German rivalry and inflamed public opinion in Germany in the cause of national prestige.

The Balkan Crisis : In the Balkans, the national aspirations of new-born states threatened the Ottoman rule in Europe. A Panslav movement began in the Balkans under Serbia. This was supported by Russia who regarded Serbia as a sort of outpost of the Balkans calculated to strengthen her supremacy in the Near East. But Russian claims in the Balkans were contested by Austria. In 1908, she annexed the provinces of Bosnia and Herzegovina which greatly enraged Serbia. This also proved a serious setback to Russia's prestige. Though Russia had been humiliated, she began in 1909 the reconstruction of her armed forces on a large scale. In 1912, a league was formed between Greece, Serbia, Montenegro and Bulgaria. Its object was to prevent any further increase in the threatening Austo-German control of the peninsula. The two great Powers-Austria and Russia-most interested in the Balkans-intervened. An international conference which met at London in May 1913 restored peace by creating an independent Albania and compensating Serbia with territory in the interior. 'The first round is won', the Serbian Premier remarked, 'now we must prepare for the second, against Austria'. The creation of an independent Albania cut off Serbia from the sea. During the Second Balkan war, Austria planned to launch an attack upon Serbia. But she was held back by Germany and Italy. The Austro-Serbian feud was greatly aggravated. The influence of Russia in the Balkans had changed the balance of power. After the Second Balkan War, Russia was preparing further alternations in her favour. Germany could not passively watch the establishment of absolute Russian hegemony in the Balkans. The German Emperor William II recorded his sentiment in February 1914. 'Russo-Prussian relations are dead once and for all! We have become enemies'.

The Serajevo Murder and the Outbreak of the First World War

From 1911, Germany was drifting towards war. In February 1912, Lord Haldane, British Minister for War, arrived in Germany to discuss a basis for an Anglo-German alliance. But the negotiations broke down, partly on the naval question and partly because Britain would give no pledge of neutrality towards Germany in case the latter should be engaged in war with any other power. The Second Balkan War provoked new outbursts of war-like sentiments in Germany. Moltke was pressing more urgently than ever before for an early war. The Austrian Chief of Staff, Baron Conrad also believed that 'any delay meant a lessening of our chances; we could not compete with Russia in masses'.

The spark which set off the First World War was the assassination of the Austrian heir-apparent Archduke Francis Ferdinand and his wife at the Bosnian town of Serajevo on June 28, 1914. The murder was the act of a fanatic whose connection with the Serbian Government could not be proved. But Berchtold, the Austro-Hungarian Foreign Minister, was determined to force war on Serbia. On July 5, 1914, he appealed to William II for assistance with the words: 'Serbia must be eliminated as a political factor in the Balkan's... friendly settlements no longer to be thought of.' Having secured the support of Germany, Austria, presented on July 23 a 48-hour ultimatum on Serbia. On the same day, Russia gave a solemn assurance to Serbia that 'she (Russia) would in no circumstances permit Austrian aggression against Serbia'. Serbia accepted a number of the terms and expressed her willingness to refer the whole matter to the Hague Tribunal or to a conference of the powers. Austria declared this unsatisfactory and on July 28 declared war.

The determined attitude of Russia filled Germany with consternation. Moreover, the news on July 29 that Germany, could not count on British neutrality if it attacked France shocked the German chancellor, Bethmann. He, therefore, pressed Austria to negotiate with Russia to avert a calamity. But it was too late. On July 30, Russia ordered general mobilisation. On the next day, Germany began to mobilise. With this step effective diplomacy ceased. 'Once the German armies mobilised, war had to be brought on, not averted'.[1] On July 31, Germany presented Russia with a 12-hour ultimatum demanding immediate demobilisation. Russia did not comply and Germany declared war on August. As France was Russia's ally, Germany presented an 18-hour ultimatum to France on July 31 demanding that she should maintain her neutrality. When France refused to promise neutrality, German declared war on France (August 3).

Britain was on the whole sympathetic to France. But the cabinet was divided and the public opinion was also uncertain. On August 2, the British Government gave assurance of protection to French coasts in the event of German attack. However, it was not France but Belgium which brought Britain into the war. On August 2, Germany occupied Luxem-burg and presented an ultimatum to Belgium requiring free passage of German troops through Belgium to invade France. King Albert refused and appealed to Britain who along with other powers had guaranteed Belgium neutrality in 1839. As the German army had actually entered Belgium, the issue had already been decided. On August 4, England sent an ultimatum to Germany demanding to respect Belgium neutrality. When the

[1] Taylor A.J.P.: *Europe: Grandeur and Decline,* p. 188.

ultimatum was ignored, England declared war against Germany on August 4. The German Chancellor Bethmann-Hollweg admitted in the Reichstag: 'Gentlemen, this is a breach of international law'. 'The lamps are going out all over Europe', said Sir Edward Grey, the British Foreign Secretary, 'we shall not see them lit again in out own life time'.

Soon afterwards Montenegro joined Serbia against Austria-Hungary. On August 23, Japan declared war against Germany. Turkey hoping to regain its lost territories, signed a secret treaty of alliance with Germany (August 1,1914). On May 30, 1915, Italy entered the war against Germany. In April 1917, America declared war against Germany. In the following months, a number of Latin American countries, together with Siam, Liberia and China took the lead of the United States. Altogether, before the guns fell silent, more than 60 nations were actively or passively involved in the war.

It is difficult to apportion the blame for the First World War to various sovereigns, diplomats and chiefs of staff. 'The war was the child of the European anarchy, of the outworn system of sovereign states. The old world had degenerated into a powder-magazine, in which the dropping of a lighted match was almost certain to produce a gigantic conflagration'. It is a mistake to attribute war to any of the Governments which, in the words of Lloyd George, stumbled into war. The catastrophe could have been prevented, in the words or Lloyd George, 'had there been a Bismarck in Germany, a Palmerston or a Disraeli in Britain, a Roosevelt in America, or a Clemenceau in authority in Paris but there was no one of that quality visible on the bridge in any great State'.[2]

Responsibility of Germany for World War I

The First World War was the unavoidable outcome of the basic instability of two states, Austria-Hungary and the Turkish Empire. It was also the unavoidable outcome of the two armed camp into which Europe was divided since 1907. The political situation was full of menacing possibilities. There were pilling up of armaments by land and sea, and Germany's naval ambitions, which deeply affected British sentiments; there was the French desire for the recovery of Alsace-Lorraine; there was the periodical trouble, of embarrassing incident like that of Morocco; there were continuous clash of interests of Austria and Russia in the Balkans, the restlessness of the Balkans themselves and the cloud of uncertainty hung over the future of Turkey. 'There were chauvinists of all nations ready to light the fuel that was heaped up.' Colonel House, the confidential adviser of the American President, Woodrow Wilson, who was on a peace mission to Europe in May 1914, found the atmosphere charged with electricity ready to ignite at any time.

The German military plans played a vital part. The German generals wanted a decisive victory for countering the 'encirclement'. Schlieffen, who died in 1913 had made it clear that any war in Europe must be a general war; it could not be localised; and he also believed that, once Germany began to mobilise, war was inevitable. The German diplomats had been told for years that only the Schlieffen plan could save Germany. 'In this sense, a dead man had the deepest responsibility of all for the European War.' In 1914, German security on the continent was at stake. She was divided from France by Alsace-Lorraine, divided from Britain by the building of her Baltic Fleet, divided from Russia by her Turkish policy. Schlieffen plan assumed that the war on two fronts, the French and

[2] Karl Dietrich: War Guilt 1914 Reconsidered in the *Origins of the First World War* (Edited by H.W. Koch), p. 369.

the Russian, could be faced and could be won, after 1909, by concentrating on the West, while Austria- Hungary held Russia. War would give Germany ascendancy on the continent and strengthen her security.

Britain went to war because her survival depended on the survival of France. 'That Britain went to war only because Germany violated the neutrality of Belgium is untrue. That without the violation of Belgium neutrality Grey would have been unable to carry Parliament into war may be true. Britain went to war because her security would be destroyed if France was defeated'? The war of 1914 could not have been averted. The Great Powers could have avoided war only by agreeing that Germany should become the dominant power of the Continent. None of these Powers decided on war. ''The three men who made the decisions—even if they too were the victims of circumstances —were Berchtold, Bethmann Hollwegg and dead man Schlieffen.[3]

Reasons for the victory of the Allied Power

At the outset the advantage lay with the central powers. Next to Russia, Germany possessed the large army which was well equipped. The German guns were famous for their precision or length of range. Though the small British army was the best trained, it was the German host which possessed most coordination and could operate as a great machine. For a short term war, the army of the Central Powers was in a advantageous position. But for a prolonged war, the greater material resources and man power of the Allies, were decisive. For Germany, the loss of her sea-borne trade dealt a shattering blow as she could not replenish her resources. The fact is irrefutable that superior sea power lay with the Allies.

Germany's plans of coordination were practically unquestioned. With regard to the fighting qualities of the troops, the German soldier had hardly the initiative of the French. The French soldier was exceptionally daring on the offensive and there was a fire camaraderie between officers and men. Series of defeat enervated the German while the fortitude of the Allies merited unstained praise. In Austria-Hungary, some of the Slavic nationalities were decidedly lukewarm. At the beginning of the war both sides were buoyed up with what they regarded as a struggle for existence. Just as the Germans believed that they were fighting in self-defense against Russian barbarism and British greed, so the allies were convinced of Germany's ambition to dominate the world. The thesis of enemy's guilt was deliberately fostered by the governments themselves from the desire to inflame a nation's fighting spirit.

Despite the collapse of Russia, the submission of Rumania, the Italian disaster and the French retreat to Marne, the position of the Central Powers had not been improved. The German submarine warfare proved to be ineffectual. Allied resistance received an impetus when in November 1917 a Supreme Allied War Council was created to coordinate the military efforts of Britain, France, Italy and the United States. The popular morale of the allied countries was heightened by the idealistic utterances of Woodrow Wilson, the American President. In his famous Fourteen points laid before the Congress on January 8, 1918, President Wilson emphasised the principles that should guide a peace settlement, with a promise to grant the peoples of Austria-Hungary an autonomous status.

By the end of 1917, Germany had became convinced that war with the Allies was not an easy affair. British blockade was sapping the resources of German economy. There were murmurs of disaffection among the German people and in July 1917 a resolution was passed in the Reichstag inviting Government to consider peace by negotiation.

---

[3] Taylor A.J.P. : *Europe, grandeur and decline*, p. 189.

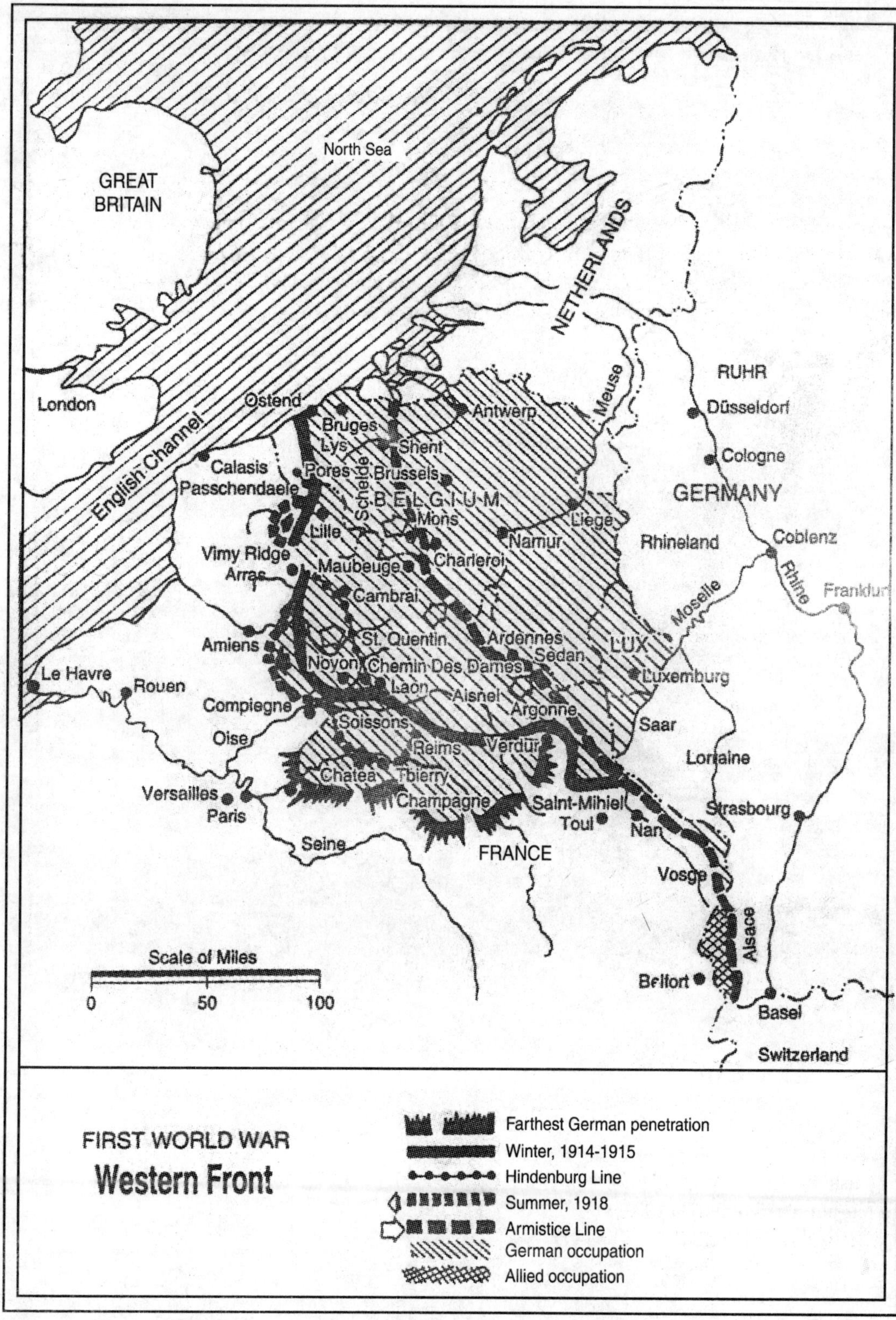
North Sea
GREAT BRITAIN
NETHERLANDS
London
English Channel
Ostend
Bruges
Lys
Antwerp
Ghent
Calasis
Pores
Brussels
Passchendaele
Scheide
BELGIUM
Mons
Lille
Liege
Namur
Vimy Ridge
Arras
Maubeuge
Charleroi
Cambrai
Meuse
RUHR
Düsseldorf
Cologne
GERMANY
Rhineland
Coblenz
Rhine
Frankfurt
Moselle
Amiens
St. Quentin
Ardennes
Sedan
LUX
Le Havre
Rouen
Noyon
Chemin Des Dames
Laon
Aisne
Luxemburg
Compiegne
Argonne
Soissons
Saar
Oise
Reims
Verdun
Lorraine
Chatea Tbierry
Versailles
Paris
Champagne
Saint-Mihiel
Toul
Nan
Strasbourg
Seine
FRANCE
Vosge
Alsace
Scale of Miles
0
50
100
Belfort
Basel
Switzerland
FIRST WORLD WAR
Western Front
Farthest German penetration
Winter, 1914-1915
Hindenburg Line
Summer, 1918
Armistice Line
German occupation
Allied occupation

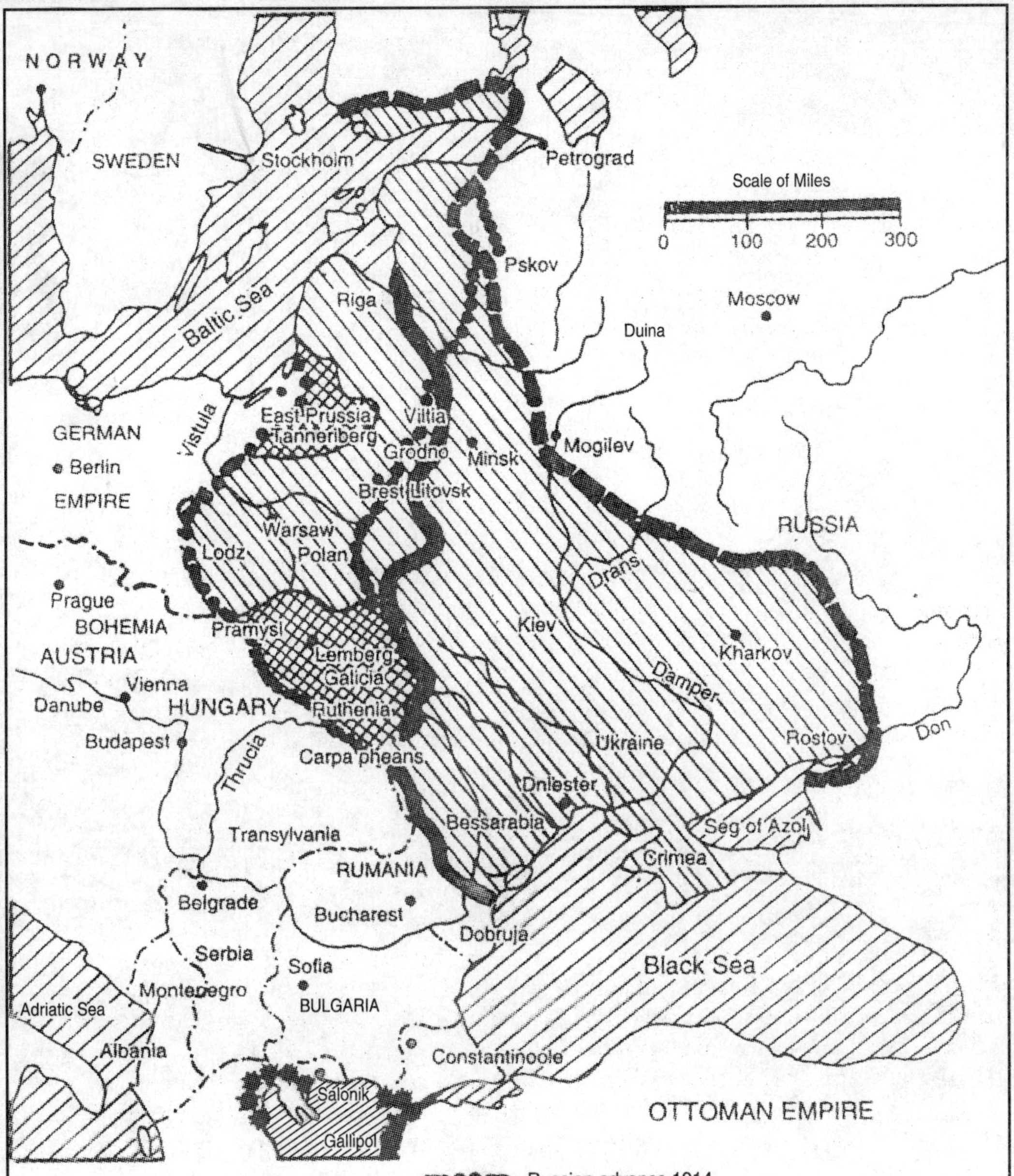

FIRST WORLD WAR
Eastern Front

The Versailles Settlement of 1919

As early as January 1918, President Wilson of the United States of America had set forth the 'Fourteen Points' as the Allied war- aims. These points emphasised the need for open diplomacy, the freedom of the seas, the removal of economic barriers, the reduction of armaments. Invaded territories in Russia, Belgium, France, Italy and the Balkan States were to be vacated and restored. Self-determination was to be granted to the peoples of Austria-Hungary and of the Ottoman Empire. Poland was to be constituted as an independent state. Finally, a League of Nations was to be created to protect the political independence and territorial integrity of all states, large and small.

A peace conference met at Paris in January 1919. In all, 32 states were represented. Two representatives from each of the big five—the United States, Britain, France, Italy and Japan formed a Council of Ten who controlled the conduct of the conference. But in effect the conference was dominated by three men-Clemenceau of France, Lloyd George of England and Woodrow Wilson of America. After four months of incessant labour, the draft of a peace treaty with Germany was adopted on May 7, 1919. German plenipotentiaries were given three weeks' time to present observations upon the draft terms. In several German memoranda, the main arguments were that 'the exactions of this treaty are more than the German people can bear', and that some of the terms were in flagrant violations of Wilson's Fourteen Points. Lloyd George took initiative in obtaining minor modifications of the draft treaty which tried to reduce harshness on Germany. On June 16, 1919 the Allies gave Germany a weeks' time to signify her acceptance of the proposed treaty. On June 23, 1919 at Versailles, near Paris, the German plenipotentiaries signed the great treaty of 440 articles.

The territorial settlement contained few surprises for the Germans. In the west, Germany ceded Alsace-Lorraine to France, the towns of Eupen and Malmedy to Belgium. To Poland, Germany surrendered her Polish districts-Posen, most of West Prussia (Polish Corridor), and a part of Upper Silesia. In order that Poland might have a seaport, the historic German port of Danzig was made a free international city. Germany agreed to the holding of plebiscites to determine the fate of East Prussia, Upper Silesia and Schleswig. East Prussia voted to remain with Germany. Upper Silesia was arbitrarily divided between Germany and Poland, and North Schleswig voted for union with Denmark while Southern Schleswig opted for Germany. The valuable coal region of the Saar was to be held by France for fifteen years. At the end of the period a plebiscite was to decide whether the inhabitants wished to belong to France or to Germany. The plebiscite, held in 1935, decided in favour of Germany.

In addition to territorial cessions in Europe, Germany surrendered all her colonial possessions. These regions were given the status of 'mandatories' and were distributed among the Allies. Britain was given a mandatory over German East Africa, which was renamed Tanganyika territory; the Union of South Africa, over German South-West Africa (Namibia); New Zealand, over the German Samoan Islands; Japan, over the northern Pacific Islands. Togo and Cameroon were divided between Britain and France. The League of Nations created a Permanent Mandates Commission to receive periodic reports on the administration of these mandated territories.

Germany recognised the independence of Belgium, Poland, Czechoslovakia and Austria, the latter being separated from Hungary. The two independent states—Poland and Czechoslovakia—promptly allied themselves with France. Thus, the creation of states in her flanks was intended to render Germany less dangerous in future.

The Treaty of Versailles provided for the disarmament of Germany. Conscription was abolished. German army was limited to 1,00,000 men; its Navy was restricted to six small warships and a number of smaller vessels. Construction of military planes, tanks, heavy artillery and submarines, was forbidden. The disarmament was to be supervised by inter-allied commissions of control. Germany was to have no fortifications or troops on the left bank of the Rhine. Germany demolished the fortifications of Heligoland and opened the Kiel Canal to all nations. The Allies expressed the fond hope that German disarmament would be followed by general disarmament.

The treaty also provided for the trial of the German' Emperor who had taken refuge in Holland. Article 228 made provision for trial of German war criminals before Allied military tribunals: By special dause—the 'warguilt'clauses—Germany was compelled to acknowledge the responsibility for bringing on the war and to promise reparations for all damages done to the civilian population. The total figure for reparation was not laid down in the treaty as it was apprehended by Lloyd George that 'if figures were given now, they would frighten rather than assure the Germans'. A Reparation Commission was formed with powers to determine Germany's capacity to pay.

Criticism of the Treaty

The Treaty of Versailles was a dictated peace of victor powers on a vanquished nation. It was also not based on principles of equity and justice. Truly did Wilson observe: 'the real case was that justice has shown itself overwhelmingly against Germany'.

The most serious defect of the settlement was that the principle of self-determination was not adhered to in the case of Germans. The creation of an independent Poland and the cession to Poland of a large slice ,of Silesia, resulted in a geographically divided Germany. People in Germany agreed to the cession of Alsace and Lorraine to France, but they could not reconcile to the reshaping of the German-Polish frontier. Germany was not allowed the benefit of self-determination in the case of Sudetenland which was included in Czechoslovakia. German Austria was not allowed to become a part of the German Republic.

The reparation terms were the most unwise penalties inflicted upon Germany. Economically Germany was crippled when she was deprived of large territories and her rich mineral resources. Lloyd George remarked later 'was it sensible to treat her (Germany) as a cow from which to extract milk and beef at the same time'? J.M. Keynes, the noted economist, was the most vocal critic of the reparation question. He demonstrated that Germany had little capacity to pay. Winston Churchill described the reparation clauses as 'malignant and silly to an extent that made them obviously futile'.

The Allies tried to provide security to Europe by reducing not only German armament, but also by carrying out a general disarmament programme. But the victors showed little inclination to implement the policy. While Germany's military strength was almost reduced to nullity, England continued to maintain a powerful navy. France kept a large army poised along the Rhine and Poland raised an army more than twice as large as that of Germany. From the beginning Germany was determined to evade the disarmament clause cleverly and she found ample opportunity to do so through the instrumentality of General Von Seeckt, who became the chief of the German army.

The settlement created a power vacuum in Europe. Germany was greatly weakened, politically and economically, but still possessed considerable potential strength. Russia became a Communist State and found certain parts of the settlement anything but satisfactory. Another weakness of the treaty was that on March 19, 1920, it failed to secure the ratification of the American Senate. Only a greatly weakened France, with the half-hearted support of Britain, was left to counteract Germany's potential strength. Balfour had earlier prophesied that were Poland reconstituted 'France would be at the mercy of Germany in the next war, for the reason, that Russia could not come to her aid without violating the neutrality of Poland.'

The Versailles Treaty gave little satisfaction to Italy. It came out of the war with colossal new debts. Italy's territorial gains did not measure up her expectations. She was particularly disturbed by the appearances of a new Yugoslav State in 1918. The minor concession given to Italy in East Africa and Libya failed to satisfy her territorial aspirations. Moreover, Italians had been disappointed in not acquiring Fiume, a Dalmatian port. It was not until 1924 when most of Fiume was secured by Italy. The Italian Prime Minister gave vent to his feeling on May 25, 1919:

> I cannot look forward without grave apprehensions to the future of Continental Europe; the German longing for revenge must be considered in conjunction with the Russian position. We can thus see even now that the settlement to be arrived at will lack the assent of more than half the population of the European continent. If we detach from the block on which the new European system will have to rely for support forty million Italians, and force them into the ranks of the malcontents, do you think that the new order will rest on a firm basis?

The Treaty of Versailles rested on fragile foundations. After the peace settlement, both Britain and France moved along divergent paths. While the British advocated a soft policy towards Germany after 1920, the French, anxious to keep Germany weak, advocated another. Wilson who had sought to make the Treaty of Versailles, the foundation of international democracy, and had expected a radical change in the German attitude, found instead people burning with revenge. Thus "the statesman had not been equal to the grandeur of events. They had made a peace which was no peace. Human nature, it was widely felt, had failed. Europe had not been made safe for democracy. The bright exhilaration of victory was soon blotted out by the fog of disillusion, resentment and despair"[4].

League of Nations

The scheme for a League of Nations for the preservation of peace was first mooted by President Woodrow Wilson in his Fourteen Points. The scheme was elaborated by Lord Robert Cecil and General Smuts of England and Hurst and Miller, legal advisers of British and American legations respectively. After discussions at the Paris Peace Conference (1919) the Covenant of the League of Nations was adopted on 28 April by the Congress as a whole. Wilson made the Covenant an integral part of the Treaty of Versailles.

The League of Nations was not a government of any kind but an association of nations to promote international co-operation and to achieve international peace and security. Members of the League bound themselves to respect and preserve the territory of one another against aggression. Every members state undertook not to go to wa: without first offering the League the chance for the settlement of the dispute and not to declare war until three months had elapsed after the League had pronounced the verdict. In the event of any member resorting to war in violation of its obligation under the Covenant, the League was to recommend military measures (sanction) against the offending party. All treaties contrary to the League were to be abrogated. The League was to recommend the reduction of armaments, to administer Danzig and the Saar and to supervise mandated colonies.

---

[4] Fisher H.a.L.: *A History of Europe,* p. 1169

The League had three principal organs: The Assembly, the Council and the Secretariat. In addition to these there was a World Court, called the Permanent Court of International Justice empowered to settle disputes which might be referred to it. Similarly, there was an International Labour Organisation designed to further interests of labour all over the world.

The Assembly was a general body in which every nation had three members but had only one vote. The Assembly was to meet once every year in September. It discussed various matters affecting the peace. It controlled the budget, admitted new members to the League, selected non-permanent members to the Council and in conjunction with the Council elected judges to the International Court. The Council was a small body which was to meet thrice in a year. It was made up of four permanent and eleven non-permanent members, the latter being elected from time to time by the smaller states. The Council was charged with the important task of mediating in international disputes as well as to approve sanctions against an offending state. It nominated the Secretary-General, carried out the recommendations of the Assembly and prepared plans for disarmament.

The Secretariat comprised the administrative machinery of the League. The Secretary-General was appointed by the Council though the formal approval of the Assembly was necessary. The Secretariat was divided into different sections each of them being headed by a director.

At the time of its establishment in 1920 the League had forty one member which rose to fifty in 1924. It was ironical that the United States, whose President had sponsored the organisation, did not become a member. Germany was not admitted until 1926, nor the Soviet Union until 1934. By 1935 there were 62 members: 28 in Europe, 21 in America, 8 in Asia, 3 in Africa and 2 in Australia. Japan and Germany later on withdrew from the League. Soviet Union was expelled from the League in 1939, when the League was already in collapse. The outbreak of the Second World War brought its formal existence to a close.

Achievements of the League of Nations

Despite its weakness, the League was able to solve some minor disputes. It settled disputes between Finland and Sweden over the Aaland islands (1920); between Poland and Germany over their boundary in Upper Silesia (1921); between Greece and Italy over the island of Corfu (1923); between Greece and Bulgaria over border incidents (1925); between Peru and Columbia over a border province (1933).

The League performed immensely important services regarding nationalist minorities and mandated territories. Thus Germany's former colonies lost by the Treaty of Versailles and Turkey's former dependencies were placed under separate mandates controlled by the League. It supervised the repatriation of 400,000 prisoners of war. It successfully administered Danzig and the Saar and conducted plebiscites impartially. A number of technical organisations dealt with world problems of health, narcotics, white-slave traffic, communications and trans-port. One of its greatest services was to rescue Austria from economic ruin. It rendered useful service with such problems as refugees and leprosy. It also promoted cultural cooperation among the nations by bringing together scholars and scientists from all parts of the world. The International Labour Office worked efficiently to improve the general position of labour. The Court of International Justice successfully arbitrated a number of disputes.

The League of Nations gave greater weight to the small powers whose representatives provided many of its most impressive figures like Benes of Czechoslovakia and others. The League brought into focus the new Irish Free State. Sweden and Norway provided the great personalities of Branting and Nansen, the latter of whom was for many years the League of Nations High Commissioner for Refugees. Thus, the League of Nations was able to fulfil the aspirations of General Smuts. In a famous pamphlet, *The Leagues of Nations, A Practical Suggestion*, Smuts urged that the League should be 'part and parcel of the common international life of states... an ever visible, living, working organ of the polity of civilisation.' Finally, 'in its purposes and principles, its institutions and its methods, the United Nations bears at every point the mark of the experiences of the League. In judgements upon the records of the League and all that it did, this truth must always be borne in mind.'

Failure of the League of Nations

In spite of its early promise, the League failed to fulfill the expectations of its most enthusiastic supporters. The rules of equality and unanimity gave even the smallest state of power of veto which prevented effective action in any emergency. The League also lacked the legal power to enforce peace. Members were free to ignore if they wished the recommendations of the Council. The absence of three major powers—United States, Russia and Germany—undermined the effectiveness of the League as an international organisation. In addition, the League appeared to be an organisation of those who were victorious in the First World War.

In the first years of the League's operation, the French Government sponsored two schemes for strengthening the League. The first was the Draft Treaty of Mutual Assistance of 1923. It proposed that once the Council had declared that a member state was the object of aggression, all other members would be obliged to come to its assistance. The second was the Geneva Protocol of 1924 which provided that all disputes of a legal character should be submitted to the Permanent Court of International Justice, whose decision would be binding. Both failed as a result of opposition of the British Government and the Dominions.

The League failed to curb the aggression and restlessness of the Great Powers. In 1931, Japan invaded Machuria and set up a puppet state known as *Manchukuo*. This was an open challenge to the League. A Commission was appointed under the auspices of the League which recommended that Manchuria would be autonomous under China. But Japan ignored this recommendation and in 1933 withdrew from the League. The question of sanctions to compel Japan to respect' the wishes of the League was never raised. The League had been successfully defied.

In 1935, Italy under Mussolini invaded and occupied Abyssinia. At once 50 nations assembled in the League, named Italy as an aggressor and put into force limited economic sanctions against her. But this limited policy of sanctions operated slowly on Italy as it did not include the prohibition of oil. In a few months Italy had crushed Abyssinia and defied fifty nations. The League also demonstrated its weakness by its failure to prevent Germany from occupying the demilitarised zone of Rhineland in 1936.

The Spanish Civil War (1936-39) was another instance of the incapacity of the League to take effective action in the interest of peace. The League failed to prevent the Spanish conflict from developing into a general European War. In March 1938 Germany occupied and annexed Austria without the League doing anything to deter her. In 1939-40 the League failed to protect Finland from Russia, although the latter was expelled from the League. During these years, there was a general feeling that some revision of articles of the Covenant ought to be undertaken. "But the fundamental question at issue was whether the League should still be armed with some sort of coercive measures ... or whether it should henceforth be merely machinery for facilitating consultation and cooperation."[5]

In respect of disarmament, the League in 1925 created a special Commission to study the problem. The Commission soon found that while nations were quite ready to agree to sacrifices by their neighbours, each country was reluctant to make sacrifices in the interests of national security. When in 1932, after several years of preparatory work, a general conference was called at Geneva in February 1932, it revealed total disagreement. President Hoover proposed in vain a cut of one third in the armies of all countries. The British Prime Minister, Macdonald, urged in vain a standard army of 200,000 men for each of the major powers. In October 1933, Germany, now dominated by Adolf Hitler, withdrew from the conference, resigned from the League and proclaimed her intention of arming.

Thus in the political sphere the League failed in its main purpose. The fundamental weakness of the League was to be found in the unwillingness of nations to subordinate their own interests to the peace of the world. 'What was everybody's business in the end proved to be nobody's business. Each one looked to the other to take the lead, and the aggressors got away with it.' The League's founders overlooked the forces of nationalism. While they had the power, Italy, Japan and Germany refused to be bound by the limitations imposed on them by the Covenant of the League. Britain and France were the only major Powers left to support the weak fabric of the League and even they were the hesitant supporters of the League. Cecil, one of the British founders of the League, wrote: 'Influential officials in the Foreign Office did not conceal their suspicion of the League. The League was officially tolerated. It was never liked.' As a matter of fact the League' existed to facilitate and to encourage co-operation among states. It could not make them co-operate if they did not want to'.

Locarno Treaty

Austen Chemberlain of Britain suggested that the covenant of the League of Nations might be supplemented by special arrangements 'Knitting together the nations most immediately concerned, and whose difference might lead to a renewal of strife, by means of treaties framed with the sole object of maintaining, as between themselves, an unbroken peace."

Meanwhile during 1922-23, Berlin had several times suggested to Paris the negotiation of frontier guarantees, anti-war pledges and arbitration projects. Each time France had been lukewarm to the proposals. Despite these setbacks, Germany, through Foreign Minister, Gustav Stresemann, in February 1925, once more broached the subject. In October 1925, the delegates from Germany, France, Britain, Italy, Belgium, Poland, and Czechoslovakia assembled at the Swiss lakeside town of Locarno. On October 15, 1925 the conference was brought to a happy conclusion by the signing of a complex set of documents constituting the Locarno pact.

(*i*) A treaty of mutual guarantee of the Franco-German and Belgo-German frontiers between Germany, Belgium, Britain and Italy.

(*ii*) Arbitration treaties between Germany and Belgium and between Germany and France.

(*iii*) Arbitration treaties between Germany and Poland and Germany and Czechoslovakia.

(*iv*) A Franco-Polish and Franco-Czechoslovak treaty for mutual assistance in case of aggression by Germany.

[5] *The New Cambridge Modern History,* Vol. XII, (1968), p. 260.

Locarno was widely hailed as a precursor of a new era in world history. Austen Chamberlain described it with justifiable pride as 'the real dividing line between the years of war and the years of peace.' It struck for the first time a fair and impartial balance between France and German needs. It completed the process by which Germany was brought to the League of Nations in 1926 which increased new prestige and authority to that organisation. The sense of improved security which Locarno implanted in the minds of Frenchmen and German was important. The fear of British intervention had the effect of restraining the political aggressors of both sides. Locarno also opened a prospect for a reconciliation between France and Germany, whose age-long hostility had endangered the peace of Europe. For the first time since the war, Germany had entered into treaty relations with the former enemies; she had accepted the loss of Alsace-Lorraine as final.

Dawes Plan

The payment of reparation by Germany after the First World War created a serious international problem. A proposal was adopted for the appointment of an international commission of experts to study the whole problem of German reparation. On November 30, 1923 the French Government agreed to participate and the Reparation Commission appointed a Committee, consisting of two representatives each from the United states, Britain, France, Italy and Belgium to study various facts of Germany's financial problems. The committee, presided over by the American General, Charles G. Dawes, met in Paris in January 1924 and presented its report on April 9.

Emphasising Germany's need for the resources of her whole territory, the report pointed out the two requisities of a stabilished currency and a balanced budget. The Dawes Committee recommended the creation of a new currency Rentenmark at the same parity, the Reichsmark, which would be controlled by a Bank of issue independent of the German government. Germany was to pay amounts rising in five years from 1000 million gold marks of £50 million to 2,500 million gold marks (£125), to be raised partly in the German budget, and partly from state railway bonds and industrial debentures. Payments were to be made in German currency, and that the responsibility for the transfer of these sums into foreign currencies should rest with the Allied Governments. There was to be an 'Agent for Reparation Payments' in charge of the whole plan. Finally Ruhr should be evacuated. For the double purpose of creating a gold reserve requirements of the new bank and of helping her to pay reparations in 1924-25, Germany should receive a foreign loan of 800 million gold marks.

On August 16, 1924, necessary agreements for carrying out the Dawes Plan were signed. On September 1, 1924 the plan became effective. Evacuation of the Ruhr began at once. Under the supervision of Agent General Seymour Parker Gilbert, a United States financier, the plan worked well. German business picked up and reparation payments were promptly made. Above all, the Dawes Plan eased diplomatic tension between the Allies and Germany, and between British and France. But the Dawes Plan had serious flaws. It provided for annual payments, but it failed to prescribe their duration or to fix the total amount of Germany's indebtedness. Worse still, the Dawes Plan set up the dangerous precedent of depending on foreign loans. German borrowing increased by leaps and bounds and the influx of capital was astonishing. "Few people had the insight to realise that Germany was paying her debts out of American money, and that her solvency depended on the continued popularity of German loans in Wall Street."

Young Plan

The Dawes Plan was not a final settlement of the reparation problem. It was 'framed to facilitate a final comprehensive agreement as to all the problems of reparation and connected questions.' One of these connected questions was the occupation of the Rhineland. In September 1928, an agreement was reached among the Allied Powers in regard to the early evacuation of the Rhineland and for the appointment of a committee of financial experts to work out a final settlement of the Reparation problem.

The committee of financial experts met in Paris in February 1929 under the chairmanship of the leading American expert, Owen D. Young. The committee was known after him as the 'Young committee'. After deliberations lasting for four months, the committee submitted to the governments the 'Young Plan.'

The Plan contemplated a new indemnity bill to be paid over a period of 58 years. For the first 37 years, Germany was to make annual payments averaging £100,000,000 followed by 22 smaller annual payments. The payments were divided into two categories, unconditional and conditional. About one-third of each annuity was to be treated as an unconditional obligation. In the case of conditional obligation, German government was entitled to postpone transfer into foreign currencies for a maximum period of two years. The sums payable were to be paid in Reichsmarks. A Bank of International Settlements was created which was to act as trustee for the creditor countries and to act as the agency for the receipt and distribution of funds. By abolishing the Reparation Commission and other agencies of foreign control, the Young Plan gave financial autonomy to Germany. On May 1930, ratification of the Young Plan, came into effect.

Washington Treaties (November 12, 1921 - February 1922)

The Washington Conference which was called on the American initiative constituted the chief post-war developments in the Far East. The treaties signed at the Washington conference were as follows:-

(1) Limitation of naval armaments, the main business of the conference, was accepted on a five, three ratio for Britain, the United States and Japan, with the proviso that no Anglo-American naval bases would be developed east of Singapore or west of Hawai.

(2) The Anglo-Japanese Alliance (1902) was superseded by a Four-Power Treaty between Britain, America, France and Japan. They agreed to respect each other's rights in relation to their insular possessions in the Pacific, and consult together in the event of any controversy between them regarding these rights or any one of them threatened by the aggressive action of any other Power. The Four-Power Treaty was little more than a diplomatic device to end the Anglo-Japanese alliance.

(3) The most important part of the Conference related to the position of China. By the Nine-Power Treaty (America, Britain, Belgium, France, Italy, China, Japan, the Netherlands and Portugal) all the powers bound themselves to respect the sovereignty, independence and integrity of China, to provide the fullest opportunity to China to establish a stable government in China, to maintain the principle of equal opportunity for the commerce of all nations and to refrain from taking advantage of conditions in China for seeking any special right or privilege.

(4) By a separate agrement between Japan and China alone, Japan agreed to restore to China Kiachow territory, Shantung and the post of Tsingtao. Britain eventually restored Weihaiwei.

Though the decisions of the conference were described as 'a blessing to all mankind' the settlement lacked any means of enforcement to maintain the arrangements it proclaimed.

Kellogg-Briand Pact

The most important milestone in the history of international relations after the Treaty of Locarno was the Kellogg Briand Pact. On April 6, 1927, French Foreign Minister Briand had send a message to the American people in which he suggested that the 10th anniversary of the entry of the United States into the war might be celebrated by a mutual agreement in favour of 'the renunication of war as an instrument of national policy.' The suggestion was followed in June by the despatch to Kellogg, American Secretary of State, of a draft treaty embodying this idea.

Instead of confining the pact only to two powers, Kellogg after a long delay, replied with a counter-proposal that the suggested pact should be universal. Briand agreed. Eventually on August 27, 1928 representatives of the six great powers (America, Britain, France, Germany, Italy and Japan), the other three Locarno powers (Belgium, Poland, Czechoslovakia) and the British Dominions and India met in Paris and signed the pact. This was known as the Kellogg-Briand pact or the pact of Paris. Most of the independent states were invited to adhere to the pact.

In the first article, the signatories condemned 'recourse to war for the solution of international controversies and renounced it as an instrument of national policy in their relations with one another.' In the second article the states agreed that 'the settlement or solution of all disputes or conflicts of whatever nature of whatever origin may be, which may arise among them, shall never be sought except by pacific means.' The third and last article outlined the terms of ratification and adherence. Within a few years, 65 nations, including the Soviet Union, signed the pact.

The pact of Paris was not a far reaching event. It renounced only wars of aggression. War was not outlawed (1) when resourted to in self-defence, (2) in the execution of obligations assumed under previous treaties and (3) in fulfilment of responsibilities under the League Covenant or Locarno agreements. Though the pact condemned aggressive wars, it made no provision for punishing the guilty. There was not even provision for consultation among the signatory powers in case of a breach of the pact. Nevertheless, the Pact of Paris was an important landmark. The universal repudiation of war as an instrument of policy seems to have a unique importance. It constituted a great step forward on the road to international security.

LONG ANSWER TYPE QUESTIONS

1. What were the causes of the First World War?
2. How did the Moroccon crisis create international tension before 1914?
3. Discuss the immediate cause of the First World War. Name the principal participants of the war.
4. Analyse the provisions of the Treaty of Versailles.
5. What were the reasons for the victory of the Allied power?
6. 'The Treaty of Versailles was a dictated peace of victor powers on a vanquished nation'. Examine the truth of the statement.
7. Discuss the achievements and failures of the league of Nations in preserving peace.
8. Describe the provisions of the Locarno Treaty. Why was it hailed as a precursor of a new era in world history?

9. How far was the Reparation problem of Germany solved by Dawes Plan and Young Plan?
10. What was Kellogg-Briand Pact? Discuss its importance.

SHORT ANSWER TYPE QUESTIONS

11. Critically examine the Colonial rivalry among the European powers in the last quarter of the nineteenth century.
12. Discuss the circumstances leading to the formation of the Triple Alliance and Triple Entente.
13. What was Agadir Crisis?
14. How did Balkan crisis of 1912-13 contribute to the outbreak of the First World War?
15. How far Germany was responsible for the outbreak of the First World War?
16. Analyse the territorial settlement of the Treaty of Versailles.
17. What were the chief causes of dissatisfaction of Germany to the Versailles Settlement.
18. Describe the chief organs of the League of Nations.
19. What were the causes of the failure of the League of Nations in maintaining world peace?
20. Discuss the significance of the Washington Treaties (1921-1922).
21. Analysis the importance of the Kellogg-Briand Pact.

OBJECTIVE TYPE QUESTIONS

22. Who were the members of the Triple Alliance?
23. Who were the members of the Triple Entente?
24. When did the First World War start?
25. Who was the author of the Fourteen Points?
26. What was 'Serajevo Murder'? When did it take place?
27. Why did England join the First World War?
28. Name the two German colonies given as mandates to Britain.
29. What were the principal organs of the League of Nations?
30. When did Germany join the League of Nations?
31. What was Dawes Plan?
32. What was Young Plan?
33. When did the Pact of Paris take place?

IMPORTANT DATES

1. 1822 : Triple Alliance between Germany, Austria and Italy
2. 1985 : Dual Alliance between France and Russia
3. 1902 : Anglo-Japanese Alliance

4. 1904 : Anglo-French Ententc
5. 1906 : Algeciras Conference
6. 1907 : Triple Entente between France, Britain and Russia
7. 1912 : First Balkan War
8. 1913 : Second Balkan War
9. June 28, 1914 : Murder of Archduke Francis Ferdinand at Serajevo
10. August 4, 1914 : Outbreak of the First World War
11. April 6, 1917 : Entry of the United States in the War
12. June 28, 1919` : Treaty of Versailles
13. April 28, 1919` : Foundation of the League of Nations
14. October 15, 1925 : Locarno Pact
15. August 16, 1924 : Dawes Plan
16. May 17, 1930 : Young Plan
17. November 12, 1921 : Feb 1922: Washington Treaties
18. August 27, 1928 : Kellogg-Briand Pact or Pact of Paris

UNIT - IV

THE WORLD BETWEEN TWO WARS

Background to the Bolshevik Revolution of 1917

Compared to other European nations, Russia was politically backward. During the 18th and 19th centuries, when Western Europe was struggling for constitutional governments, Russia was a thoroughly absolute state. In 1861, Alexander II (1855-81) by the Edict of Emancipation abolished serfdom which kept more than forty million people in bondage to landowners or state. The abolition of serfdom failed to achieve the desired result. The condition of the Russian peasant was 'both better and worse.'

Tsar Nicholas II (1894-1917), a young man of twenty-six, was weak in character and was overshadowed by the influence of his wife and her favourities, espectially the monk Gregory Rasputin, The beginning of the 20th century witnessed the revolutionary movement in full swing. Strikes, demonstrations and mass meetings were of daily occurence. In July 1904 the revolutionaries assassinated Plehve, Minister of the Interior. The representatives of zemstovs meeting at Petrogard in November 1904 drew up the 'Eleven Points.' They demanded inviolbility of person, freedom of conscience, of speech and of the press and the immediate summoning of a constituent Assembly to prepare a constitution. The defeat of the Russian armies and navy in the battles with the Japanese (1904-5) utterly discredited the Government.

The accumulated tension exploded at St. Petersburg in January 1905. On January 22, 1905, took place the massacre of the pacific strikers. A wave of strikes gripped the country. In the face of this crisis, the Tsar issued a Manifesto on October 30, 1905. The October Manifesto guaranteed personal liberties and established a moderately popular franchise for the election of the Duma. The period of constitutional experiment when the first Duma met in 1705 and the last Duma which was dispersed by the Tsar in 1916 was a painful reading.

The Bolshevik Revolution of 1917: Its Causes

The autocratic government of Nicholas II continued in an atmosphere of growing corruption. The economic and social structure of the country remained unchanged. About 30,000 landlords were still in possession of most of the lands. One-third of the peasantry was without any land. The technical level of agriculture was extremely low. More than one-third of the farmsteads possessed no implements at all. The average yield of grain per acre was extremely low. The grinding poverty was increased by the annual tributes which the peasantry had to pay to the landlords. The landlord's share was often

50 per cent of the crop. More than half a century after the emancipation of the serfs traces of serfdom were still existent.

Agricultural poverty was followed by industrial backwardness. On the eve of the war, Russia's production of iron and coal was insignificant in comparison with Germany, Britain and the United States. She was deficient in electrical and machine- building industries and had no machine-tool industry, chemical plants and motorcar factories. In 1914 Russia's industrial workers made up less than 15 percent of the population. They worked from 12 to 16 hours a day and their average pay was only $ 150 a year. Unions were forbidden by law until the opening years of the twentieth century. Even then the unions that were allowed, were, in fact, government-controlled unions. To counter these unions certain labour leaders created a new organisation called the Soviet. Actually the Soviets held secret meetings to discuss revolutionary ideas.

But of itself misery does not lead to successful revolution. An intellectual background is necessary for bringing revolutionary upsurge. In 1820 Pushkin published the *Ode to Liberty*. One of the most outstanding of the westernizers was Alexander Herzen (1812-70). He advocated a voluntary socialism that would provide material comfort for the exploited masses. Another aggressive rebel was Mikhail Bakunin (1814-76). He found mankind's salvation in the destruction of all conventions and institutions. Another celebrity was Nikolai Chernyshevsky (1828-89) who emphasised the need to rely on thorough going revolution, in order to usher in the reign of true justice and liberty. But the most eloquent exponent of Marxism in Russia was George Plekhanov (1857-1918). His most influential disciple, Lenin, not only interpreted Marxist philosophy, but made it the basis of the revolution in Russia.

It has often been what the Russians call 'a jolt from outside' that has often brought about some radical changes in the domestic sphere of Russia. The Napoleonic Wars led to the first political movement in Russia-that of the Decembrists in 1825. The Crimean War of 1855-56 led directly to the emancipation of the serfs. The Russo-Japanese War of 1904-5 led to the institution of a representative legislative assembly. The First World War was to lead to the Revolution of 1917.

The last of the Czars, Nicholas II, who had come to the throne in 1894, proved himself utterly incompetent. He submitted himself to his dominating wife Czarina Alexandra and an unscrupulous monk, Rasputin. It has been observed that Rasputin was 'the axle on which revolved the destinies of Russia'. But it was Russia's participation in the First World War which proved to be her undoing. For Russia was not equal to a struggle such as this. Her losses in the first ten months of the war were reckoned as 3,80,000. The winter of 1915-16 was outstanding for casualties and sufferings for the Russians. Men went about muttering that 'everybody steals, and Christ himself would steal if his hands were not nailed to the cross'. In December 1916 Rasptuin was murdered.

During the winter of 1916-17, popular disaffection overtook Russia. Patriots complained that the government was hampering the prosecution of the war. The subject nationalities grew restless. There were riots of peasants. At the beginning of March 1917, there were widespread strikes in the national capital of Petrograd. On March 8, International Women's Day, a band of housewives attacked the bakeries. On the next day, demonstrators, breaking through police cordons, demanded bread. On March 10, all factories and industrial establishments in the capital were closed down. On March 11, the Tsar issued an edict disbanding the Duma, and ordered the general commanding the Petrograd garrison to suppress the movement immediately. On March 12, the situation deteriorated further. The local garrisons joined the revolutionary cause. Late in the afternoon, delegates of factories and representatives of the Socialist parties organised a Soviet of Worker's Deputies. By the following morning, the Soviet became the only de facto power in existence.

On March 14, the Duma, despite the Tsar's attempt to dissolve it, set up a Provisional Government headed by Prince Lvov. On March 15, the Tsar abdicated in favour of his brother, grand Duke Michael. But the Grand Duke refused to accept the throne and Russia virtually became a Republic.

From the beginning, the Provisional Government clashed with the Soviets. The Provisional Government, representing the upper and middle classes, hoped for the restoration of a constitutional monarchy. They were determined to continue the war. The Soviets, on the other hand, spoke in the name of the toiling masses. They were inclined to believe that the present revolution was the long-awaited bourgeois revolution and a proletarian revolution would come some day.

Meanwhile in early April 1917 Lenin returned to Russia from his exile in Switzerland. Lenin, who was a pillar of the Bolshevik Party, combined 'a variety of qualities, enormous scholarship, the passionate temperament of the revolutionary, tactical genius and great administrative ability'. In his so-called April thesis Lenin described that the revolution in the first stage had given power to the bourgeois, which would, in the second stage, transfer power to the workers and the poor peasants. The end in view was not a parliamentary republic, but 'a Republic of Soviets of Workers', poor peasants and Peasants' Deputies all over the country, growing up from below'.

The struggle between the Provisional Government and the Soviet for supremacy made the situation more complex. The slogans of the Bolsheviks were: 'Peace' now; 'Bread' for the cities; 'Land' to be given to the peasants and all power to the Soviets. The Bolsheviks staged a rising in July, but it proved to be premature and Lenin fled to Finland. While continuing the war, the Provisional Government postponed the crucial land question. The peasants attacked the land-owners and seized the land. On July 15, the Provisional Government fell. A new Government under Kerenesky was formed. But it became apparent that Russia could not sustain both war and revolution at the same time. The Russian troops mutinied. Kerenesky planned to summon a Constituent Assembly. Lenin countered by demanding an All-Russian Congress of Soviets. By gaining Bolshevik pre-dominance in the Petrograd Soviet and in most provincial Soviets, Lenin, who had returned, staged a successful coup d'etat on the night of November 6-7, 1917. But the brain behind the operation was Leon Trotsky (1879-1940), who displayed uncommon strategical ability. Kerenesky fled abroad and Lenin became the head of the new government of the Soviets. Communism had come to Russia.

Impact of the establishment of the First Socialist State on International Relations

The Revolution of 1917 is an epoch-making event in the history of the world. Marx and Engels visualised the proletarian revolution sweeping all over Europe. By a systematic appeal to peace, the Bolsheviks hoped to lead the European masses toward general revolution. The example and propaganda of the Bolshevik Revolution helped to found Communist parties in different countries. These were federated in 1919 in a Third International (Comintern) with headquarters at Moscow. Through the Comintern, Russia directed the policies and activities of Germany, France, Italy and most other countries on the European continent. The Indian Communist Party was formed in 1925 and Manabendra Nath Roy (M. N. Roy) was the first Indian to be elected to the Communist International.

The Bolshevik Revolution ushered in a great socialist movement and created panic in the capitalist world. As a matter of fact, the Fascist revolution after 1920 was the outcome of hatred and fear of Communism. The impact of the Bolshevik Revolution was felt not only in western Europe but also in the colonial world. It opened an era of nationalist struggle against the colonial rule. By propagating the doctrine that the last of capitalism is imperialism, the Bolshevik Revolution became eloquent champion of racial equality and freedom. The Bolshevik Revolution influenced the Chinese nationalist revolution.

The example of the Bolshevik success inflamed imaginations everywhere. European labour became militant and tried to forge the unity of workers as a whole. Socialism, as opposed to imperialism, emerged as a great force for order and stabilisation in Western and Central Europe. Moreover, the success of Russia's economic planning gave great encouragement to various countries of the world to reach the goal of economic progress.

At the XVII Congress of the Communist Party in January 1934, Stalin observed the strength of Soviet Communism:

> Marxism has achieved complete victory on one-sixth of the globe-has achieved in the very country in which Marxism was considered to have been utterly destroyed. It cannot be regarded as an accident that the country in which Marxism triumphed is now the only country in the world which knows no crises and unemployment, whereas in all other countries, including the Fascist countries, crisis and unemployment have been reigning for four years now.

Lenin and the Reconstruction of the Soviet Union

In mid-1890, there were 20 Marxist groups in St. Petersburg alone. To this group belonged Vladimir Uyich Ulyanov (Lenin) who had been expelled from the University of Kazan for his revolutionary activities. In 1898, the Russian Social Democrat Worker's Party held its first Congress at Minsk. It was poorly attended and some members of the party were arrested. Lenin was already in exile in Siberia. So it was that Plekhanov, Zasulich and others organised Russian Marxism from outside Russia. 'League of Russian Social Democrats Abroad' was located in Switzerland. Lenin became the first editor of the party newspaper Iskra (the Spark). At the second party Congress that met in Brussels in 1903, doctrinal differences split the party into two factions-Bolsheviks and Mensheviks. Both believed in the basic tenets of Marxism. Both believed that the fall of the imperial regime would be followed by a period of bourgeois democratic government before socialism could usher in. But whereas Lenin and the Bolsheviks argued that this period of bourgeois rule must be regarded as a purely transitional rule, the Mensheviks regarded it as a period of long duration. Through his brilliant pamphlet *What is to be Done* published in 1902, Lenin advocated that the socialist movement must be led by an elite of professional revolutionaries. This implied a small party with a centralised and disciplined structure. On the other hand, the Mensheviks argued for a more comprehensive party.

Lenin was the pillar of the Bolshevik Party which, since 1912, had been a party distinct from the Mensheviks. After the beginning of the Revolution, Lenin came back to Russia. Soon after, there began a sharp conflict between Lenin and the Provisional Government led by Kerenesky. After temporary eclipse of power Lenin with the help of Trotsky seized power in the beginning of November 1917. 'The cause for which people has struggled: the immediate offer of a democratic peace, the abolition of the Landlords' property of the land, workers' control over production and the formation of a Sóviet Government—this cause is now secure. Long live the revolution of soldiers, workers and peasants'. Lenin was opposed to the continuation of the war. In order to consolidate the communist rule in Russia, Lenin advocated peace. By a narrow margin Lenin had his way, and the Treaty of Brest-Litovsk was signed in March 1918.

From War Communism to New Economic Policy

From 1918 to 1921, during the period of War Communism, the Supreme Council of National Economy (Vesenkha) regulated the Soviet economy in all its aspects. Established on December 15, 1917, it developed several departments and a hierarchy of regional and local bodies through which it worked. The most burning problem of the Soviet economy was the procurement of food. Deliveries of food by the peasants became compulsory. The practice promoted the despoiling of the rich. In June 1918 the method of requisitioning grain and other supplies was systematised. Industry was nationalised and a ban was enforced on private trade and private manufacture. Central control of production was not effective. Production of large-scale industry dropped in 1920 by twelve per cent of its pre-war level: Agricultural production declined by a third. The result was the collapse of the Soviet economy in 1920 and famine in 1921. Forty million persons suffered from malnutrition and at least five million died. The situation not only threatened the essential economic base of the regime, but also engendered discontents and opposition to the Bolsheviks. At the end of February 1921, a widespread labour unrest broke out in Petrograd. In March, sailors of the great naval base at Kronstadt mutinied which was suppressed only by ruthless military action.

Lenin with a deep sense of realism adjusted his policy to meet these obstacles. In October 1921, he frankly described 'the defeat we have suffered on the economic front at the beginning of 1921, in our attempt to make a transition to communism (was) much more serious than any we have suffered at the hands of Kolchak, Denikin or Pilsudski'. In 1921, Lenin proclaimed a New Economic Policy-generally known in the abbreviated form as the NEP. It was a temporary halt in the revolutionary policy of socialism, a step back in order to move two steps forward later. The policy of forced grain collections was abandoned. The peasant was allowed to trade on the open market with whatever surplus he might have. This measure was supplemented by others-to restore a limited market economy in food and other consumer goods, to permit revival of the handicraft and cottage industries, and to make possible the operation of small industrial and commercial enterprises. The state retained complete control of banking, foreign trade and large-scale industry.

Hardly had the NEP been able to produce favourable economic results, when Russia was stricken with worst famine in 1921. It not only took human lives by millions, but it also caused a shortfall in foodgrain of several million tonnes. With effective help from American Relief Administration and other foreign sources, the disaster was finally overcome: In 1922 and 1923, food production was satisfactory. There was revival of small-scale industry; although heavy industry, which remained under state control, took long periods for recovery.

The NEP served its purpose successfully. By the end of 1922, Soviet Russia made rapid progress. But in 1923, a sharp crisis-the so-called 'Scissors Crisis' developed in the Soyiet economy. Industrial prices rose dramatically at the expense of agricultural prices. At the twelfth Party Congress in April 1923, Trotsky produced a diagram which showed how the 'scissors', representing the blades of agricultural and industrial prices, had opened more and more widely. In October 1923, the scissors opened to their widest extent, the ratio of industrial prices to agricultural prices was three times as high as in 1913. The crisis was overcome by the establishment of a system of price controls, under which prices on industrial goods were brought down.

By the summer of 1924, a growing confidence was visible in Soviet economy. The recovery of Russian agriculture in the years of the mid-twenties was rapid. Industry steadily revived. The currency reform was completed in March 1924, when the gold-based currency was adopted, and the old Soviet rouble notes withdrawn. Foreign trade, managed by a separate commissariat, reached favourable figures for the first time in the year 1923-24. Of exports, 75 per cent were agricultural products, including grain; of imports, nearly 75 per cent were taken by industry. "These impressive results been achieved under the regime of NEP and could have not been achieved without it; they were hailed as a triumtphant vindication of NEP".[1]

The U.S.A. in inter-war Period : The Republication Era (1921-33)

After the First World War, the United States adoped a policy of isolation. In the Presidential election of 1920, the Republican nominee, Warren G. Harding was elected. In July 1921 the Congress declared the War to be 'at an end.' A few months later the treaties of Berlin, Vienna, and Budepest were signed and ratified. Despite his indifference to the League of Nations, President Harding urged membership in the World Court just to enable the United States to play a significant role in the selection of judges.

In the Far East, the United States could not afford to remain passive onlooker. The close of the war enabled Japan to dominant power in the Pacific. By the Treaty of Versailles she had acquired from Germany the leased territory of Kiaochow. Moreover Japan's aggressive policy towards China and her bid for naval supremacy affected the foreign policy of the United States.

In the latter part of 1921, the United States invited Britain, Japan, France and Italy together with other powers (China, the Netherlands, Portugal and Belgium) 'to participate in a conference on the limitation of armaments, in connection with which Pacific and Far Eastern questions would also be discussed.' The conference continued from November 1921 to February 1922 and concluded seven treaties. Two of these dealt with naval disarmament, the remaining five the Pacific and Far Eastern Questions.

The Five Power Treaty concluded between the United States, Britain, Japan, France and Italy agreed to respect each other's rights in the Pacific and to consult together in the event of any controversy or any threat to them from the aggressive action of any power. Thus the United States for the first time was drawn into European alliance after their rejection of the League convenant. The Five Power Treaty drew up an extensive programme of naval disarmament by fixing naval parity between Britain and the United States and hte strength of Japan in Capital ships at 60 per cent of the British and America figures.

In the domestic sphere, the Harding administration inaugurated 'a policy of normalcy.' This was a happy combination of two policies—one, freedom of private enterprise and the other generous subsidies to private enterprise. In 1921 the Congress lowered the surtax maximum on the largest incomes to 50 per cent. In 1922, the Congress passed a Tariff Act which authorised the President to increase or decrease the Tariff rates upto 50 per cent to protect the United States from the competition of foreign countries. Between 1921 and 1923 several measures were passed to give relief to farmers. But in the face of mounting competition from Canada, Australia and Russia, these measures failed to alleviate the country's agricultural problem.

---

[1] Carr E.H.: *The Russian Revolution from Lenin to Stalin* 1917-29 (1979), p. 59

After Harding's death on August 2, 1923, Calvin Coolidge became President. Coolidge believed that 'the business of America is business." He made economy his goal. He was an embodiment of thrift and caution. In 1924, the income tax was further reduced and a highly restrictive immigration law, was adopted. The Secretary of State, Herbert Hoover, encouraged American business to look abroad for expanding markets. In domestic spheres, however, the situation was far from comfortable. Communists were active in fomenting strikes.

Herbert Hoover assumed office in 1929 under auspicious circumstances. He was a hard working and a man with a high sense of duty. But soon he showed his incapacity as a leader. In politics, he was conservative, and in business a neo-mercantilist, favouring high tariffs. In the matter of the tariff, the government lowered the rates on about 250 items, but raised on about 900 items. The Act was passed in the fact of the opposition of economist and other experts. The efforts of the government to provide relief were equally unsuccessful.

1929 Economic Crash

In the beginning, Hoover boasted "We in America are nearer to the final triumph over poverty than ever before in the history of any land." But the final triumph eluded Hoover when financial collapse occurred in October 1929. On October 24, the stock market in Wall Street crashed. Sound stock like the American Telephone and Telegraph, General Electric, and General Motors lost their market value. The spiral of depression affected business houses, banks, factories leading to mass unemployment. Foreign trade declined to an unprecedented loss. After the crash in the United States, disaster quickly gripped Europe. First came collapse in Austria and finally the economic depression became worldwide.

The causes of depression were manifold. In the first place, the productive capacity of the nation far exceeded than its capacity to consume. In the second place, the tariff and war-debt policies of the Government severely curtailed foreign market for American goods. With the world-wide depression of the early 30s, the market collapsed. In the third place, easy credit policies had led to an inordinate expansion of credit and unrestrained speculation. Finally, the chronic agricultural depression and industrial unemployment and concentration of wealth in great corporations produced an unhealthy national economy.

In order to speed up economic revival, the President proposed an international moratorium from mid-1931 to mid-1932. To meet mounting unemployment, the government allotted large sums for the construction of public buildings and highways. National and local taxes raised. Since 1932 the Congress enlarged the credit facilities of the Federal Revenue System. The insolvency of many railways and the threatened insolvency of many banks, forced the Government to underwrite the credit structure. One instrument of that underwriting was the creation of a Reconstruction Finance Corporation. It was authorised to lend money for three years for financing agriculture, commerce and industry and for exportation of agricultural and other products. All these remedial measures failed to solve the pressing problem of economic malaise of the country. By 1932, the number of unemployed had risen to over 12 million; over 5 thousand banks had collapsed, form prices dropped to the lowest point in history and national income fell from 80 billion in 1929 to 40 billion. The Americans turned hopefully to a different leadership. In 1930, Democrats swept the congressional elections and in the elections of November 1932 Franklin D. Roosevelt won by a large majority.

Roosevelt's New Deal

When Roosevelt assumed office on March 4, 1933, the country was on the verge of complete the collapse. He met the crisis with boldness and vigour. In his inaugural address, Roosevelt declared that 'there was nothing to fear but fear itself.' He prophesied that the nation would 'revive and prosper' and promised a 'New Deal.' He sought from the Congress "broad executive powers to wage a war against the emergency". To many contemporaries, the New Deal appeared like revolution. But in a sense, it was deeply conservative and it aimed to protect the essentials of American democracy. In philosophy, the New Deal was democratic, in method evolutionary. For fifteen years, the legislative reforms had proceeded haltingly, but now they burst upon the country with great fury leaving a precious legacy to future generations.

The New Deal was made up in part of measures for recovery and relief, and in part measures for reform. In the realm of relief the government gave Federal loans to sick business. It inaugurated a programme of public works in order to stimulate business and provide employment. It set up elaborate systems of conservation of natural resources and financed long overdue improvements. On June 16, 1933, the National Industrial Recovery Act was passed. The Act provided for fair competition in industry, contained protective clause for labour and outlined a works programme. To integrate the recovery measures, the President created an executive council known as the National Recovery Administration (NRA). The 'Codes of fair competition' by which NRA became best known, were originally planned for big industries. But every type of business insisted on being protected against 'unfair competition.' Labour too wanted guaranteed wages and limitation of working hours. The NRA., however proved a failure.

In matters of reform, the New Deal reopened the banks under strict supervision and with government guarantees of bank deposits. It abandoned the gold standard and devalued the dollar. It controlled the selling of stocks and bonds and other securities. It broke up the great holding companies. It formulated codes of fair practices for business. It raised tax on the income of the rich and of corporations.

The New Deal paid particular attention to agriculture, labour, social security and administration. The government made money payments to farmers who set a part of their land for 'soil conserving' crops. By 1940 nearly six million farmers had joined in this programme. A Farm Credit Administration made credit available at almost nominal rates of interest. In the field of labour the New Deal enacted a whole series of epoch-making laws. The National Recovery Act of 1933 attempted to spread work, shorten hours, raise wages, end child labour and guaranteed the right of collective bargaining. The Wagner Act of 1935 set up a Labour Relations Board to adjudicate all labour disputes. In 1935 set up a series of Social Security Acts providing pensions for the aged, and unemployment insurance. Among its most significant achievements were the creation of Tennesse Valley Authority which undertook to make the project a comprehensive laboratory for social and economic experimentation. In administrative sphere, the Hatch Act of 1939, prohibited political activities on the part of government employees and struck at the corruption and extravagance of political parties.

The value of relief expenditure, the mounting cost of administration brought about a steady increase in the national deficit and in taxes. As time went on, governmental activities expanded so much that it was feared that it might undermine the liberties of the people. President Roosevelt rebutted the criticism by defending New Deal measures—measures which fostered economic well-being. In a broadcast to the nation in 1938, he said:

"Democracy has disappeared in several other great nation, not because the people of those countries dislinked democracy, but because they had grown tired of unemployment and insecurity. Finally in desperation, they chose to sacrifice liberty in the hope of getting something to eat. We in America know that our democratic institutions can be preserved and made to work. The people of America are in agreement in defending the liberties at any cost, and the first line of defence lies in the protection of economic security".

Western Europe Between the Two Wars : Rise of Nazism in Germany

Germany's defeat in the First World War brought about the downfall of the Hohenzollern Empire. Germany became a Republic—generally called the Weimar Republic and Ebert—a prominent Socialist, became its President. The Weimar constitution of the new German Republic was thoroughly democratic. While it retained the federal organisation it lessened the powers of the several states and strengthened those of the central government. The executive authority was vested in a President, elected by the people for seven years, and in a Chancellor and ministry responsible to the Reichstag. The constitution included a detailed bill of rights, provisions of a proportional representation of all parties and for a National Economic Council.

The Weimar Republic had to encounter serious difficulties. In 1919, a communist uprising occurred in Berlin and hundreds were killed. The next year monarchist rebels attacked the government. For various reasons the Weimar Republic did not endure long. Germany was burdened with enormous amount of reparation for damages to the victorious allies. There was inflation which reached a climax in 1923, when a basketful of notes would not buy a dozen eggs. To economic distress was added the tyranny of injustice. The French occupation of the Ruhr caused Germany deep humiliation. In 1924, the first attempt was made to reduce the burden of Germany's war debt under the Dawes Plan. The operation of this plan was achieved in 1929 by the Young Plan under which Germany was required to complete payment of her debt within the next six decades.

In 1925, President Ebert died and Field Marshal von Hindenburg was elected President of the Republic. During the years, 1923-29 German foreign policy was controlled by Stresseman. In the words of Lord D' Abernon, he, "raised Germany from the position of a stricken and disarmed foe into that of a diplomatic equal." To D' Abernon, Stressemann seemed like a German Winston Churchill. "Probably he remained an intense, even a romantic nationalist, but he saw that German nationalism might be better served by subtle diplomacy than by showing one's teeth." Under his leadership, Germany signed the Locarno Treaties (1925), joined the League of Nations (1926) and accepted the Pact of Paris (1928) that outlawed war as an instrument of national policy. His death in 1929 had far-reaching consequences.

Hitler in Germany: Rise of Nazi Party: Its Organisation

The advent of the Great Depression in 1929 served to bring about the weakness of the Weimer Republic. Adolf Hitler who had established the National Socialist or Nazi Party in 1920 found his opportunity in an atmosphere of discontent and frustration. In 1923 having failed to seize political power, he went to jail and wrote *Mein Kampf* in which he told how Germany's wrongs would be righted.

A political genius as Hitler was, he combined in his own person indomitable will and self-confidence, a superb sense of timing, a mastery of the arts of propaganda. Hitler had tremendous resources of patience and remarkable intuitive power. He directed his attack against the Versailles Treaty, the Young Plan, the League of Nations and the parliamentary democracy.

On emerging from prison, Hitler rebuilt his party of National Socialists, called Nazis in short. The party had a number of organs, like the political organisation which looked after foreign affairs, labour relations, agriculture, justice, and national economy. There was also a separate propaganda division in which Hitler took prominent interest, a department to study defence questions and a youth organisation. He organised the party's para-military forces, the storm Troopers (the S.A.). There was also a second elite force, the Schutzstaffel or S./S. Originally designed as a personal bodyguard of Hitler, this body found its permanent chief in Heinrich Himmler. They adopted a brown- shirt uniform and the emblem of a black swastika on a red field. At the head of the elaborate organisation stood Hitler himself. He maintained his control of the party by sheer strength of will. Most of his close associates—Hess, Goebbles, Goering—regarded him with awe and veneration. Hitler sought to strengthen his influence among the people, especially the middle-class youths who turned to National Socialism after 1929.

After a slow growth during the years 1925-29, the party gained considerably after 1929. The economic depression and the growing unemployment generated a sense of frustration among the people who sought salvation in National Socialism. In the elections of 1930, the Nazis made their first breakthrough by winning 107 seats to become the second largest party after the Socialists.

The period from 1930 to the end of January 1933 was a testing period for Hitler. The Nazis did all in the their power to discredit Weimar Republic. Early in 1932, the Chancellor, Bruning suggested that President Hindenburg's term be extended by the Reichstag. Hitler opposed this suggestion. In March 1932 elections were held. Hindenburg and Hitler both were candidates. Hindenburg won and a few weeks afterwards Bruning resigned. Bruning's system of government by emergency decree had accomplished little. The President selected as the new Chancellor Papen in June 1932. But the new government enjoyed no support in the *Reichstag*. The effect of the two elections which Papen induced Hindenburg to call in July and November 1932 to secure some support in the parliament were the coffin nails of democracy. The Nazis in July won 230 seats and 37 per cent of the vote; in the election of November 1932 they secured 33 per cent. As no party gained control of the Reichstag, Papen resigned on November 17. Hindenburg now invited Hitler, as the head of the largest party, to form a government. But when Hitler demanded dictatorial powers, the President turned to General Kurt von Schleicher. But the new chancellor too had failed to control either the country or the Reichstag. In January 1933 Hindenburg appointed Hitler to the Chancellorship.

Hitler had power; but he had not unlimited power which he wished to possess. He needed some pretext for frightening the other parties into giving him dictatorial power. He got it on February 27, 1933 when the Reichstag building caught fire, presumably through the initiative of the Nazi agents. Hitler laid the blame on the Communist Party; 4000 Communist members were arrested. Then he induced the President to sign on February 28 an emergency decree suspending personal liberties and political rights. In the elections of march 5,1933, Hitler failed to secure an absolute majority. But on March 23, Hitler passed an Enabling Act which granted him dictatorial power for four years. Hitler was in the saddle. He abolished all opposition parties and took over all the machinery of state power. On August 2, 1934, Hindenburg died and Hitler assumed the offices of both President and Chancellor. He became the head of State (Fuehrer) and Commander of the Armed Forces.

Rise of Fascism in Italy

The victory of communism in Russia encouraged the rise of totalitarian movements in Europe which promised to keep the countries free from Marxist ideas. This was the case in Italy which surrendered itself to the dictatorship of the Fascist Party after the First World War. Moreover, the parliamentary system of government had long been under fire from reactionary quarters. Universal suffrage, remarked Tolstoy, was no more than a method whereby prisoners elect their prison guards. By 1928 parliamentary system of government had been replaced by dictatorship in Italy, Spain, Portugal, Hungary, Austria, Yugoslavia, Poland and Lithuania. This was due to the unsettled social and economic conditions after the First World War.

Fascism was a movement designed to secure the support of the masses for a leader who had no faith in parliamentary system of government. Fascism could not brook the existence of other parties. It stood for 'strength through unity' at the expense of civil liberties. The cult of the leader was deliberately fostered. It was a totalitarian response to new social forces and the discontents real and imagined.

The most notable example of Fascism was the one established by Mussolini in Italy. The aftermath of World War I made unexpected changes in Italy. Fascism in Italy grew out of national resentment of Versailles Settlement. Italy had joined the First World War as an ally of England and France which had promised substantial territorial gain. Although territorial gains had been made in the north and north-east, they fell far short of what had been promised. Particularly irritating was the creation of the 'international city' of Fiume. Indemnities from both Austria and Germany amounted to virtually nothing. Moreover, War costs had brought the economy close to bankruptcy. Returning War veterans could find no jobs. In September 1919 d' Anunzio, with a number of soldiers, seized Fiume. The government was neither strong nor bold enough to subdue him. In the late month of 1920, workers in the industrial cities of the north occupied some factories. Landlords and industrialists became alarmed at the possibility of socialism.

The situation called for vigorous action by the authorities. Their response was ineffective. In the Parliamentary election of 1919, the three largest parties were the Socialists, the Catholic Popular Party and the Liberals. The Socialists were disunited and split into several groups. The Catholic Popular Party, also lacked cohesion. As for the Liberals, they were opposed to government action in economic spheres. In these circumstances, the first post-war governments headed first by Francisco Nitti and then by Giolitti, accomplished little. The budget was unbalanced, the public debt large and the currency inflated. The balance of trade was highly unfavourable. The situation was ripe for the emergence of a new leader, Benito Mussolini.

Rise of Mussolini

Mussolini, son of a blacksmith, was born on July 29,1883. He taught at school for some time. In 1902 he went to Switzerland, engaging in socialist journalism. Expelled from Switzerland, he returned to Italy in 1904 to serve in the army. His subsequent participation in socialist agitation cost him an imprisonment in 1908. Shortly afterwards he went to the Austrian district of Trent (Trentino) where he edited a newspaper in support of revolutionary socialism and of Italian cause. After his expulsion from Trent, he returned to Italy. He denounced parliamentary system of government and advocated violence. In 1911, he was jailed by the Italian government for his attacks upon government policy in North Africa. In 1912, he became editor of *Avanti*, the official paper of the Italian Socialist Party. But when he began to propagate idea of nationalism and urge intervention in the war, he was made to resign from *Avanti.* Thereupon, Mussolini founded his own paper, *Il Popolo d' Italia* at Milan and campaigned for intervention. He served in the army from 1915 to 1917. After being wounded, he returned to patriotic journalism.

Mussolini observed the weakness of parliamentary government after the war. In March 1919, he founded at Milan the fasci (bundle) which gave rise to a network of similar fasci all over Italy. The new organisation was at first more a movement than a party. Unemployed war veterans, passionate nationalists and exploited peasants—all joined the Fascists. After September 1920, the Fascists took the lead in a violent campaign against socialists and communists. They broke up socialist and communist meetings and burned trade union halls. By these actions, the Fascists won the sympathy of employers and others who feared revolution. In April 1921, some 35 fascists were elected to the Chamber of Deputies. In November of the same year, the Fascist political party was organised with a graded hierarchy and rigid discipline. Fascists wore black shirts in imitation of Garibaldi's Red Shirts. The Fascist militia, *squadristi*, bound by an oath to Mussolini, was founded.

The Fascist movement gathered momentum during 1921- 22 while its opponents—Liberals, Socialist and Catholic—remained divided. The government, first led by Bonomi and then by Facta, failed to form a stable ministry. In August 1922, the Socialists declared a general strike which irritated the public who was tired of strikes. The Fascists declared open war on socialism and destroyed all socialist and union headquarters in Genoa and other key cities. Conditions were ripe for Mussolini's bid. In October 1922, Mussolini held a party conference in Naples at which he demanded that the government be turned over to him. Otherwise he would march on Rome and seize control. Then as the Liberal Prime Minister, Luigi Facta resigned on October 27, 1922, Mussolini marched with his followers on Rome. King Victor Emmanuel III asked Mussolini to form a ministry. The Fascist dictatorship of Italy had began.

Third French Republic in France

The First French Republic, associated with the glorious days of the Revolution, lasted only about a decade. The Second French Republic, an offshoot of the Revolution of 1848, lasted only for four years. But the Third French Republic, which was the child of defeat, not of revolution, proved to be enduring.

The Third French Republic was proclaimed at Paris on September 4, 1870 two days after the disastrous defeat of the French army at Sedan. A Provisional Government of National Defence was immediately installed. This government gave way in February 1871, to a National Assembly of 650 deputies. A majority of the members of the National Assembly were Royalists and only about 250 were Republicans. The Assembly chose Adolphe Thiers as head of the executive power.

Between the Government and the people of Paris serious disagreement arose over the activities of the Assembly. Armed Parisians set up a *de facto* government—the commune—that resisted the central government from March to May 1871. However, Thiers was able to mobilise a huge army and wreaked a terrible revenge. By the end of May 1871, the organised resistance broke down. After the suppression of the Commune, the National Assembly turned to the work of reconstruction. Thiers defined his task 'pacification reorganisation, the restoration of credit and the revival of industry.' The Thiers government quickly paid a war indemnity to German and secured the evacuation of German troops in 1873.

The Assembly, however, was predominantly monarchist. But the monarchists were divided into three parties, no one of which was in the majority. There were Legitimists, the Orleanists and the

Bonapartists. Thiers defended his policy of upholding the Republic. On May, 1873, the Assembly by a small majority brought about Thiers' resignation, and elected Marshal MacMohan as the new President. The divided monarchists extended Mac Mohan's term of office to seven years. But the country was tired of make-shift arrangements. Thiers' fall was provoking a republic reaction. The by-elections ran against the monarchists. On January 30, 1875, by the slender majority of one vote, France was committed to a republic. A new Constitution was enacted. France was to be a Republic. The head of the Republic was the President elected by the two Chambers—the Chamber of Deputies and the Senate—for a term of seven years. Parliamentary government on the English model was the gift of the Constitution of 1875 to France. The President had little power as the authority was vested with a cabinet responsible to the popular chamber. The principle of ministerial responsibility was borrowed from the English. But the French Cabinet—was quite different from that of the British because of the multiplicity of political parties. France had to witness cabinet crisis. Between 1873 and 1888, there were nineteen ministries in France.

During the next few years, the Republic was greatly strengthened. Most of the Republicans were anti-clerical. They viewed the Catholics as their natural opponents. Republications viewed the Church's hold on education as a threat to themselves. Between 1880 and 1885, the Government carried through a comprehensive system of education. In 1880, Minister of Education, Jules-Ferry ordered the Jesuits and all unauthorised teaching orders to disband. Primary education in state schools was made free in 1881 and an elementary education in some kind of school compulsory in 1882. State education was proclaimed in 1882 to be 'laic', i.e., divorced from all religious ideas.

Apart from the educational reforms, the government busied itself with other constructive activity. Charles de Freycinet's comprehensive programme of improving railways, canals, roads and harbours, was supported by parliament. Paris became the intellectual and artistic capital of the world and great international expositions were held here in 1878, 1889, and in 1900.

Another significant development under the Third Republic was the re-emergence of France as a Colonial Power. In 1881, Jules Ferry established a French protectorate over Tunis. In 1883-85, he compelled China to consent to the establishment of a French protectorate over its vassal states in Indo-China-Annam and Tonkin. Likewise, by effective bombardment, he secured Madagascar, the huge island in the Indian Ocean. By similar means, he brought under French control a part of Somaliland on the African Coast. In 1912, a French protectorate was established over the greater part of Morocco. By 1913, the empire of Republic France included not only Indo-China and Madagassar, but also a huge block of African territory constituting the five great administrative division of Algeria, Tunisia, Morocco, French West Africa and French Equatorial Africa, comprising an area almost 14 times the area of France.

A great threat to the Republic was the Boulanger affair. General Boulanger, a former commander in Algeria became minister of war in 1886. Stirring demands for revenge on Germany, Boulanger built up a Napoleonic image and following. Clergy, monarchists, revolutionary socialists all looked to him. Stripped of his office, he was elected to the Chamber of Deputies by many constituencies. When the moment for his coup d' etat arrived, Boulanger proved himself a poor Bonapartist. He fled to Brussels where he committed suicide in 1891.

The Third Republic came into conflict with the strongholds of monarchism—the army and the Church. In 1894, Captain Alfred Dreyfus, a Jewish Officer, was arrested for leaking military secrets to Germany. A secret court martial condemned him to life imprisonment. But in 1896, a new chief of the Intelligence Section, Georges Picquart, furnished evidence that the real culprit was Major

Esterhazy. Luckily for Dreyfus, a small band of Deputies like Clemenceau and Jaures, as well as writers like Anatole France and Emile Zola, took up his cause and vindicated his innocence. The mystery of the case deepended when a second court martial still found Dreyfus guilty but reduces his sentence to 10 years. Dreyfus was pardoned in 1899 and fully exonerated in 1906.

The Controversies between Church and State had been chronic throughout the French history. It has been said in 1902: "clericalism is to be found at the bottom of every agitation and every intrigue from which the Republican France has suffered during the last 35 years." Emile Combes who in 1901, succeeded Waldeck—Rousseau as Premier was an extreme anti-Clerical. In 1901, an Association Law passed which required that all congregations must apply for legal authorization or be dissolved. By the end of 1902, 12,000 schools conducted by unauthorized congregations had been closed. In 1904, a law was passed forbidding all congregations to give teaching of any kind. In 1905, by a law the church was wholly separated from the State. It declared that the Republic ensured freedom of worship and guaranteed its free exercise. "Thus by the separation of church and state France broke with the European tradition of Concordats, by which the state officially recognises religion; she adopted the American system which leaves the Churches to be organised by private initiative. This was a revolution in the ecclesiastical regime of France."

The Third Republic was distinguished by the creation of universities, by the foundation of more specialized schools such as Ecole des Sciences Politiques, and by a great improvement in the facilities for scientific study.

The experiment of National Government in England

In the general electrons of May 1929 the Labour Party regained power and Ramsay MacDonald once more became the Prime Minister. But it was by a slender majority the Labour had won with 288 seats, against the Conservatives 260 and the Liberals 59. The efforts of the government to solve domestic problems proved ineffective when Britain was overtaken by the World depression of 1929. The Chancellor of the Exchequer, Snowden adopted a policy of rigid oxthodoxy and tried to meet the budget deficit. A small team consisting of J.H. Thomas, Thomas Johnston, Sir Oswald Mosley and George Lamburg was formed to deal with the problem of unemployment. But Philip Snowden contented himself with palliative measures—the Housing Act of 1930, to speed up slum clearance, and the Agricultural Marketing Act of 1931, to help the farming community. The situation, however, did not improve. Destitution was widespread and the fiscal position of the country was imperilled by heavy withdrawals of gold from the Bank of England. In July 1931 the Government warned a deficit of £120 million and proposed increased taxes and drastic cut to government expenditure, specially the unemployment benefits. This created panic and the value of the pound slumped. MacDonald resigned on August 24, 1931. But the King asked him to form a national government. The new ministry as formed under MacDonald's leadership, comprised four Labourites, four Conservatives and two Liberals. As Prime Minister MacDonald solicited the cooperation of his party to support the Coalition. But the Labour Party opposed the National Government.

The National Government reduced government salaries and unemployment benefits, but the budget showed no signs of improvement. Foreign bankers began to withdraw gold and in 1931 Britain went off the gold standard. The new government went to polls to ratify its mandate. It appealed to the country for a 'doctor's mandate' to cure the financial ills of England. The election of October 1931 returned the government with a massive majority. 654 National Government candidates were returned out of 615 members of parliament. As the Conservative alone had secured 472 seats, it became the mainstay of the National Government.

The new government under Mac Donald's leadership, included four National Labourites, five National Liberals and eleven Conservatives. Neville Chamberrlain replaced Snowden as Chancellor of the Exchequer and the Liberal Sir John Simon as Foreign Secretary. The Government made a determined effort to bolster up confidence in the country. It abandoned the gold standard and allowed the pound to find its own level. In 1932, Chamberlain introduced Tariff Reform; he abandoned free trade principles and levied preferential duties on imports. To support farm prices, the government passed legislation that guaranteed a minimum price for some grains. Other legislation standardised the wages of industrial workers and stabilized price levels of various manufactured goods. Expenditure on social service rose. For a time, Britain was on the road to recovery. In foreign policy the government abandoned the pacific policy.

In 1935 Mac Donald resigned owing to ill health. In the election campaign of 1935, Stanley Baldwin promised to the electrorate, 'I give you my word that there will be no great armaments.' Baldwin won the elections with 387 seats. The Conservative Leader, Baldwin became the Prime Minister with Sir Samuel Hoare as Foreign Secretary, Neville Chamberlain as Chancellor of the Exchequer, and Anthony Eden as 'Minister for League of Nations Affair.'

ESSAY TYPE QUESTIONS

1. Discuss the various causes that led to the Bolshevik Revolution of 1917.
2. What were the consequences of the Russian Revolution of 1917 with special emphasis of its international significance.
3. Write a critical estimate of Lenin and his economic policy.
4. Analysis the different phases of Russian history from War Communism to New Economic Policy.
5. Trace the development of the U.S.A. in inter-war period.
6. Discuss the causes of the economic crash in America in 1929. How did the U.S.A. tide over the difficulties?
7. What is New Deal? Discuss the achievements of the United States of America during the period of the New Deal?
8. Account for the rise the Fascism in Italy.
9. Trace the rise of Mussolini.. How did he consolidate his position?
10. Narrate briefly how Hitler captured power in Germany.
11. Discuss the achievements of the Third Republic in France.
12. How did the National Government in England tackle the domestic problems?

SHORT ANSWER TYPE QUESTIONS

13. Discuss the role of the intellectuals to the outbreak of the Revolution of 1917.
14. What was New Economic Policy? Who was the propounder of the policy?
15. Discuss the achievements of the New Economic Policy.
16. What were the causes of the 1929 economic crash in U.S.A.
17. Discuss the significance of the New Deal in America.

18. What was Fascism? Account for its rise in Europe.
19. How did Mussolini establish dictatorial powers at home?
20. Give a pen picture of Germany after the First World War.
21. What were Nazi ideals? How did Hitlar organise the Nazi party?
22. Why the period from 1930 to 1933 was called a testing period for Hitler?
23. Trace the development of the French Colonial empire under the Third Republic.

OBJECTIVE TYPE QUESTIONS

24. In whose reign did the Russian Revolution of 1917 take place?
25. Who inaugurated the Five-year Plan and when?
26. What do you mean by NEP?
27. When was the Indian Communist Party formed?
28. Who was the first Indian elected to the Communist International?
29. Name the two factions of the Communist Party.
30. Who inaugurated the New Deal?
31. Who founded the Fascist Party and when?
32. Who wrote the *Mein Kampf*?
33. Who controlled the foreign policy of Germany during the period 1923-20?
34. Who were the close associates of Hitler?
35. When did Hitler assume the offices of both President and Chancellor?
36. Who was Alfred Dreyfus?
37. When was the National Government formed in England? Who became the head of the government?

IMPORTANT DATES

1.	September 4, 1870	:	Third French Republic
2.	1917	:	Russian Revolution
3.	1921	:	New Economic Policy proclaimed by Lenin
4.	1924	:	Death of Lenin
5.	1929	:	Economic Crash
6.	March 4, 1933	:	Franklin D. Rooservelt becomes president of U.S.A.
7.	March 1919	:	Foundation of Fascist Party
8.	October 1922	:	Fascist rule under Mussolini in Italy
9.	January 1933	:	Hitler became Chancellor
10.	August 1934	:	Hitler combined Presidency with Chancellorship
11.	August 1931	:	National Government in England under Mac Donald
12.	1935	:	Stanley Baldwin became the Prime Minister of England

UNIT - V

THE SECOND WORLD WAR

Foreign Policy of Hitler: Repudiation of the Versailles Treaty: German Rearmament

The basic principles of Hitler' s foreign policy formulated in *Mein Kampf* was the acquisition of new living space in Eastern Europe which was essential to the future of the German race. In another book which Hitler wrote in 1928 and which was not discovered until after the Second World War, he repeated the basic foreign policies for Germany-complete passivity, revision of the Versailles Treaty to restore the boundaries of 1914 and a 'clear far-seeing territorial policy'. As Mussolini claimed for Fascism a new ideology which made all else subordinate to the State, so Hitler evolved a complete doctrine of racialism. The doctrine presented Germans as the 'master race' (Herrenvolk) with a historic destiny to rule the world once it had purged itself of contamination by Jews, Socialists and Communists. Younger generations, fascinated by this doctrine and believing that historic destiny on their side, gathered round Hitler. Moreover, the idea of war with France had run like a red thread through all his statements concerning foreign policy ever since 1919. European powers were not unconcerned about the aims of Hitler's policy. Sir Horace Rumbold, the British ambassador to Berlin since 1928, was perhaps the first foreign observer to perceive that Hitler was a serious threat to his neighbours and to the peace of the world.

The limitation of armaments imposed on Germany by the Treaty of Versailles proved to be galling to Hitler and the latter wanted equality of status in armaments. By participating in the Disarmament conference that had begun in Geneva in 1932, Hitler persuaded other powers to grant Germany equality of status in armaments. Fully aware that the other Powers were reluctant to reduce their forces to Germany's level, he insisted that all controls must be lifted. The French, supported by the British Government, refused to yield. This gave Hitler the excuse he needed. In October 1933, Hitler withdrew from the Disarmament Conference and from the League of Nations as well.

After concluding German-Polish Pact in January 1934 and bringing Saar to the Reich by a plebiscite in January 1935, Hitler proceeded to repudiate the military restrictions of the Versailles Treaty. On March 7, 1935, the British Government published a White Paper relating to the question of defence. This drew attention to the fact that 'Germany was rearming openly on a large scale, despite the violations of the Treaty of Versailles'. On March 9, the foreign governments were officially notified of the existence of a German airforce. On March 16, Hitler reintroduced conscription and placed the peace-strength of the German army at 12 corps and 36 divisions or 550,000 men.

The British Government made an official protest. In a conference at Stress on April, 11, 1935, Britain, France and Italy condemned Germany's repudiation of her obligation under the Versailles Treaty. Moreover, to counteract Germany's growing influence, France concluded an alliance with Soviet Russia on May 2, 1935. But the efficacy of the Franco-Soviet alliance was almost destroyed by the Anglo-German naval agreement of June 18, 1935. This now permitted Germany to develop the formidable pocket battleships and submarines. All Germany undertook was to limit her naval strength to 35 percent of British strength. The Anglo-German Naval agreement legitimised Hitler's repudiation of the arms clauses of the Versailles Treaty.

Taking advantage of Italy's Ethiopian adventure, Hitler on March 7, 1936 sent his troops into the demilitarized zone of the Rhineland. The Rhineland invasion was perhaps the biggest gamble of his career. France alone could not take any action as she could expect no assistance either from Soviet Russia or Italy. Britain was deeply pacifist and was more concerned with Italy than with Germany. Hitler had reasons to be jubiiant. "The world belongs to the man with guts! God helps him".

Formation of Rome-Berlin- Tokyo Axis

Hitler had tried to cultivate good relations with Britain and appointed Ribbentrop as German ambassador in London. Ribbentrop tried in vain to bully the British into an alliance, in accordance with which they would give Germany a free hand in the East. But Britain received the proposal with coldness. Meanwhile, the Spanish War had consolidated a partnership between Hitler and Mussolini. In July 1936, German-Italian discussion took place on the possibility of replacing Locarno. In the same month, an agreement between Germany and Austria lessened Italian misgivings about Hitler's policy. Agreements were reached in October 1936 when Italy's Foreign Minister Ciano visited Berlin. This was the basis of Rome-Berlin Axis.

A month latter in November 1936, Germany and Japan signed an Anti-Commintern Pact. It was a joint agreement to combat international communism and invited the participation of other states. A secret protocol, signed on October 24 bound the signatories to support each other diplomatically, if either were involved in war with the Soviet Union. A year later, in November 1937, the Anti-Commintern Pact was strengthened by Italy's adhesion and a Berlin-Rome-Tokyo Axis created. Thus, a new balance of power was set-up between Germany, Italy and Japan on the one side and France, Britain and Soviet Union, on the other.

Policy of Appeasement: Russo-German Non-Aggression Pact

On November 5, 1937, in a secret talk with his military chiefs, Hitler gave them a clear idea of his foreign policy. Germany would have to acquire living space (Lebensraum) in Eastern Europe which would be possible only by the use of force. The first stages of the solution were to be the absorption of Austria and the destruction of Czechoslovakia. Hitler was aware that in carrying out a policy 'German policy would have to reckon with the two hateful antagonists England and France'. The new British Prime Minister, Neville Chamberlain, who succeeded Stanley Baldwin in May 1937 pursued a policy of appeasement towards Germany. In November 1937, the new Foreign Secretary, Lord Halifax visited Hitler. He admitted that certain changes in Eastern Europe, notably in Ausula, Czechoslovakia and Danzig, could not probably be avoided in the long run. This green signal Hitler could hardly afford to ignore.

On March 12, 1938 Hitler invaded Austria and annexed it to the German Reich. Chamberlain's policy of appeasement became manifest when he signed an agreement with Italy in April 1938. Italy promised to get out of Spain as soon as possible and to stop anti-British propaganda. Britain promised in return to work for general recognition of Italy's conquest of Ethiopia. By this agreement, Chamberlain expected to alienate Italy from Germany.

But no sooner was Italy appeased than Germany made further demands. Hitler demanded a further slice of Czechoslovakia-Sudetenland where more than three million Germans lived. In March 1938, France and Soviet Union pledged to assist the Czechs if they were attacked. But Chamberlain refused to give any assurance to maintain Czech independence against German aggression. For a few days the crisis was acute and war seemed imminent. Chamberlain made an appeal for peace. On September 28, Chamberlain invoked the aid of Mussolini in proposing a four-Power conference to settle the Sudeten question. On the following day, Chamberlain, Daladiar, Hitler and Mussolini met at Munich. The pact was signed on October 1,1938. Sudeten province and the 'Little Maginot Line', the only effective defence of Czechoslovakia was handed over to Hitler. A separate agreement, signed by Hitler and Chamberlain, stipulated that any differences between their two countries in future would be settled by negotiation. 'Peace in our time', 'Peace with Honour', Chamberlain announced on his return from Munich. 'A total and unmitigated defeat', replied Churchill in the House of Commons on October 5, 1938. It was only six months after the Munich Pact, Hitler conquered the whole of Czechoslovakia. Chamberlain's policy of appeasement was at as end.

The Munich pact convinced Stalin that Britain and France were now concerned to direct Germany's' expansion eastward and against Russia. Since Russia controlled the balance of power in Europe, Stalin could afford to make terms with Germany. As Hitler had eyes on Poland, Stalin could expect large share of Polish territory in any partition of Poland. This would create a buffer between Soviet Union and Germany and encourage Hitler to direct his main attack against the West. Moreover, Hitler was deterred from any military action unless he was sure of the attitude of the Soviet Russia. On August 23,1939 Germany and the Soviet Union, acting through Foreign Ministers Ribbentrop and Molotov, signed a Non-Agression Pact for ten years' duration. Each Power promised not to attack the other 'either individually or jointly with others'. A secret protocol provided for a division of territory between the two powers. Germany was to have Lithuania and Western Poland, the Soviet Union was to have Finland, Estonia, Latvia, the eastern part of Poland and Rumanian province of Bessarabia. Now Hitler had nothing to fear on his eastern front.

Attack on Poland (September 1, 1939) — Beginning of the Second World War

On March 21, 1939 Hitler seized from Lithuania the port of Memel. In April, Italy occupied Albania. Simultaneously, Hitler demanded from Poland Danzig and the narrow corridor that separated East Prussia from the rest of Germany. Poland refused to accept these terms. She was fortified by the British offer of an Anglo-French guarantee against aggression, which Chamberlain, the British Prime Minister, made in the House of Commons on March 31. On April 6, Poland accepted the Franco-British guarantee as a mutual obligation and one week later Britain and France guaranteed the independence of Greece and Rumania. In May, Britain signed with Turkey a mutual assistance pact.

As things were looking ominous, Britain introduced conscription. Germany countered this by denouncing the Anglo-German Naval agreement of 1935. Germany also drew closer to Italy. On May

22, 1939 Foreign Ministers Ciano and Ribbentrop signed a 10-year alliance at Berlin, the so-called 'Pact of Steel'. It provided for immediate military aid in case either signatory became involved in hostilities. On the following day, Hitler confidentially reported to his chief advisers that Poland must be attacked 'at the first suitable opportunity'.

After concluding a Non-Aggression Pact with Russia on August 23, 1939, Hitler proceeded swiftly. On August 25, Britain signed a formal alliance with Poland. On August 31, the German Government broadcast a sixteen-point proposal for the settlement of all German-Polish differences. At dawn on September 1, Germany without declaring war, sent its army and planes to Poland. Both Britain and France sent warning notes to Berlin on the 1st. Fifty hours later, on September 3,1939, after a German refusal to withdraw from the territory it had already occupied, Chamberlain declared war against Germany. Within a few hours France also declared war. Thus, 25 years after the outbreak of the First World War, Europe entered the Second World War.

Aggressive Nationalism of Italy

Imperialism and militarism were the two conspicuous features of Fascist Italy. Mussolini expressed his disappointment at the Peace Settlement of Versailles. He asserted that Italy must be an expanding power and that 'imperialism is the basis of life for every people which tends to expand economically and spiritually'. He did not like to be thwarted in his policy of expansion and hence he violently disliked the League of Nations. 'Fascism', he said in 1921, 'does not believe in the vitality and the principles of the so-called League of Nations'. He introduced universal compulsory service and increased air and navy. In 1932, he dismissed his foreign minister Grandi and assumed direct control of the army, navy and air forces of Italy. ''Words are very fine things", he told his Black Shirts in 1930, 'but rifles, machine-guns, warships, airplanes and cannon are still finer things. They are finer because right without might is an empty word". He created a press and propaganda bureau in 1934 under the supervision of his son-in-law Nobile Galeazzo Ciano.

In the 20s, Mussolini's conquests were meagre. In Libya and Somalia, his troops fought savagely to reduce armed tribesmen. After prolonged fighting they were subjugated. In the Balkans and the Middle East, he could do little because of Anglo-French opposition. In 1923, by defying the League of Nations, he seized the island of Corfu from the Greeks. But Britain and France intervened and he had to withdraw. But he obtained the disputed port of Fiume from Yugoslavia in 1924. In 1926, he established a virtual protectorate over Albania and forcibly occupied this country in 1939.

Ever since the establishment of Fascist dictatorship, Mussolini had been anxious to win for Italy a commanding position in the Mediterranean and particularly to bring the East African country of Ethiopia under Italian sway. The independent African Kingdom of Ethiopia lay between Eritrea and Italian Somaliland and was reputed to possess mineral wealth. Italy already enjoyed certain rights there. In 1925 an agreement between Italy and Britain, while granting to the latter free water rights in northern Ethiopia, promised to Italy certain concessions in the rest of the country. Ethiopia vainly protested to the League of Nations against this foreign spheres of influence in the country. In 1928, Italy concluded with Ethiopia a treaty of perpetual friendship and arbitration. After the accession of Haile Selassie as Emperor, Ethiopia refused the requests of Italy for concessions and favours. In December 1934 there occurred a clash between the Abyssian forces and Italian troops near the village of Walwal. The Italian government demanded an apology and a substantial indemnity from the Ethiopian government. In January 1935, Mussolini secured from France an agreement that Italy should have a free hand in Ethiopia. Britain was intent on maintaining friendship with Italy.

Early in 1935 Ethiopia appealed to the League and pleaded for arbitration in accordance with the Italo-Ethiopian treaty of 1928. At League Council's suggestion, representatives of Britain, France and Italy met at Paris (August 1935). Britain and France agreed to give Italy extensive economic rights in Ethiopia. Mussolini, however, rejected the offer. The League, therefore, took up the matter once more and appointed a neutral committee of conciliation. The conciliation committee drafted a plan for the international development of Abyssinia with a recognition of Italy's special interests. Though the Emperor Haile Selassie accepted the plan in principle but Mussolini rejected it.

Britain took up a stem attitude towards Italy as she feared that Italy's Abyssinian venture might endanger British pre-dominance along the Red Sea and in north-eastern Africa. The new British Foreign Secretary, Sir Samuel Hoare, emphatically declared at the Assembly on September 11, 1935 of the British Government's intention to carry out its obligation under the Covenant. But on October 3, 1935 without declaring war, Mussolini launched an attack and captured Adowa. This time the League Council acted promptly. On October 7, it declared Italy an aggressor nation and agreed to impose economic sanctions against her. The sanctions caused some distress in Italy, but they failed in their purpose. Sanctions were not imposed on oil–Italy's prime need while the latter obtained war materials from Germany. Britain and France avoided putting such pressure upon Italy as might involve them in war. In December 1935, Sir Samuel Hoare had consulted M. Laval and the latter said in the French Chamber of Deputies:

> We found ourselves instantaneously in agreement upon ruling out military sanctions, not adopting any measure of naval blockade, never contemplating the closure of the Suez Canal-in a word ruling out everything that might lead to war.

In December 1935, Hoare and Laval agreed on a plan whereby Italy was to keep most of the extensive territory she had acquired by that date, while Abyssinia was to get in exchange a narrow corridor to the Red Sea through Eritrea. The Chamberlain Cabinet, in the face of public outcry, repudiated it. Hoare resigned and was succeeded by Eden. When Foreign Secretary Eden proposed oil sanctions in early 1936, French Foreign Minister Flandin suggested a policy of appeasement. In May 1936, the Italians captured the capital Addis Ababa and the whole country was formally annexed to Italy. King Victor Emmanuel III assumed the title of Emperor of Ethiopia. Italy thus defied the League though the latter declined to recognise Italy's conquest. Haile Selassie went into exile in Britain until he recovered his Empire during the Second World War.

Aggressive Nationalism of Japan

The end of the First World War placed Japan in a serious economic crisis. The influence of the army increased with the appointment of General Baron Tanaka in 1927. In the late 20s Japan was beset with various problems. The domestic depression of 1926 was followed by a bank crisis of 1927. The worldwide depression hit early in 1930. The value of Japanese export dropped 50 per cent from 1929 to 1931.

Far more serious than the depression was the Manchurian incident of September 1931. For economic reasons, Japan had to maintain her hold over China. By the end of 1931, the whole of Manchuria was in Japanese hands. Meanwhile, the army was gaining control in the decision-making functions of the cabinet. The Prime Minister, Inukai Tsuyoshi, unsuccessfully sought to restrain the army in Manchuria. Therefore, he and others of his government were assassinated by Ultra-nationalists on May 15, 1932. During four years of government from 1932 to 1936, there emerged patriotic societies. Frustrated army officers joined patriotic societies. On February 26, 1936, some junior officers with 1400 troops staged a coup in Tokyo itself. But the mutiny was crushed after four days and its leaders executed. The period after the February revolution of 1936 in Japan was the growing influence of the army. In December 1936, Japan signed the Anti- Comintern Pact with Germany. Japan considered Soviet Union as her only serious rival in the Far East. The last thing Japan needed was a full-scale war with China. A clash between Japanese and Chinese troops near Peking in July 1937 developed into a full war with disastrous results for Japan.

War became the national cause and the Japanese army obtained full national support. The imperial Headquarters were formed in November 1937 to coordinate planning and operations between the army and the navy. The National Mobilisation Law of April, 1938 provided for the control of resources, labour prices and for censorship of the press. Political parties were ended and a totalitarian state emerged.

Breakdown of the System of Collective Security and the League of Nations

The provisions made in the convenant of the League of Nations for joint action against aggression supplemented by such agreements as the Locarno and the Kellogg-Briand pacts, envisaged the maintenance of peace and tranquillity in international reations. But the policy of collective security required military action which was seldom appreciated by the nations. 'A policy of collective security which shirked military action could never give security against men like Mussolini or Hitler.'

By 1936, the League as an agency of collective action was already a battered instrument. In 1931 Japan invaded Manchuria and set up a puppet state known as Manchukuo. This was an open challenge to the League. A Commission was appointed by the League, headed by an Englishman, Lord Lytton to investigate the dispute between Japan and China. The report of the Commission condemned the Japanese aggression and recommended that China should be sovereign in Manchuria. In February 1933 the Assembly of the League accepted the report and a month later Japan withdrew from the League. The weakness of the Collective Security system had been exposed and the confidence of the smaller powers in the League had been shaken.

Any hope that remained of the effectiveness of the League was destroyed on October 3, 1935 when Italy invaded Ethiopia. At once 50 nations assembled in the League Assembly, named Italy as an aggressor and put into force limited economic sanctions against her. Mussolini at first was surprised by the vigour of the League's reaction. But his apprehension was lessened when the limited policy of sanction operated slowly on Italy as it did not include the prohibition of oil. The early collapse of Ethiopian resistance in May 1935 decided the issue. It became clear that nothing short of military sanctions would affect the issue. In July 1937, the Assembly decided to lift the sanctions and in December Italy gave notice of withdrawal from the League. The League also demonstrated its weakness by its failure to prevent Germany from occupying the demilitarized zone of Rhineland in 1936.

The Spanish Civil War (1936-39) was another instance of the incapacity of the League to take effective action in the interest of peace. The League failed to prevent the Spanish imbroglio from developing into a general European war. In March 1938, Germany occupied and annexed Austria without the League doing anything to deter her. In 1939-40, the League failed to protect Finland from Russia, although the latter was expelled from the League. During these years, there was a general feeling that some revision of articles of the convenant ought to be undertaken. "But the fundamental question at issue was whether the League should still be armed with some sort of coercive powers .... or whether it should henceforth be merely a machinery for facilitating consultation and co-operation."[1]

Thus, in the political sphere the League failed in its main purpose. The fundamental weakness of the League was to be found in the unwillingness of nations to subordinate their own interests to the peace of the world. The League's founders overlooked the forces of nationalism. While they had the power, Italy, Japan and Germany refused to be bound by the limitations imposed on them by the Covenant of the League. Britain and France were the only major powers left to support the weak fabric of the League and even they were the hesitant supporters of the League.

The Outbreak of the Second World War

British Policy of Appeasement: Since 1919, Britain had refused to assume any burden for the preservation of peace. Without her support such plan of Collective Security as the Geneva Protocol of 1924 had little chance of success. The Chamberlain Government believed that Hitler had legitimate grievances and once these grievances were removed, the possibility of war need not arise. This policy of appeasement marked the final collapse of the doctrine of Collective Security.

Hitler's Policy of Aggression: When Hitler assumed supreme power in 1934, he made no secret of his intentions. He meant to reverse the verdict of Versailles, redeem Germany's honour and establish her unchallenged dominance in Europe. At first he proceeded with caution. In March 1935, he introduced conscription and began to rearm openly on a large scale in violation of the Treaty of Versailles. In March 1936, Hitler occupied the demilitarised Rhineland. In November 1936, Germany and Japan signed an Anti-commintern Pact. In 1937, Italy joined the pact and thus was formed the Rome-Berlin-Tokyo Axis. In November 1937, Hitler announced that Germany's basic need was greater living space to be attained only through military conquest. In March 1938 Hitler marched troops on Austria and annexed it. Thereafter, Hitler demanded Sudetenland, a portion of Czechoslovakia where three million Germans lived. The situation seemed ripe for the outbreak of a war. But Chamberlain, the British Prime Minister, was opposed to war. He seemed ready, to believe that by permiting Germany to annex Sudetenland, Hitler would be appeased and there would be no war. At the Munich Pact (October 1,1938), Hitler got a free hand to annex the Sudetenland. But it was only six months afterwards, Hitler conquered the whole of Czechoslovakia.

Hitler's Demand on Poland : On March 21,1929 Hitler seized Memel, a port of Lithuania. In April, Italy occupied Albania. Simultaneously, Hitler demanded from Poland, Danzig and the narrow corridoor that separated East Prussia from the rest of Germany. This was too much for Chamlberlain. On March 31, he guaranteed Polish independence and France did likewise. On April 6, Poland accepted the Franco-British guarantee as a mutual obligation.

As the situation worsened, Britain introduced conscription. On May 22, 1939 was signed a 10-year alliance between Italy and Germany, the so-called 'Pact of Steel' which provided for immediate military aid in case either signatory became involved in hostilities. Meanwhile, attempts were made, though half-heartedly, by the Western Powers, to draw Soviet Union with them. But on August 23, the world was surprised by, the news of the German-Soviet Non-Aggression Pact. Events moved swiftly. At dawn, on September I, 1939, Germany, without declaring war, attacked Poland.

[1] The New Cambridge Modern History. Vol. XII (1968), p. 260.

Fifty hours later, on September 3, Britain declared war against Germany. France jointed in the war at once.

Historians differ in their interpretation of the causes of the war. Some trace the basic cause to harsh terms of the Treaty of Versailles imposed on Germany at the end of the First World War. Others blame the policy of appeasement pursued by Britain and France in the 1930s the climax of which was reached in the Munich Pact of 1938. The British historian, A.J.P. Taylor has argued that Hitler's aims were moderate and justifiable. Most historians, however, ascribe the responsibility of the Second World War to Hitler's policy of aggression. 'The Second World War was Hitler's War. He planned it, began it and ultimately lost it'.

Course of the War

The Second World War began in Europe in September 1939 between Germany on one side and England and France on the other. Until the entry of the United States into the war in December 1941, the war remained essentially a European war. Italy remained neutral; Russia, too, remained neutral owing to Nazi-Soviet Pact of August 23, 1939. The war affected most of the nations in the world. The war was certainly global in character for it saw prolonged fighting in the Pacific as well as m the Atlantic, in Asia and Africa as well as in Europe.

The first phase of the war lasted from September 1939 until April 1940. It was one of unbroken German victories against Poland, Scandinavia and the Low Countries. The events of the second phase of the war (1940-41) were Italy's declaration of war against France, the defeat and fall of France, the Battle of Britain and the war in North Africa. The third phase of the war began in June 1941 and lasted until November 1942. The chief events were the German invasion of Soviet Russia, the Japanese war against the United States and the Allies and the Allied landings in Morocco and Algiers. The fourth phase of the war (1942-44) was a phase of preparation for the final repulse of Germany, Italy and Japan. The final phase of the war (1944-45) witnessed the liberation of France and the surrender of Germany and Japan.

Axis Victories

The Second World War began on September 1,1939 with a devastating attack on Poland. In less than a month Poland capitulated. On September 28, a German-Russian pact was signed at Moscow which partitioned Poland. Russia took the eastern half while Germany took the western half which contained Danzig and the Polish corridor. It was not long afterwards Russia occupied the Baltic Republic of Estonia, Latvia and Lithuania. Finland resisted until March 1940 when she ceded certain strategic areas to the Soviet Union. Meanwhile, Poland's allies, Britain and France, were powerless to help. France had a large army but she settled down behind a great system of fortification—the Maginot Line—on the Franco-German frontier.

The comparative lull in the war (October 1939-March 1940) which the Germans called 'sitting war' was suddenly broken when on April 9, 1940, Hitler struck against Denmark and Norway. Denmark was occupied in one day. Assisted by the Allies, Norway held on for several weeks until it surrendered. The British disaster in Norway led to the resignation of Neville Chamberlain on May 10, 1940. He was succeeded by Winston Churchill who inspired confidence and gave new direction to the war.

On the very day when Churchill became Prime Minister, Hitler suddenly attacked Netherlands and Belgium. The Netherlands Government asked for a armistice within five days. Hitler also gained a complete victory over the Belgians in 19 days. The end of Belgian resistance placed 3,40,000 British and French soldiers, who had been sent to help Belgium, in a critical condition. Harried by the Germans in the south, they were pushed into the vicinity of Dunkirk, with only the sea at their back But thanks to the combined power of navy and air force, the brave rearguard action of the French and the hundreds of little boats, the Allied troops evacuated from Dunkirk (May 27- June 4,1940).

The battle for France began at once. On June 10, 1940, Italy declared war against France. The French fell back in disorder and on June 14, the Germans occupied Paris. Renaud, the premier who had succeeded Daladier in March, resigned and was replaced by the 84-year old Petain. The new government asked the Germans for an armistice which was granted on June 22, 1940. The German occupied all northern and western France, but permitted Petain to retain a nominal government at Vichy. For Hitler the war seemed over: France had fallen, Britain was isolated, Russia was his ally.

The fall of France left Britain exposed to German attack separated only by the narrow water of the English Channel. Happily for Britain, Hitler made no serious efforts to cripple Britain. It seemed that Hitler became distracted by thoughts of an attack on Russia. Nevertheless, in early July 1940, German *Luftwaffe* made air attack on Britain as preparation for a possible invasion. More than 20,000 civilians were killed in London alone. Yet the German air attack on Britain failed. By the spring of 1941, Britain was retaliating with her efficient Royal Air Force which had shot down 2,400 German planes. Perhaps England would not have held out if the United States had not furnished massive aid. In March 1941, Congress passed the Lend-Lease Act. Under the terms of the Act, Britain received from the United States vast quantities of goods of various kinds to meet both civilian and military needs.

Spread of the War: Involvement of Russia, Japan and America

Despite the German-Soviet alliance, Hitler had taken the decision in June 1940 for a final break with Russia. In the beginning of 1941 Hitler had prepared 'Operation Barbarossa', a strategic plan for the invasions of Russia. He was freed from any immediate threat of invasion from the West. He was confident that the conquest of Russia would force the capitulation of Britain; it would enable him to command the immense resources of Russia and would bring to realisation his Pan-German quest for expansion in the East. Finally, Hitler believed that a war on Communism might lead to an ideological split in both Britain and the United States.

On June 22, 1941, without warning Hitler sent three large army groups across Russia's western frontier. In July, London and Moscow signed a military pact. By November, vast Russian spaces were under Nazi control. But the Germans were still not quite victors. By adopting a scorched-earth policy and guerilla tactics, the Russians harassed the Germans. The Germans failed to capture the key cities of Leningrad, Moscow, Sebastopol and Stalingrad. Further the worst winter halted German sweep. Russian counter-offensive stepped up and Hitler ordered a limited withdrawal in mid-January 1942.

In the spring of 1942, Hitler planned a new offense which was to concentrate on Caucasus oilfields. Deprived of their chief oil resources, Hitler believed, the Russians would finally have no alternative but to capitulate. Despite the resistance of the Russians, the German army occupied the Don along its whole length in July and Sebastopol fell. But Hitler split his forces between the double objectives of the Caucasus and Stalingrad. Exhausted by .the immense distances with their supply line over-lengthened, the Germans failed to capture Stalingrad and cross the Caucasus. In mid-October 1942, Hitler decided to break off the offensive.

Japan which was an ally of Germany and Italy, was preparing to attack American possessions in the Pacific. Her ambition was to rule an empire that would stretch from the mid-Pacific to the western limits of China. It would include the Dutch East Indies, the Philippines, Malaya, Indo-China, Burma and Thailand—areas that contained about one-half of the world's population. In July 1941, Japan took advantage of the fall of France to obtain military and naval bases in French Indo-China. The United States and Great Britain were alarmed. But while Tokyo was carrying on pretended negotiations with Washington, a Japanese fleet with 360 aircraft struck at the American fleet at Pearl Harbour in the Hawaiian Islands on December 7, 1941. The next day America and Britain declared war on Japan. On December 10, 80 Japanese bombers from their base at Singapore struck at the British battleship *Prince of Wales* and the armoured *Cruiser Repulse* near Singapore, and both ships were sunk.

By the end of December 1941, the Japanese were in Siam and were threatening Burma. They captured Guam and Wake Island from the Americans and Hong Kong from the British. Singapore fell on February 15, 1942. Rangoon was evacuated on March 7, Mandalay on May 1, and a week later the Japanese armies reached Akyab on the Bay of Bengal. Thus, by June 1942, the Japanese armies occupied the Dutch East Indies, Malaya, Singapore, Burma, the Philippines, much of New Guinea and the Solomon Islands. They had made what one writer has called 'the most rapid stupendous conquest in modern times'. But the limits of Japanese expansion had been reached. In May 1942, the Americans won a naval victory over Japan in the Battle of the Coral Sea, off the Solomon Islands. Exactly a month later the Japanese suffered another decisive defeat in the battle off Mid-way Island. In August, American marines landed at Guadalcanal in the Solomon Islands and held it against repeated Japanese counter-attacks. By early February 1943, the Japanese were forced to withdraw from Guadalcanal.

Defeat of Italy: Mussolini's Fall-Allied Invasion of Italy

For many months after the fall of France in June 1940, fighting between the belligerants was confined to North and East Africa. In August 1940, the Italians seized British Somaliland. The Italian attack on Egypt opened in September. In December 1940, the British in Egypt, under general Wavell, counter-attacked and took 1,30,000 prisoners. Between January and May 1941, the British troops overwhelmed the Italian garrisons in Somaliland, Eritrea and Ethiopia and restored Haile Selassie to the throne.

Meanwhile in March 1941 the Germans shipped men and materials under an experienced tank commander, General Rommel, to the assistance of the Italians. Within less than a month, the Allies were ousted from Libya, except that the garrison in Tobruk, which held out until relieved in November by General Sir Claude Auchinleck. In May 1942, Rommel embarked on a new full-scale offensive. In June, he captured Tobruk and advanced to El Alamein, only 60 miles west of Alexandria.

The advance of the Axis forces under Rommel posed a great threat to the Suez Canal. Churchill dismissed Auchinleck and put General Montgomery in command of the Eighth Army. Montgomery re-equipped the troops with new and heavier tanks sent from the United States. The decisive battle of El Alamein was fought in October 1942. One thousand massed guns opened with an intense barrage. Then British armoured tanks advanced. Unable to break through, Rommel ordered a general retreat. He lost some 60,000 men, 500 tanks and 1000 guns. As Churchil observed later 'upto Alamein we survived. After Alamein we conquered'. Within a few weeks Tobruk and Benghazi were again occupied by the British. In January 1943, Tripoli fell and the Allied forces were within striking distances of Tunis, the gateway to Italy.

Meanwhile the Anglo-American forces under General Dwight Eisenhower landed in Morocco and Algeria on November 8, 1942. The Allies hoped to close in on Tunis before German reinforcements could be concentrated there. During January and February 1943 powerful attacks were launched against American forces along the Algeria-Tunisia border. But by early March they had checked the assault and effected junction with the British forces under Montgomery on April 7. On May 6, the Allies won a decisive victory. More than 2,50,000 Germans and Italians were taken prisoner. It was a decisive Axis defeat as within a week the entire Axis forces in Africa surrendered. It made possible the next steps—an attack by the Allies upon the Balkans and upon Italy. Moreover, the North-African campaign broke the morale of Italy and was the prelude to the collapse of Mussolini's regime.

The invasion of Italy began in early July. On July 9, 1943, the Allied forces numbering about 13 divisions, landed on the coast of Sicily and quickly overcame the Italian defence. On July 19, 1943, 700 Allied planes bombed Rome. On the same day Mussolini met Hitler and asked for more German reinforcements. Mussolini's popularity had fallen to low-water mark. On July 25, 1943 King Victor Emmanuel dismissed Mussolini and had taken him into custody. The King entrusted the government to Marshal Badoglio who opened secret negotiations with the Allies. On September 3, Badoglio signed an armistice, amounting to unconditional surrender. The Allies crossed from Sicily to the Italian mainland. Despite the resistance of the Germans, the Allied forces captured Naples by October 1. Meanwhile the Nazis had freed Mussolini from prison and the latter set up a puppet Fascist republic. At last on June 4, 1944 the Allied forces entered Rome.

Allied Invasion of Europe on D Day (June 6, 1944)

Russian Offensive : The Axis defeat in Italy was followed by the liberation of Russia. Early in 1943, the Russians continued to push the Germans back to the Ukraine. The German General Paulus who had begun the siege of Stalingrad with 300,000 men, surrendered with ragged remnants of 123,000 officers and men on February 2, 1943. After the victory of Stalingrad, the Red Army recaptured Rostov, Kursk and Kharkov. In July 1943, the Germans began their great offensive on the eastern front. But these were soon lost by a Russian counter-offensive. The Russians pushed forward until, by March 1944, the Axis forces were expelled from most of the Ukraine. Meanwhile, in the north Leningrad had succumbed after a siege of nearly two years and a half. By mid-May l944, the Crimea was again in Russian possession.

Second Front in France : After the entry of the United States into the war, the Soviet Union demanded the opening of a second front in Western Europe only to engage the Germans on two sides. Though the Allies agreed in principle bat could not implement the strategy owing to events in North Africa and lack of resources. In November 1943, Churchill, Roosevelt and Stalin met at Teheran when the latter emphasised the need for a major second front-preferably in France. Churchill was in favour of operations in the Mediterranean and the Balkans 'the soft underbelly of Europe'. But Roosevelt and Stalin overcame Churchill's objections. General Dwight D. Eisenhower was appointed Supreme Allied-Commander to conduct Operation Overlord 'aimed at the heart of Germany

SECOND WORLD WAR
Eastern Front

SECOND
WORLD WAR
Western Front
German advances
Allied advances
Major aerial conflict
Scale of Miles
0 100 200 300
Narvik
FINLAND
Helsinki
Leningrad
U.S.S.R.
Norway
SWEDEN
Oslo
Stockholm
Riga
April
1940
North Sea
Baltic
Great
Britain
Denmark
Copennagen
Warsaw
1940-1942
IRELAND
Hamburg
Potsdam
Berlin
POLAND
Atlantic Ocean
Netherlands
Coventry
1941-1945
Dresden
London
Rotterdam
Dunkirk
Ostend
Bonn
Spring
1945
Prague
Calais
Remagen
CZECHOSLOVAKIA
Cherbourg
Le Havre
Winter 1944/45
Abbeville
Falaisa
July 1944
Lexemburg
Vienna
Budapest
Paris
HUNGARY
AUSTRIA
Summer 1944
Switzerland
Spring 1945
Belgrade
FRANCE
Milan
Bolorna
YUGOSLAVIA
Lyon
Bordezaue
Turin
Florence
Winter 1944/45
Fall 1944
Italy
Adriatic sea
Marseille
Nice
Fall 1944
Albania
Summer 1944
Rome
Winter 1943/44
Anzio
Greece
Cassino
Fall 1943
Naples
Madrid
Portugal
SPAIN
Lisbon
Palonia
Summer 1943
Gibraltar
Mediterranea Sea
Malta

and at the destruction of her armed forces'. Stalin promised to open a simultaneous offensive on the Eastern Front

At last in the early morning of June 6, 1944 the invasion time or D-Day arrived when the Allied forces, under the command of Eisenhower, landed on the Normandy beaches of France. This was the greatest water-borne invasion of Europe. Ten thousand planes, four thousand ships to ferry troops and supplies, eighty warships to guard the armada, and artificial harbours to provide port facilities contributed to success. In mid-August, the United States Seventh Army, landed near Cannes in southern France. By the end of August, the Allies had two million men in France. Paris fell to the Allies on August 25. After liberating France, the Allied forces pushed into Belgium and Luxemburg, freed Brussels and Antwerp and entered Germany on September 11, 1944—ninety seven days after D-Day.

Collapse of Germany: Hitler Commits Suicide (Apri1 30,1945)

Even in the midst of defeat, Nazi Germany made a determined bid to recover its power. In mid-November 1944, a general offensive was launched by all six Allied armies on the Western front. It yielded little result at heavy cost. In mid-December, the Germans under their experienced commander, Marshal Von Runstedt, struck back at the heavily forested area of Ardennes. Soon a whole sector of the Allied line in Belgium and Luxemburg was thrown into confusion: a great 'bulge' opened which had to be closed at all costs. In the so-called 'Battle of the Bulge', Runstedt cut 50 miles through American lines and reinvaded Belgium. Supplementing this effort, Hitler employed small, unpiloted aircraft bombers which did considerable damage to the civilian population of London. Next were the long-range rockets—so-called V-2—against which no effective defence could be found in time. But the Nazi offensive proved to be temporary. By the end of January 1945, the Germans were again driven out of France with the loss of 120,000 men. The Ardennes offensive had exhausted Hitler's last reserves—it hastened rather than delayed the fall of Germany.

The opening of the Second Front in June 1944 brought great advantage to the Russians. After overrunning Rumania, Bulgaria, Poland, Russian forces reached by January 31,1945 the Lower Oder, only 40 miles from Berlin. Meanwhile in early February, 1945 Churchill, Roosevelt and Stalin met at Yalta in Crimea. Here a general plan for the destruction of Germany was approved. In early March, Eisenhower's armies began a general advance towards the Rhine. They were followed by the British to the North and the French to the south. On April 11, the Allied armies reached the Elbe, only 60 miles from Berlin.

In March and April, 1945, Russian armies under Generals Zhukov and Konev took Danzig and Vienna, overran Czechoslovakia and rushed towards Berlin. By April 25, Berlin had been encircled by the armies of Zhukov and Konev. On the 27th Konev's forces joined the Americans on the Elbe. On April 30, 1945, Hitler shot his mistress and himself in a bunker in Berlin. Goebbles and his family also took their own lives. On May 2, after desperate street-by-street resistance by the Germans, Berlin capitulated. On May 7, 1945, the Third Reich, under Admiral Karl Doenitz, surrendered unconditionally to the Allies. It was a formal ending of the Second World War. For the real ending took place on August 14, 1945 when Japan surrendered on the terns laid down by the Allies.

End of War in the Pacific: Surrender of Japan

The victory of Guadalcanal in February 1943 by the Allies marked the beginning of a protracted war in the Pacific. All the great island cluster groups in the Pacific West of Hawaii still remained under

Japanese control. Since the Pacific extends over more than half the surface of hte globe, the strategy of the war involved the conquest of two key areas—the Philippines and the Burma. If the Philippines could be re-taken, offensive operations by air and sea could be launched *via* Formosa and Okinawa, against Japan itself. Reconquest of Burma would open the way into China. At the same time efforts were made of using China as a base for a successful Allied invasion of the Japanese homeland.

American and Australian troops under General MacArthur spent most of 1943 and 1944 along the New Guinea Coast. The autumn of 1944 marked the beginning of two great Allied campaigns in the Public. The one, under Rear Admiral Lord Louis Mountbatten involved the reconquest of Burma and the other by General MacArthur involved the reconquest of the Philippine Islands. On October 19, 1944, the United States Sixth Army with 250,000 men moved towards Leyte, the centre of the Philippine Archipelago. There took place the greatest naval battle of the war. It was a decisive American victory and made possible the conquest first of Leyte and eventually of the whole of hte Philippines. In November 1944, the first major strike was delivered on a Japanese Island, Honshu. In January 1945, MacArthur made a surprise landing on Luzon, the largest of the islands. Manila fell on February 23, 1945.

Meanwhile, the Americans conquered Iwo Jima in February and Okinawa in April in preparation for the eventual invasion of Japan. The shock of the news along with Moscow's repudiation of the neutrality pact with Japan, precipitated the fall of the Japanese cabinet on April 5, 1945. The war had come to the doorstep of Japan as the airfields were within less than 400 miles of Japan. Since November 1944, Japan had been under heavy and continuous bombardment by the super fortress, B-29. By the end of May more than 185,000 had been killed and injured at Tokyo while 3 million rendered homeless. In May 1945, the British recovered most of Burma

The collapse of Japan was imminent. Emperor Hirohito—became convinced that further fighting was futile and that they should sue for peace. Eventually it was decided on June 20 that Prince Konoye should be sent on a mission to Moscow to negotiate for peace. On July 17, 1945 at Potsdam in Germany, President Truman of U.S.A., Premier Attiee of Britain and Chiang Kai-Shek of China issued a declaration demanding unconditional surrender of Japan as an alternative to complete destruction. Japan rejected the demand.

The anticipated entrance of the Soviet Union in the war lest she might gain an advantageous position in the Far East led President Truman to take the hard decision of using atom bomb to hasten Japan's collapse. On August 6, 1945, the first atomic bomb was dropped on Hiroshima in Japan which destroyed half of the city and caused 80,000 deaths. Two days later, on August 8, Moscow declared war on Tokyo and sent troops into Manchuria and the Japanese half of the island of Sakhalin. On August 9, a second atomic bomb was dropped on Nagasaki in Kyushu, destroying the whole municipal area and killing 10 thousands of people. On the following day, Japan offered to surrender unconditionally which was accepted by the Allies on August 14. But the formal armistice was not signed until September 23,1945.

Causes of the Defeat of Axis Powers

The German attack on the USSR rapidly transformed the diplomatic balance. This opened the way for Great Britain to join the Soviet Union and to rebuild a new version of the diplomatic system of the First World War. An Anglo-Soviet Treaty of Mutual Assistance was signed to Moscow on July 12, 1941. The German-Soviet Pact was formally annulled. But the crucial point was the participation of the U.S.A. in the war as 'Without the USA, the Allied powers amounted to little than a club for invalids.' The Japanese bombers attack on the US Pacific fleet at Pearl Harbour on Hawai on

December 7, 1941 unlocked the door of the Grand Alliance. The Big Three with war winning trio of Churchill, Stalin and Roosevelt—were in business. The German, however, did not anticipate the participation of the USA in the war. They were counting on finishing the war before the Americans could intervene.

In the initial stage, the Grand Alliance could achieve little against German hegemony in Europe. The immediate tasks were to secure the lines of communication, to obstruct Germany's advance, to cripple Germany's war industries and to devise offensive action in the future. Aerial bombing on main German cities did not achieve the expected results. Western operations to supply the Soviet Union with war materials gathered pace from 1941. With the opening of a second front in Europe, German offensive in the East was to a certain extent lessened. War in Italy and Anglo-American landings on the Western extremities of North Africa spelled danger for the German armies.

Having survived the initial onslaught of 1941, Soveit Russia deployed inexhaustible strength of Red Army buttressed by the T-34, the best tank of the war. They were helped by the wilderness and the weather as well as the brilliant generalship of Marshal Zhukov. The battle of Stalingrad where the German army surrendered in February 2, 1943 flashed round the world, giving heart to anti-Nazi resistance movements. In the spring of 1943, the Red Army launched general offensive which rolled back the Nazi enemy. The tide, to use Churchill's metaphor, had turned.

From mid-1943, the Grand Alliance held the leverage. The Reich, though fighting stubbornly, was under siege. The Soviets held the initiative on land. The Anglo-Americans held mastery of sea and air. The combined resources of American technology, of Russia manpower, and of the British Empire were too much for Hitler to bear. For political and strategic coordination, the 'Big Three' organised three personal meetings—at Teheran (December 1943), at Yalta (February 1945) and at Postdam (June 1945). The Americans bore the chief brunt in carrying on the simultaneous war against Germany and Japan.

The Red Army's offensive of 1943-45 kept the Germans on the tenterhook of suspense. They began in the Baltic States, Byelo-Russia and Ukraine and ended with the siege of Berlin. They were organized in colossal concentration of men and material in front of the Germans' over-stretched lines and then unleashed in irresistible fury. In each of these movements, the basis tactic was to envelope the points of resistance. The Soviet drive into Central Europe was the beset tactical military operations crushing the German opposition beneath its wheel. The Soviet advance into the Balkans in August 1944 changed the complexion of the war.

In the west, the Second Front was finally opened on June 6, 1944, D-Day when the Allied troops landed on their beaches of Normandy. Operation Overlord involved not only the greatest technical feat of the war but also the concentration of colossal resources 156,000 men, 2,000 warships, 4,000 landing craft, 10,000 war planes. The Allied army surprised the German defenders, bombarded by heavy shells from unseen warships, and mercilessly strafed from the air. The Germans had nothing to do but run for safety. After that, the Allies' road was clear for the race of Paris and the drive for the Rhine. On July 20, 1944, an attempt was made to assassinate Hitler. The French resistance worked closely with the American command forcing the German garrison to surrender. However, In December 1944, in the 'Battle of the Bulge', the Germans made the last major armoured counter attack in the Ardennes. The terminal conquest of Germany took place in January to May 1945 amidst harrowing scenes of heavy bombardment reducing every German city to hecatombs of rubble and corpses. "Just as doctors will debate the exact moment of human death, in heart, brain, lungs, or limbs, so it is with bodies politic. In the case of the Third Reich, the siege of Berlin ensured suffocation; the suicide of the Fuhrer on 30 April prevented all chance of recovery; the general surrender of 8/9 May marked the last twitch."

ESSAY TYPE QUESTIONS

1. Account for the rise of Fascism in Italy.
2. Trace the rise of Mussolini. How did he consolidate his position?
3. Give an account of Mussolini's foreign policy.
4. Narrate briefly the gradual steps by which Hitler captured power in Germany.
5. Discuss the basic principles of Hitler's foreign policy. Write in brief his expansionist policy till the conclusion of the Munich Pact.
6. Why did Britain and France follow a policy of appeasement towards Germany?
7. What were the causes of the Second World War?
8. Narrate the course of the Second World War till the fall of France (June 1940).
9. How were Russia, Japan and America involved in the Second World War?
10. Narrate the circumstances leading to the fall of Italy in 1943.
11. Trace the history of the Second World War from D. Day (June 1944) to the fall of Germany.

SHORT ANSWER TYPE QUESTIONS

12. What was Fascism? Account for its rise in Europe.
13. How did Mussolini establish dictatorial powers at home?
14. Discuss the causes and effects of Italo-Ethiopian War.
15. Give a pen picture of Germany after the First World War.
16. What were Nazi ideals? How did Hitler organise the Nazi party?
17. Why the period from 1930 to 1933 was called a *testing period* for Hitler?
18. In what way did Hitler repudiate the Treaty of Versailles?
19. Trace the circumstances leading to the formation of Rome-Berlin-Tokyo Axis.
20. Discuss the circumstances leading to the conclusion of the Munich Pact.
21. What were the chief features of Japanese militarian after the First World War?
22. What were the causes of the breakdown of the system of Collective Security and the League of Nations?
23. What were the immediate cause of the Second World War?
24. What led to the collapse of France?
25. Analyse the causes and effects of German invasion of Russia.
26. How did Japan get involved in the war? Trace the course of her victories till 1942.
27. Describe, in brief, the involvement of Axis and Allied forces in Africa in the Second World War.
28. What was 'Second Front'? What was its effects on the course of the Second World War?
29. Describe the last phase of the war that brought about the collapse of Germany.

30. Narrate the circumstances leading to the fall of Japan.
31. What were the causes of the defeat of the Axis Powers?

OBJECTIVE TYPE QUESTIONS

32. Who founded the Fascist Party and when?
33. Who wrote the *Mein Kampf*?
34. When and why was Munich Pact signed?
35. Who were the Axis Powers?
36. What was Anti-Commintern Pact? When was it signed?
37. What was the meaning of Lebensraum?
38. What was 'Pact of Steel'? When and between whom was it signed?
39. When the between whom was the ten-year Non-Aggression Pact signed?
40. When did the Second World War start?
41. What do you understand by the Axis Alliance?
42. What was 'Operation Barbarossa'?
43. When did the Allies declare war against Japan?
44. What was D-Day?
45. Who was the Chief Commander of the Allies to conduct D-Day?
46. When did Hitler commit suicide?
47. When did the Second World War come to an end in Europe?
48. When and where were atom bombs dropped?
49. When did Japan surrender?

IMPORTANT DATES

1.	March 1919	:	Foundation of Fascist Party
2.	October 1922	:	Fascist rule under Mussolini in Italy
3.	January 1933	:	Hitler became Chancellor
4.	August 1934	:	Hitler combined Presidentship with Chancellorship
5.	January 1934	:	German-Polish pact
6.	January 1934	:	Franco-Soviet Pact
7.	May 1935	:	Rome-Berlin Axis
8.	November 1936	:	Anti-Commintern Pact between Germany and Japan
9.	November 1937	:	Rome-Berlin-Tokyo Axis
10.	March 1938	:	German annexation of Austria

11.	October 1938	:	Munich Pact
12.	August 1939	:	Russo-German Non-Aggression Pact
13.	Sep. 1, 1939	:	Hitler's attack on Poland
14.	May 27-June 4, 1940	:	Battle of Dunkirk
15.	June 22, 1940	:	Fall of France
16.	June 22, 1941	:	German invasion of Russia
17.	December 8, 1941	:	America and Britain's declaration of war against Japan
18.	September 3, 1943	:	Unconditional surrender of Italy
19.	June 6, 1944	:	D-Day: Allied Invasion of Europe
20.	April 30, 1945	:	Suicide of Hitler
21.	May 7, 1945	:	Unconditional surrender of Germany
22.	August 6 and August 9, 1945	:	Dropping of atom bombs on Hiroshima and Nagasaki
23.	September 2, 1945	:	Surrender of Japan

UNIT - VI

THE COLD WAR

Background to the Cold War

Just before his suicide in 1945, Hitler had made the statement "With the defeat of the Reich, there will remain in the world only two powers capable of confronting each other—the United States and the Soveit Russia. The laws of both history and geography will compel these two powers to a trial of strength." The harmony that had existed between the Western countries and Russia disappeared after the end of the Second World War. It became clear that the ideological differences between the two groups were too deep to be removed by any cooperation. The Anglo-Americans feared the permanent Soviet domination of Eastern European and the threat of Communist influence in the democracies of Western Europe. The Soviets, on the other hand, were determined to maintain control of Eastern Europe. In February 1946, Stalin declared that communism and capitalism could never live in peaceful co-existence.

In his assessment of the World politics, George F. Kenan, the senior U.S. diplomat in Moscow, emphasised on February 22, 1946 the deep-rooted animosity of the communists to the capitalist world. Kenan's advice was unequivocal-instead of offering the tempting bait of accommodation, which would never work in any case it was better to concentrate, instead, upon checking the spread of Soviet power. The Kremlin, he insisted, would yield only to superior force. On March 5, 1946, Winston Churchill, the British war time leader, gave vent to his feeling by observing "From Stettin in the Baltic to Trieste in the Adriatic, an iron curtain has descended across the continent." Christian civilization itself, Churchill warned, was now imperilled by Communist expansions.

The strategy of the West now crystallized as a policy of containment. The United States devised a strategy aimed simultaneously at containing the Soviet influence and reducing the appeal of communism. American officials determined that the United States must assume a supervisory role so as to prevent the virus of Communist influence into the eastern Mediterranean and into the oil-rich Middle East. On March 12, 1947, U.S. President told Congress in his appeal for the Greak-Turkish aid package: 'At the present moment in world history, nearly every nation must choose between alternative ways of life.' After cataloguing the perfidies of the Soviet Union, though never directly naming it, Truman concluded with the exhortation that 'it must be the policy of the United States to support free people who are resisting attempted subjugation by armed minorities or by outside pressure.' That commitment was quickly dubbed the Truman Doctrine. The Truman Doctrine symbolised a declaration of ideological Cold War along with a declaration of geopolitical Cold War.

In June 1947, the United States publicity announced the second major phase of its diplomatic offensive, Secretary of State George C. Marshall, promised US aid to all European countries willing to coordinate their recovery efforts. British Foreign Minister Ernest Bevin and French Foreign Minister Georges Bidault responded favourably to Marshall Plan. Other Western European governments seized a golden opportunity to help alleviate serious economic problems and thwart Soveit expansion. The Marshall Plan eventually provided £ 13 billion in assistance to Western Europe, helping economic recovery there, encourage European economic integration, and restore an important market for American goods. Stalin, fearful that the European Recovery Programme would be used to loosen Russia's grip on its satellites, cautioned them to keep aloof from the Plan. Soveit Foreign Minister warned that the Marshall Plan would 'split Europe into two groups of states.'

The Soviet reaction to Marshall plan was quick. In September 1947, at a conference in Poland, the Soviets established the Communist Information Bureau (Cominform) as a means of tightening control over their satellite states in Eastern Europe. Decrying the Marshall Plan as a part of a concerted strategy to forge a Western alliance against the Soviet Union, chief Russia delegate, Anderei Zhdanov said the world was now divided into two camps. A Soviet-sponsored coup in Czechoslovakia, in February 1948, followed. Along with brutal repression of the non-communist opposition in Hungary, the Czech coup crystallized East-West split.

It was against this background the Brussels Pact of April 1948 was formed. The mutual security agreement between Britain, France and the Benelex group (Belgium, Netherlands and Luxemburg) was formed. It set up permanent organisation for joint military action in the event of an armed attack in Europe. The Pact, Bevin hoped, could serve as the basis for a broader Western alliance. It was meant 'to keep the Americans in, the Soviets out, and the German down.' The North Atlantic Treaty Organization (NATO) met the needs identified by Bevin. Signed in Washington on April 4, 1949, NATO brought together the Brussels signatories, Italy, Denmark, Norway, Portugal, Canada, Britain, France and the United States in a mutual security pact. Each of the member-states consented to treat an attack on one or more as an attack on all. Eventually, Russia and the Communist states of Eastern Europe formed a similar organisation under the terms of the Warsaw Pact (1954). Thus, a basic tension grew up between the two powers blocs which may be termed a 'Cold war' opposed to a 'hot' or shooting war. It foreshadowed the outbreak of another global conflict. In the world of Friedmann: 'A world divided into two camps is still a world living under shadow of war.'

Berlin Crisis

The Cold War reached its peak during the Berlin crisis of June 1948 - May 1949. On June 24, 1948 Soviet occupation forces in the eastern zone blocked Allied road and rail access to the western zones of Berlin. By isolating the western enclave in that divided city, located 125 miles within Soviet-occupied eastern Germany, Stalin wanted to derail the establishment of the separate West German state he so feared. U.S. government advocated sending an armed convoy along the access routes to assert Allied rights, but neither the British nor the French was prepared to risk war. Truman responded by initiating a round the clock airlift of supplies and fuel to the two million embattled residents of West Berlin. Perhaps Stalin hoped to drive the Allies from Berlin or to prevent the setting up of a West German State. In the event, the blockade only frightened the Western powers into stronger new measures. On April 4, 1949, the foreign ministers of the United States, Britain, France, Belgium, the Netherlands, Luxembourg, Italy, Portugal, Denmark, Iceland, Norway and Canada founded the North Atlantic Treaty Organisation (NATO) providing for mutual aid in case of attack

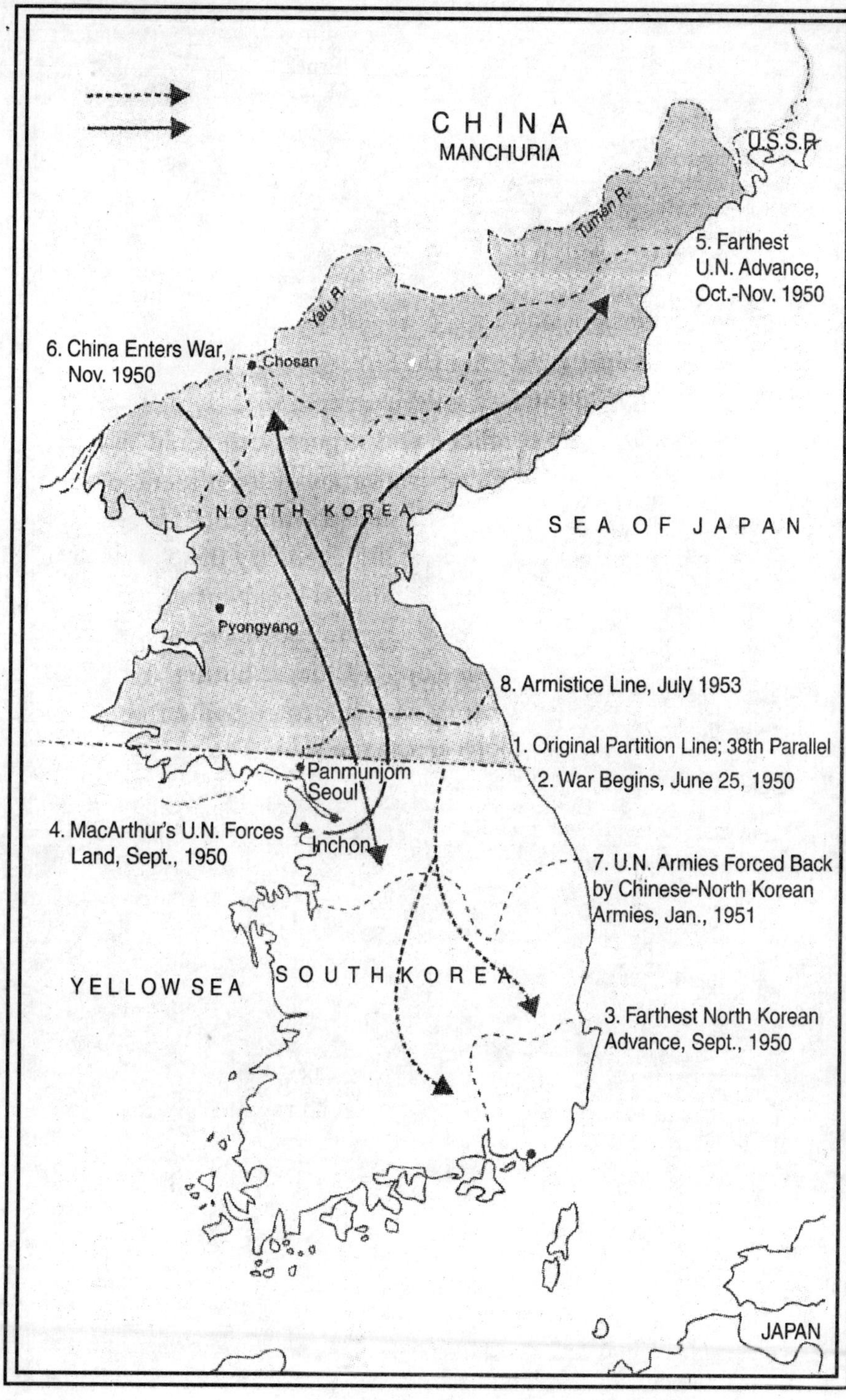

The Korean War, 1950-3

against any member. On May 8, 1949, the West German parliamentary Council adopted a constitution and on May 23, the Federal Republic of Germany came into being. On May 12, Stalin finally called off what had turned into an ineffectual blockade. The Soviet countered by creating the German Democratic Republic (October 7, 1949) in their occupation zone. Europe's Cold War lines were now clearly demarcated, the division of Germany between west and east reflecting the broader division of Europe into American-led and Soviet-led spheres.

Korean War

In 1910, Japan annexed Korea. After the outbreak of the Sino-Japanese War (1937) and of World War II in the Pacific (1941), Japan attempted to obliterate Korea as a nation. Japan's surrender in August 1945 ended 36 years of Japanese rule over Korea. The Cairo Declaration issued in December, 1943 by the United States, Britain and China pleaded independence for Korea in due course. During the autumn of 1945, Soviet and American troops entered Korea and divided it along the 38 parallel into two occupation zones. The Moscow Conference of December 1945 established a joint U.S.-U.S.S.R. Commission to Korea for the settlement of the question of a unified Korea. But the attempt ended in fiasco. The United States presented the question of Korean unification to the United Nations in September 1947. In November, the U.N. General Assembly adopted a resolution that called for general elections in Korea under the observation of a UN temporary commission on Korea. Those elected were to form a National Assembly and arrange with the occupying powers for the withdrawal of their troops from Korea. The U.S.S.R., however, prevented the Temporary Commission from entering the Northern zone. The south, however, held elections under the supervision of the Temporary Commission on May 10, 1948. Shortly afterwards, a constitution was adopted and Rhee was elected President on July 20. Finally, on August 15, the Republic of Korea was inaugurated with Seoul as the capital, and the military government came to an end. Meanwhile on November 18, 1947, the Supreme People's Assembly of North Korea set up a committee to draft a constitution. The new constitution was adopted in April 1948 and on August 25, election for members of the Supreme People's Assembly were held with a single list of candidates. Kim II Sung was appointed premier. On September 9, 1948, Democratic People's Republic of Korea was proclaimed with the capital at P' Youngyang.

The division of Korea left a trail of bitterness among the people. The U.S. occupation forces completely withdrew from Korea by June 1947. In 1949-50, the United States authorised substantial military aid which was yet to reach when North Korean troops invaded the South. The Soviet occupation force left North Korea in December 1948. By a reciprocal aid agreement with North Korea in March 1949, the U.S.S.R. agreed to furnish heavy military equipment. By June 1950, North forces numbered 135,000 including a tank brigade. On June 25, 1950, North Korean troops launched a full-scale invasion of the South.

On June 26, 1950 the UN Security Council condemned the invasion of South Korea. On June 27, U.S. President Harry S. Truman issued the order for U.S. air and naval force to resist Communist aggression in Korea. But Seoul fell on June 28. The UN approved the creation of a united command in Korea, and General Douglas Mac Arthur was appointed commander. Ultimately, 16 UN member states sent armed contingents, but U.S. and South Korean troops bore the brunt of the fighting.

The North Koreans continued to advance despite the presence of U.S. troops in the field. On September 15, Mac Arthur counter-attacked and soon UN forces were driving through North towards the Yalu river border with China. On October 7, 1959, the UN General Assembly adopted a U.S. resolution to establish a unified, democratic Korea. In November, however, contrary to Mac Arthur's predictions, Chinese forces attacked across the Yalu. By the new year, UN armies had retreated south of the 38th parallel, but Mac Arthur was in favour of the escalation of the war. British Prime Minister Attlee strongly opposed the extension of the war or the use of nuclear weapons. By April 1951 the UN forces had recaptured Seoul and regained the 38th parallel.

The effects of the Korean war reverberated around the World. Europeans feared that Korea was a division and that Stalin's real aim was to attack in Europe. Accordingly, America agreed in September 1950, to contribute U.S. divisions to a NATO army under the command of General Eisenbower. As American and public resentment became hostile towards the continuance of the war, President Truman sought a negotiated peace. Mac Arthur tried to undermine this policy by observing that "there is no substitute for victory," where upon Truman dismissed him for insubordination. American Senate held hearings on the propriety of the "limited war" strategy. Marshall defended the President, arguing that a wider war in Asia would expose Europe to attack, while General Omar Bradley opined that Mac Arthur's plans would "involve us in the wrong war, at the wrong place, at the wrong time and with the wrong enemy." Mac Arthur retorted that limited war was a form of appeasement.

Truce negotiations opened on July 10, 1951 after the Chinese had dropped their demand for withdrawal of all foreign troops from Korea and admission of the people's Republic to the UN in place of Nationalist China. The talks broke off in August, then resumed at Panmunjom in October. Bitter fighting continued for two more years each side trying to gain tactical advantage. The talks centred on two issues—the demarcation line between North and South Korea and the repatriation of more than 150,000 Chinese and North Korean prisoners of war. After hinting that the United States might resort to use of the atomic bombs, the newly-elected President Dwight Eisenhower achieved an armistice signed at Panmunjom on July 27, 1953. The United Nations proposals, by and large, were accepted. The military line became the boundary between North and South Korea and a demilitarized zone was created that extended along each side of the boundary. In addition, commissions were established to enforce the cease-fire. A Neutral Nations Commission for Repatriation was entrusted with the repatriation of prisoners.

The war resulted in roughly 4,000,000 casualities including civilians. During the war, 2/5th of Korea's industrial facilities were destroyed and 1/3rd of its homes devastated. After the war, the UN Korean Reconstruction Agency (UNKRA) was established to carry out economic aid to South Korea with most of the contributions provided by the United States. The UNKRA came to an end in 1958, but UN emergency relief and aid from other international agencies continued.

The Cuban Missile Crisis

The Cold War passed through several distinct phases. In the 1950s when the USA had a superiority in the nuclear arsenal, the Soviets could not risk a major clash. At the Moscow meeting in January 1951, whilst the Americans were tied down in Korea, Stalin gave a clarion call to the leaders of the Soviet bloc to prepare for a Third World War. But the plan was never carried out. First Britain (1952), then France (1960) developed independent nuclear capacity.

In the late 50s, the situation underwent rapid changes. From the successful detonation of an atomic bomb the Russians began to build up a massive arsenal of medium and long-range missiles. Moreover, in 1957 it announced the successful orbiting of an object in space—the first Sputnik. However, with the emergence of Khrushchev as Russia's chief policy maker in 1956, tension between the two superpowers began to ease. In April 1956, the dissolution of the Comminform was announced. However, a recurrence in 1961 of the Berlin crisis embittered the relations of the two powers. By then migrations from East Berlin to West Berlin had reached gigantic proportions. Khrushchev demanded an end of Western occupation. A violent show-down seemed to be inescapable. A meeting between him and President Kennedy in Vienna (1961) did not resolve the issue, but it helped to avert the crisis.

In the midst of this crisis, the Soviets uniltaterally broke the moratorium on nuclear testing. Soviet technology had also perfected a smaller warhead for the new Soviet missiles now ready to be deployed. Khrushchev tried to redress the balance by insinuating 42 medium-range missiles into Cuba, whence they could reach any part of the Unites States. He hoped to strike a bargain in negotiations with the USA leading to a neutralized Germany, which in turn might help Moscow persuade the Chinese to cease their own nuclear programme, Instead, the ploy brought the world to the brink of war. On October 14, 1962, U-2 spy planes photographed the missile sites in Cuba. Two days later Kennedy convened a secret crisis-management committee that favoured a surgical air-strike to destroy the sites. The President, however, opted for a palliative measure; naval blockade to prevent Soviet freighters from reaching Cuba and an ultimatum demanding that the bases be dismantled and the missiles removed. On October 18, Soviet ambassador Andrey Gromyko met with Kennedy and denied that the U.S.S.R. had any sinister motive with respect to Cuba. On October 22, Kennedy informed the nation of the crisis and asked Khrushchev to pull back from "this clandestine, reeckless, and provocative threat to world peace." For two days the world was kept in suspense, and on the 24th Soviet ships in transit changed their course from Cuba. On the 26th, Khrushchev offered to withdrew the missiles in exchange for a U.S. pledge never to invade Cuba. The next day the Soviets broached a fresh demand that the United States withdraw its own missiles from Turkey. On the 28th, the Soviets agreed to dismantle the Cuban bases in return for a no-invasion pledge. Several months later, the United States quietly removed its missiles from Turkey.

The Cuban missile crisis heightened the prestige of Kennedy and the United States and was attributed to American superiority in nuclear weapons. In fact, neither side was willing for a show-down, and it was probably the overwhelming U.S. superiority in conventional naval and air power that left the U.S.S.R. no option but retreat. However, it should not be construed as an unmitigated American victory. Kennedy's pledge never to overthrow Castro by force meant that the United States would have to tolerate whatever mischief he might contrive in the future. Nevertheless, Kennedy warned that the United States would never tolerate any expansion of Communism in the hemisphere. Conversely, the Cuban missile crisis bolstered Soviet determination never again to be humiliated by military inferiority. Khrushchev and his successors accordingly began the largest military build up in history which tried to reach parity with the United States in nuclear forces. On the other hand, the Cuban missile crisis marked the final frustration of Khrushchev's efforts to force a German peace treaty.

Emergence of the Third World

The see-saw struggle for global power and influence between the United States, the Soviet Union and their respective allies gave birth to the very term "Third World". A political catchphrase that branded the poor, non-white and uncommitted areas of the planet, Third World originally connoted an areas of contest between West and East. Cold War pressures sometimes exacerbated, on other occasions, facilitated the transition from colonialism to independence. The superpower conflict impinged upon the process—from the South and South-East Asian freedom movements of the mid and late 1940s which opened the decolonization area.

The formation of new, post-colonical states throughout much of Asia, Africa and the Middle East and parts of the Carribean unfolded against the backdrop of the Cold War. The shape, cohesion and vitality of the Third World were affected significantly by the Cold War.

For several reasons, the developing nations of the Third World emerging from decades of Western Colonical rule, became a focal point of Soviet-American competition during the 1950s. The US Government recognised that the resources and markets of Third World areas were essential to the health of the World capitalist economy. The Soviets made a concerted bid for friends and allies among the Third World's uncommitted nations in order to weaken Western strength. Utilizing diplomacy and generous development loans, the Kremlin sought to gain influence and access to resources among the Afro-Asian nations. According to the American Secretary of State, Dean Rusk, the increasing interest of the Soviet in the developing world, demonstrated that the Soviet-American struggle had shifted from 'the military problem in Western Europe to a genuine contest for the underdeveloped countries.' He warned that 'the battles from Africa, Lain America, the Middle East Asia, are now joined, not on a military plain to the first instance, but for influence, prestige, loyalty, and so forth, and the stakes there are very high.'

The Cold War presented aspiring Third World leaders with a complex range of problems. This became evident during the anti-colonial struggles in early post war South-East Asia. He Chi Minh and Sukarno each appealed to the United States for assistance immediately following Japan's surrender. Yet each was quickly disheartened. Ho, founding member of the Indo-China Communist Party, turned to the Soviet Union and the People's Republic of China for backing, which he began to receive early in 1950. Sukarno, on the other hand, proved his anti-communist bias by suppressing an internal communist revolt.

The bids for national self-governance mounted by Vietnamese and Indonesian nationalists illustrate clearly the importance of Cold War dynamics inside Third World countries. In the essentially bipolar world, all Third World independence movements, faced the pressure of one or the other ideological camp. In their bid for independence, the Third World sought support from one or the other of the two blocs. The pressure of the superpower conflict cast its shadow over the Third World.

With independence, newly-established Third World states faced an acute set of dilemmas. Some actively sought alignment with the Unites States. In the mid-1950s Pakistan became a formal ally of the United States. The US connection afforded Pakistan protection from India, its principal regional rival. Like their counterparts in Pakistan, Thailand also sought an American connection. The Third World nations that opted for Western alignment did so more for domestic reasons than out of a fear of communism. Such varied countries were Iraq, Iran, Saudi Arabia, Turkey, Pakistan, the Philippines, Ceylon, South Korea and Thailand.

A group of Third World leaders believed that important national goals could be more effectively advanced without any formal commitment to either West or East. Indoncsia's Sukarno, Egypt's Gamal abdel Nasser, Ghana's Kwame NKrumah and India's Jawaharlal Nehru, sought for a neutral stand for their nations from either of the Cold War power blocs. 'Once foreign relations go out of our hand into the charge of somebody else,' warned Nehru, 'to that extent and in that measure you are not independent,' Nehru was convinced that his young nation could raise its international stature and influence in world councils by assuming the role of a third force in international affairs. By remaining unattached to the American or Soviet spheres of influence, Indian planners calculated that they might be able to attract needed development assistance from both camps. 'Even in accepting economic help,' a realistic Nehru confided ' it is not a wise policy to put all our eggs in one basket.'

ESSAY TYPE QUESTIONS

1. Enumerate the course of Cold War. How far was it responsible for the rise of a bipolar world war?
2. Analyse the causes of the Korean War after the end of World War II. What were its consequences?
3. How far the strategic considerations of the superpowers were responsible for the end of the Cold War?
4. Trace the emergence of the Third World in the second half of the 20th century? What were the problems faced by the Third World countries?
5. Analyse the genesis of the Cold War.
6. What led to the Berlin Crisis of 1948-49? What were its effects in the global scenario?
7. What led to the Cuban crisis of 1962? How was it resolved?
8. Analyse the course of events that led to the end of the Cold War.
9. How far the World countries were influenced by superpowers?

OBJECTIVE TYPE QUESTIONS

10. What was Truman Doctrine?
11. What was Marshall Plan? What were its objects?
12. When was NATO formed? What were its objects?
13. What is SEATO?
14. When did the Cuban missile crisis occur?
15. When was the Nuclear Test Ban Treaty signed? Who were its signatories?
16. When did the Soviet Union collapse? What were its results?
17. Who were the leaders of the Third World countries that advocated non-alignment as their basic goals?

IMPORTANT DATES

1. March 12, 1947	:	Truman Doctrine
2. June 1947	:	Marshall Plan
3. March 1948	:	Brussels Treaty
4. 1949	:	NATO
5. 1954	:	Warsaw Pact
6. October 1962	:	Cuban Missile Crisis
7. 1963	:	Nuclear Test Ban Treaty
8. 1972	:	SALT I and SALT II agreements

UNIT - VII

The Challenge of Communism

Rise of Communist China and its Impact on International Relations

The most momentous event in the post-war world was the birth of the People's Republic of China. The event was a direct consequence of the Second World War in that it was precipitated by the defeat of Japan. Civil war broke out in China between the Nationalist Kuomintang led by Chiang Kai-Shek and the Chinese Communist Party (CCP), led by Mao Zedong (Mao Tse-tung). The Kuomintang, after nearly 40 years of power, had become corrupt and inefficient. It was no match for the Communists which had coherent policy and mass support. By the end of 1949 Chiang was forced to the island of Formosa (or Taiwan) with the remnant of his forces. In September 1949, Mao Zedong proclaimed the People's Republic of China with Chou-En-Lai as premier and Foreign Minister of the new regime.

In a series of speeches Chairman Mao stated that his aim was to create a socialist society. These objectives could be achieved by forming a coalition of elements of urban middle class with workers and peasants, under the leadership of the CCP. During the period, 1949-52, the CCP made great strides towards bringing economic growth and political strength. The determination of the Chinese troops against UN forces on the Korean peninsula in 1950-53, raised the prestige of China in international affairs. In the three years of war, a 'Resist America, Aid Korea' campaign, China enforced emergency at home. Regulations for the suppression of counter-revolutionaries (February 20, 1951) authorised police action against dissidents. At about the same time China dispatched troops to Tibet.

Under the Agrarian Reform Law of June 1950 the property of rural landlords was confiscated and redistributed which satisfied the peasants. The property of traitors, 'bureaucrat capitalists' was also confiscated. Programmes were also begun to increase production. By the beginning of 1951, the revolutionary agenda of the Communists begun to be felt in the cities. In late 1951 and early 1952, three major political campaigns carried communism to key urban groups. The Three Antis Campaign targated communist cadres who had become close to China's capitalists. The Five Antis campaign aimed at the capitalists themselves. The thought Reform campaign humbled University professors and marked a turning point in the move from Western to Soviet influence in structuring China's University curriculum.

By 1952, the new government had already increased the quantity of 33 major industrial products, 26 per cent above pre-war levels. Consequently, a Five-Year Plan along Soviet lines was set for 1953-57 in the hope of doubling output. This period was regarded as highly successful. A strong central governments' apparatus helped to foster rapid development of heavy industry. In 1953 China experimented with voluntary forms of agricultural collectivization. A campaign was launched to organize small collectives, called lower level agricultural producers' cooperatives, averaging 20 to 30 households. In July, Mao called for an acceleration to lower level, and then to higher level agricultural producers' cooperatives in the countryside. By 1956, 88 per cent of China's peasant house-holds were organised into advanced cooperatives.

The socialist transformation of agriculture, industry and commerce went relatively smoothly. However, several problems began to appear. It was found that agricultural sector was not growing fast enough to provide additional capital for its own development. Moreover, Soviet assistance had been available to China as loans and not grants.

The Communist leadership's policies towards the intelligentsia underwent a change. In 1955 began an intensive thought reform movement. Party leaders publicly discussed the role of intellectuals in the new tasks of national construction and adopted the line of 'let a hundred flowers blossom, a hundred schools of thought contend.' The 'hundred flowers' line encouraged free ranging discussion and inquiry.

In May 1958, the Eighth Party Congress announced the general line of socialist construction and the Great Leap forward. In August 1958 People's Commune was popularised. Rural cooperatives and collective farms were merged into large communes. The objective was to develop a large labour force to implement an ambitious programme of industrializations supported by increased food production. But the policy was not successful. After 1959 China experienced a severe combination of floods and drought. Despite the grave situation, China's worst problem was bad policy. The people's communes were too large to be effective. So, the programme was revised in 1962. Individual Farming was revised.

Mao personally lost considerable prestige over the failure of the Great Leap. He was in fact deeply troubled during 1961-65. Moreover, he began to lose faith in Soviet socialist revolution after Stalin's death in 1953. Mao took a number of initiatives in domestic and foreign policy during the mid-1960's. Enormous efforts continued to be made to revive the economy. The most important set of measures Mao took concerned the People's Liberation Army (PLA) which he and Lin Biao tried to make into a model organization. In 1966, Mao announced his 'Cultural Revolution' by which he intended to use the youth to save the Revolution. In May 66, Mao secretly assigned major responsibilities to the army in cultural and educational affairs. During the following months Mao encouraged the Red Guards to attack all traditional values and 'bourgeois' things.

The period from mid 1966 to early 1969 constituted the Red Guard phase of the cultural Revolution. A movement began against the Cultural Revolution. January 1967 witnessed the overthrow of provincial CCP Committees. The country was dragged on to the verge of civil war. By the summer of 1967 large armed clashes occurred throughout urban China. The resulting anarchy and chaos threw the economy into doldrum. The military tightened its grip on the entire society and Defence Minister Lin Biao was named as Mao's successor. Lin Biao declared martial law and many leaders died under the martial law regime of 1969. Soon differences arose between Lin Biao and Mao Zedong. Finally in September 1971 Lin was killed after an abortive assassination plot against Mao. During 1972, Mao suffered a serious stroke. In early 1973, Deng Xiaoping who had been purged by the radicals during the cultural Revolution, was brought back to power. From mid-1973, Chinese politics were swayed between Mao's wife, Jiang Qing and her followers later dubbed the Gang of Four - and the supporters of Zhou En-Lai and Deng. During the summer of 1974 to the late fall of 1975, Deng sought to put the four Modernizations of agriculture, industry, science and technology and defence at the top of the country's agenda. To further this effort, Deng continued to rehabilitate victims of the cultural Revolution. Mao did not like this and criticised Deng's policies. Zhou died in January 1976 and Deng was formally purged with Mao's backing in April. Many of Deng's followers also fell from power. Mao died in September 1976 and the Gang of Four was purged in October. With Mao's death and the purge of the gang of Four, the Cultural Revolution had come to an end.

The CCP leadership tried to bring some order to the country. Deng was rehabilitated in the summer of 1977. The leaders adopted an ambitious 10 years plan in early 1978 to achieve rapid economic growth. Henceforth, China began to participate in international economy. The leaders became convinced that large amounts of capital could be acquired from abroad to speed up the country's modernization. In late 1978, China formally agreed to establish full diplomatic relations with the United States. China's leaders also formally adopted the Four Modernizations as the country's highest priority. Numerous experiments were undertaken with regard to finance, banking, planning, urban economic management and rural policy.

By the mid-1980s China was in transition. Economically, financial decentralisation combined with other factors led to inflation and encourage corruption. There was widespread unrest within the country in late 1986 and again on much large scale in the spring of 1989. From May 1989 the students of Beijing began to hold demonstration in the city's Tiananmen Square. The government viewed the event as a challenge to the Communist Party's authority. The government used the army on June 3 and 4 to disperse the students in the Tiananmen Square. Thousands of students who had assembled in the square for peaceful demonstration were gunned down. China reverted to more conservative economic, political and cultural policies. In 1992, however, Deng Xiaoping sought to renew the efforts at economic reform. In November 1993, the CCP encouraged market reform processes.

New members are admitted to the United Nations on the recommendation of the Security Council and by a two-thirds vote of The General Assembly. The admittance of new members, however, has often created controversy. The most contentious application for membership, however, was that of the People's Republic of China. The matter was placed before the General Assembly at every session from 1950 to 1971. The United States successfully opposed efforts to admit the People's Republic and to expel Nationalist China (Taiwan). Finally, in 1971, the United States, in an effort to improve its relationship with China, refrained from blocking the Assembly's vote to admit the People's Republic. As a result, Nationalist China's membership and permanents Security Council seat were given to the People's Republic.

China economy had stagnated in 1976 owing to political turmoil and Mao's successors were anxious to set things in proper perspective. The leaders adopted an ambitious 10 year plan in early 1978 and used the Government's resources to raise the rate of investment and achieve rapid economic growth. One of the major changes of 1978 was China's participation in the international economy. China's leaders became convinced that large amounts of capital could be acquired from abroad to speed up the country's modernization. In late 1978, China formally agreed to establish full diplomatic relations with the United States. In the late 1970s, China enacted numerous law to create an attractive environment for foreign capital.

In the three years of war, a 'Resist America, Aid Korea' campaign translated the atmosphere of external threat into a spirit of sacrifice. Public attention was drawn to Peking's despatch of troops to Tibet at about the same time that it intervened in Korea. In 1959, the Tibetans rose in rebellion, to which Peking responded with force. Adhering to the initial pro-Soviet line, the Chinese began to pursue a cautious foreign policy lest it might invite direct U.S. retaliation against China. It was also realized that the neutralist states in Asia and Africa were not Western puppets, and it was profitable to promote friendly relations with them. These lessons led China to take a conciliatory role in the Geneva Conference on Indo-China in 1954 and to try to normalize its foreign relations.

At the Afro-Asian Conference held at Bandung, Indonesia in April 1955, Premier Zhou En-Lai symbolized China's more active diplomatic role. His slogan 'unity with all' gained world-wide attention as he told the Bandung delegates that his government was fully prepared to achieve normal relations with all countries, including the United States. Between 1955 and 1957, however, changes in Soviet and U.S. policies caused Chinese leaders to doubt the validity of conciliatory foreign policy. China adopted a more militant foreign policy when Mao announced in November 1957 that the 'East Wind prevails over the West wind.' The change in line was necessitated by the U.S. build up anti-communist regimes to encircle China and by the lack of major gains in peaceful coexistence with Third World neutrals.

China's foreign policy since 1978 reflected the country's preoccupation with domestic economic development. In International affairs China had by large avoided disputes and encouraged the peaceful evolution of events in Asia. By 1992 China had largely regained its international standing with all the United States. But by the mid-1990s both sides had taken steps toward improved relations, and China retained its most favoured nation status in U.S. trade. China adopted policy of 'One country, two systems' in order to provide a framework for the successful negotiation with Great Britain of the return of Hong Kong and adjacent territories in 1997.

The Vietnam War and the Defeat of the USA

In the latter half of the 19th Century, Vietnam was gradually conquered by the French, who controlled it as a colony (1988-1939) and then as a possession (1939-45). In May 1941 under Ho Chi Minh's inspiration, was formed the League for the Independence of Vietnam, generally known as the Viet Minh as a nationalist party seeking Vietnamese independence from France. After the Japanese surrender in August 1945, Viet Minh seized power in Hanoi. The French, however, were determined to restore their control in Indo-China. At the beginning of 1946, there were two Vietnams - a Communist North and a non-Communist South.

In March 1946, a peaceful solution appeared to be in sight when the French and Ho Chi Minh reached an agreement. Under the agreement France would recognise the Viet Minh government and give Vietnam the status of a free state within the French Union. French troops were to be withdrawn in a phased manner over a period of 5 years. However, the policies of the two governments were totally different. While Hanoi wanted total independence, the French aimed to reestablish colonial rule. Further negotiations did not resolve the basic differences between the French and the Viet Minh. In late November 1946 the French started war. This was considered as the beginning of the First Indo-China war.

Fighting between the French and the Viet Minh continued until 1954, when the French were badly defeated in the battle of Dien Bien Phu in May 1954. An international conference in Geneva in 1954 negotiated a cease-fire. It was decided that French and the Vietnamese fighting forces under the French command could move south of the 17th parallel and the Viet Minh would go north of the 17th parallel. The agreement left the Communist-led Viet Minh in control of the northern half of Vietnam, while the non-Communist southern half became South Vietnam.

The Geneva Accord stipulated that free elections be held throughout Vietnam in 1956 under the supervision of an International Control Committee with the object of unifying the country. Viet Minh leaders appeared certain to win these elections. But South Vietnam, supported by the United States, refused to hold the scheduled elections. With the assistance of the Soviet Union and China the Hanoi Government in the north began a programme of industrialization. In the south a new government appointed by Bao Dai began to build a new country; Ngo Dinh Diem was named Prime Minister and succeeded with American support. In October 1955 Diem removed Bao Dai as Chief of State and made himself President of Vietnam.

Fearing the spread of communism, the U.S. government provided economic and military assistance to the Diem regime. But the regime became increasingly unpopular with the people of South Vietnam. With support from the north, Communist-led forces, popularly called the Viet Cong tried to seize power and reunify the country. The Diem Government received American military advisers and materials. However, popular dissatisfaction with Diem continued to grow and Diem was assassinated during a military coup on November 1, 1963. A series of unstable government followed in quick succession after Diem's death and the Viet Cong increased their activities. The survival of Saigon regime was seriously threatened.

Until 1960 the United States had supported the Saigon regime only with military equipment and financial aid. All this assistance, however, proved insufficient to halt the advance of the Viet Cong. In February 1965 U.S. President Lyndon B. Johnson ordered the bombing of North Vietnam and began to send troops into the south. By the end of 1965, 1,80,000 American troops were deployed in South Vietnam under the command of General William C. Westmoreland.

The Soveit Union reacted to American escalation by trying to reconvene the Geneva Conference and bring pressure to bear on the United States to submit to the reunification of Vietnam. China refused to encourage a negotiated settlement and insisted that the U.S.S.R. help North Vietnam by pressuring the United States. The Soviets in turn resented Peking's assertion of leadership in the communist world and had no desire to sever ties with Washington. North Vietnam was caught in a quagmire. Despite his pro-Soviet stance, real politics obliged Ho Chi Minh to favour Peking. Hence North Vietnam joined in boycotting the March 1965 Communist conference in Moscow.

Meanwhile, the United States were caught into the quagmire predicted by the De Gaulle. U.S. forces reached a peak of 543,000 men in 1969. The U.S. strategy was to employ mobility, based on helicopters, and firepower to wear down the enemy by attrition. But this did not succeed. Johnson's popularity fell steadily. Most Americans favoured more vigorous prosecution to end the war, but a growing number advocated withdrawal. Anti-war dissent grew and spread. The American foreign policy was shattered by Vietnam. Three years of intensive bombing of the north and fighting in the south, did not weaken the strength of the Viet Cong and their allies from the north. In the so-called Tet offensive of February 1968, the Viet Cong and North Vietnamese attacked more than 100 cities and military bases. U.S. President Lyndon Johnson ordered a restriction of the bombing in the north. U.S. negotiations with Hanoi began in Paris in May 1968.

The War continued under a new American President, Richard M. Nixon. He began to withdraw U.S. troops gradually. Meanwhile peace talks went on in Paris. Finally in January 1973 a peace treaty was signed by the United States and the Vietnamese parties. It provided for the complete withdrawal of U.S. troops within 60 days. The signing of the Paris agreement did not bring an end to the fighting in Vietnam. The Saigon regime made a determined effort to eliminate the communist forces remaining in the South. The North Vietnamese troops also launched a major offensive against the South. Saigon's forces retreated in panic and on April 30, 1975 the Communist entered Saigon in triumpth. On July 2, 1976, the country was officially united as the Socialist Republic of Vietnam with its capital in Hanoi. Saigon was renamed Ho Chi Mihn City.

The effects of the long conflict were severe. More than 47,000 Americans were killed in action, and more than 303,000 were wounded in the war. The North Vietnamese and Viet Cong suffered about 900,000 troops killed and wounded. In addition, more than 1,000,000 North and South Vietnamese civilians were killed during the war. In the south alone, millions of people had been rendered homeless by the war. With the Communist victory in South Vietnam and Communist takeovers in neighbouring Cambodia and Laos, the new Vietnam emerged as an important South-east Asian power. In its proportional impact on Vietnamese society, the Vietnam War, 1955-75, was the fourth most severe in the World since 1816.

ESSAY TYPE QUESTIONS

1. What were the revolutionary developments in China between 1949 and 1976? How did these developments consolidate the position of Mao Tse-tung in China?
2. What was 'Cultural Revolution'? When did it come to an end?
3. Discuss the impact of Communist China on international relations.
4. State the reasons for the outbreak of the Vietnam War. How did the United States involve in the conflict?

SHORT ANSWER TYPE QUESTIONS

5. What were the objective of Mao Tse Tung in building a socialist state in China? How far did he succeed?
6. What were the difficulties that beset Mao in his objectives?
7. Make an estimate of Mao Tse-tung as a reformer and a diplomat.
8. What were the achievements of Deng Xiaoping?
9. Analyse the main events that took place in China after the death of Mao Tse Tung.
10. In what way did the Vietnam war affect the U.S. prestige?
11. What led to the Tiananmen Square Massacre?
12. How and when did China become member of the United Nations?

OBJECTIVE TYPE QUESTIONS

13. When was the People's Republic of China proclaimed?
14. Who inaugurated the Cultural Revolution? What were its objectives?
15. What led to the Tiananmen Massacre?

16. When did the battle of Dien Phu take place? Who were the contestants?
17. What was the popular name of the Communist led forces in Vietnam?
18. When was the 'Great Leap' inaugurated? What were its objectives?
19. Who was Bao Dai?
20. What was the Tet Offensive?
21. When was the Socialist Republic of Vietnam inaugurated.

IMPORTANT DATES

1.	September 1949	:	People's Republic of China proclaimed
2.	May 1959	:	The Great Leap Forward
3.	September 1976	:	Death of Mao Tse Tung
4.	June 1989	:	Tiananmen Square Massacre
5.	1971	:	China admitted as member to the United Nations
6.	May 1954	:	Battle of Dien Bien Phu
7.	October 1955	:	Ngo Dinh Diem became President of South Vietnam
8.	November 1, 1963	:	Ngo Dinh Diem assassinated
9.	July 2, 1976	:	Socialist Republic of Vietnam proclaimed

UNIT - VIII

THE MUDDLE OF THE MIDDLE EAST

THE MIDDLE EAST IN WORLD POLITICS

Establishment of Isreal

The most important area involving European settlement in the Middle East was Palestine, part of which became Isreal in 1948. The Palestinian-Israeli problem is a complex one. Three forces interacted with each other—zionism, Arab nationalism and British imperialism. The zionist move emerged as a political force of consequence in the late 18th century under the leadership of the Austrian Jew, Theodore Herzl. He helped to found the World Zionist Organisation. He believed that the assimilation of the Jews into European societies was not possible and called upon the Jews to form a state of their own. The attraction of Palestine was too strong and it became the symbol and dream of Zionist hopes. The Zionist movement of the late 19th century had led by 1917 to the Balfour Declaration by which Britain promised an eventual homeland for Jews in Palestine. When the Balfour Declaration was issued, the Jewish population of Palestine as approximately 80,000, the Arab population was a close to 700,000. Between 1933 and 1939 almost 225,000 Jews entered Palestine. The Jewish population was further increased at the end of the end of World War II as displaced East European Jews left refugee camps to find new lives in Palestine.

Whereas the Balfour Declaration had merely promised a homeland for Jews with safeguard for the Arab population, some Jewish leaders had long favoured the establishment of an independent state. As Zionism grew, Arab nationalism also grew. With the encouragement of Amin-al-Husayni, grand Mufti of Jerusalem, Arab resentment exploded in bloody riots in 1929 and again in 1936-39. For self-protection, the Jews formed Haganah (Defence), an underground militia. The Zionist cause began to benefit from the worldwide sympathy caused by the Nazi holocaust.

From the beginning, the British esperienced enormous difficulties in governing Palestine. The most controversial issues revolved around the amount of Jewish immigration to allow, the sale of lands by Arabs to Jews and eventual autonomy of Palestine. The newly-formed Arab League in turn, pledged in March 1945 to prevent the formation of any Jewish State in Palestine. At the end of World War II the political climate in Palestine had become exceedingly tense. In 1947, the issue was placed before the United Nations, and a special committee on Palestine recommended a partition, which the United Nations supported. The United States and Britain feared that the Arabs would turn to the Soviets for aid. The Soviet hoped to hasten British withdrawal and profit from the discord following partition.

Palestinian Arabs and Jews armed for the inevitable struggle. On May 14, 1948, the new State of Isreal under the premiership David Ben Gurion proclaimed its independence. It was recognised almost immediately by the United States and Soviet Union. At the moment of partition, the number of Jews had risen to some 35 per cent of the total population of Palestine. On the day after partition the Arab League launched its attack, but the desperate Jewish defence prevailed on all fronts. The UN called for a cease-fire on May 20 and appointed Count Bernadotte as mediator, but his partition plan was unacceptable to both sides. Fighting ensued throughout the area and the neighbouring Arab States invaded Isreal. But the Arab forces were not united. The Isrealis had a better organised army. From the outbreak of the war in May 1948 until a truce was established in 1949, the Israelis repulsed the Arab armies and added substantially to their territories.

The Israeli's were far more united than their defeated Arab neighbours. The country underwent economic development. Despite its lack of natural resources, and the small size of the country, Isreali economic achievement owed much to the resourcefulness and a considerable influx of capital. For a long time, the German Government paid reparations to the new state. The United States also provided a great deal of assistance.

Palestine Question and Arab Nationalism

The Balfour Declaration of November 1917 complicated the situation when it agreed to respect the national aspirations of the Jews as well as Arabs in Palestine. Palestine had long been as Arab speaking Muslin country. But after the installation of the British administration, the Jewish immigration overflowed Palestine, increasing from a barely 70,000 in 1920 to half a million in 1938. As the mandatory of Palestine, Britain tried to work out a compromise that would give some measure of satisfaction to both Arabs and Jews.

The Palestine question became highly critical after the close of the Second World War. The situation became acute with the increased national feeling of the Arabs, the misarable plight of Jews in post-war Central Europe and their attempts to enter Palestine surreptitiously and the importance of Palestine in Near Eastern oil picture. Meanwhile, the League of the Arab States extended support to the Palestinian Arabs. The League formed at Cairo in 1945 among Syria, Transjordan, Iraq, Saudi Arabia, Lebanon, Egypt, and Yemen demanded a cessation of Jewish immigration into Palestine. Anxious to end her Palestinian obligation, Britain in the spring in 1947, sought U.N. intervention. UN special committee in Palestine suggested a partition of Palestine into three spheres—an Arabic State, a Jewish State and the city of Jerusalem with one customs Union. In November 1947, the General Assembly accepted partition plan and set up a Palestine Commission to implement the plan. The Commission after convening 75 meetings, ceased to exist in May 1948. The announcement of Britain in the early months of 1948, added fuel to the Palestine cauldron. Meanwhile, the world was startled by the declaration in Tel Aviv of a new independent state of Isreal in the midnight of May 14-15, 1948. This was immediately followed by Britain's laying down of the Palestine mandate and the withdrawal of her forces.

As civil war was raging in Palestine between Arab and Jews, the former were routed by Isreali forces by December 1948. Isreal emerged from the war with about 50 per cent more land than it had been allotted under the UN plan. After the Arab-Israeli war of 1948, the Arab States, motably Egypt, took the lead in the struggle against Isreal. An Arab summit meeting held in Cairo in 1964 led to the creation of the Palestine Liberation Organisation (PLO). Declaring itself to be the sole representative of the Palestinian people, the PLO was committed to the total liberation of Palestine,

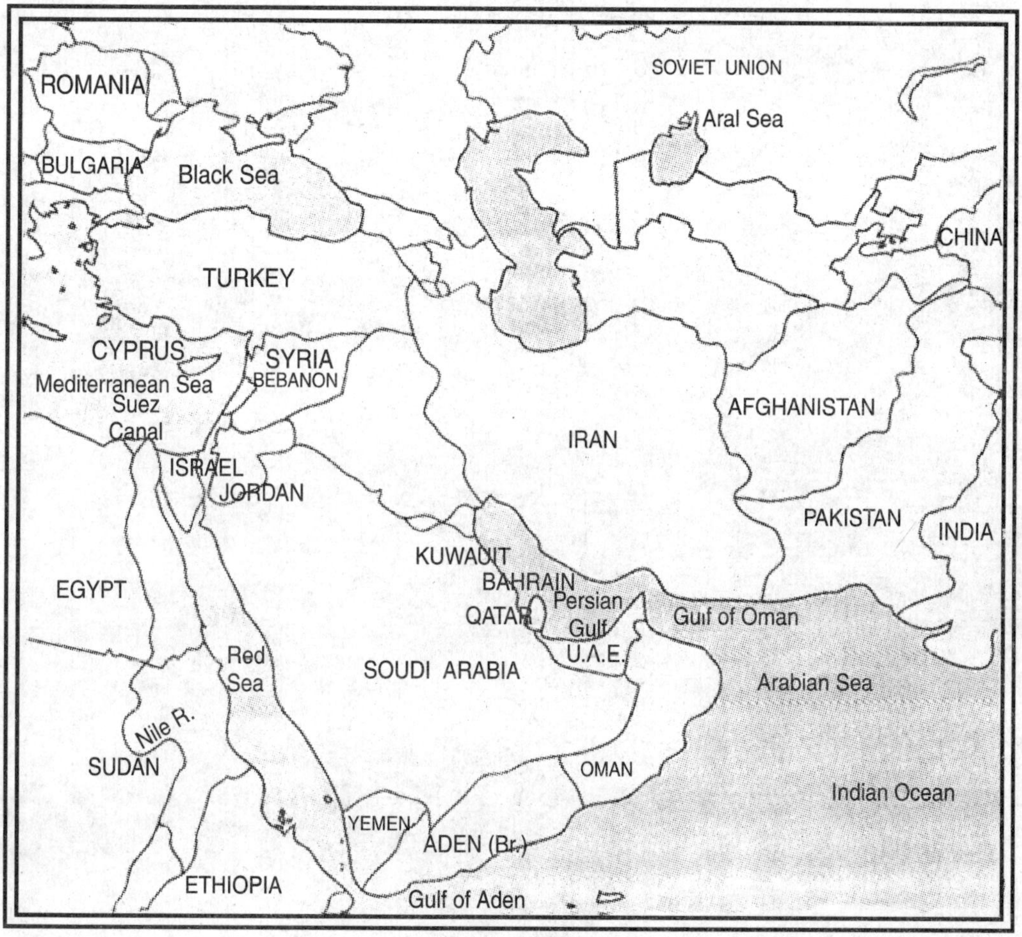

The Middle East 1956

the creation of an independent Palestinian state, and the destruction of Isreal. After 1967, the PLO emerged as an element of major importance in the Middle East. The Palestinian guerillas carried out raids and reprisals against Isreal. In the 1970s the PLO gradually gained international recognition. In 1974 at an Arab summit meeting in Rabat, Morocco, it was recognised by the Arab League as the sole representative of the Palestinian people.

In 1969, Yasir Arafat, Leader of Fatah, the largest Palestinian group, was named Chairman of the PLO. From the late 1960s the PLO organized and launched terrorist attacks against Isreal from its bases in Jordan. In 1974, the Arab heads of state recognised the PLO as the sole legitimate representative of all Palestinians. The PLO was admitted to full membership in the Arab League in 1976. The Palestinians in the occupied territories became increasingly impatient with Israeli rule. In late 1987, tensions erupted in a Palestinian uprising known as the *intifada* which continued sporadically for more than five years. In 1993, Isreal and the PLO agreed to a 'peace accord' that signified the PLO's recognition of Isreali's right to exist and Israelis recognition of the PLO as the sole representative of the Palestinian people.

Egypt Under Nasser

On July 23, 1952, Gamal Abdel Nasser and other officers staged an almost bloodless coup d'etat, ousting the monarchy. The country was taken over by a Revolutionary Command Council of 11 officers controlled by Nasser, with Major General Mohammad Naguib as the puppet head of state. For more than a year Nasser kept himself in a low profile. In the spring of 1954, in a complicated series of intrigues, Naguib was deposed and placed under house arrest, and Nasser emerged and named himself Prime Minister. That same year an Egyptian fanatic tried to assassinate Nasser at a mass meeting in Alexandria.

In January 1956, Nasser announced the promulgation of a constitution under which Egypt became a socialist Arab state with a one party political system and with Islam as the official religion. In June 1956, Nasser was elected President by an overwhelming majority of votes. The Constitution was approved by 99.8 per cent.

As Nasser assumed titular as well as actual control, Egypt's prospects looked bright. In *Philosophy of the Revolution* which he wrote in 1954, Nasser told of heroec and glorious roles which never found heroes to perform them, and outlined his aspiration to be the leader of the Arabs, then of Africans, then of the followers of Islam. In 1958, Syria and Egypt formed the United Arab Republic which Nasser hoped would someday include the entire Arab world. Syria withdrew in 1961, but Egypt continued to be known as the United Arab Republic.

But there were other accomplishments. The Aswan High Dam, built with the help of the Soviet Union, began operating in 1968; 20th century life was introduced into many villages; industrialization was accelerated; a partially successful campaign was conducted against corruption and women were accorded the rights. A new middle class began to occupy the political and economic positions once held in Egypt by Italians, Greeks, French, Britains and other foreigners. Nasser's outstanding accomplishment was his survival for 18 years as Egypt's political leader, despite the strength of his opponents.

On the negative side, Nasser made Egypt a police state in which communications media were censored and the newspapers nationalized. Political democracy in the Western sense was nonexistent, Political enemies were herded into concentration camps. The birthrate remained so high as to defeat attempts to increase the living standard.

In foreign affairs Nasser joined Tito of Yugoslavia and Jawahalal Nehru of India as an advocate of non-alignment. At the Bandung Conference in 1955, he emerged as a world figure. His refused to recognize Isreal and Egypt's defeat by Isreal in 1956 forced him to divert vast sums into defence that might have gone to implement his social revolution.

Egyption's troops supported the Republican Army in Yemen's civil war that began in 1962. But they were withdrawan in 1967, when war broke out again between Egypt and Isreal. After the Egyptian air force was destroyed on the ground and the Egyptian army forced to retreat across the Suez, Nasser attempted to resign, but a vote of confidence by the National Assembly induced him to remain in office. The Soviet Union immediately began replacing all the destroyed war equipment and installed surface to air missiles along the Suez. Nasser had accepted a U.S. plan leading to peace negotiations with Isreal when he died, in 1970, from a heart attack.

Although complex and revolutionary in his public life, privately Nasser was conservative and simple. No other Arab leader in modern times has succeeded in winning the support of the Arab masses throughout the Middle East as did Gamal Aradel Nasser. Despite the loss of two wars, with disastrous results for Egypt, his popularity was not dimmed. He became the first true Egyptian to rule the country in several millenia, giving his people the dignity denied them under foreign rule.

Suez Crisis

It was an international crisis in the Middle East, precipitated on July 26, 1956, when the Egyptian President, Gamal Abdel Nasser, rationalized the Suez Canal. The Canal had been owned by the Suez Canal Company, which was controlled by French and British interests.

The Suez crisis was provoked by an American and British decision not to finance Egypt's construction of the Aswan High Dam, as they had promised, in response to Egypt's growing ties with Communist Czechoslovakia and the Soviet Union. Nasser reacted to the American and British decision by seizing control of the Suez Canal company. He predicted that the tolls collected from ships passing through the canal would pay for the dam's construction within five years. Britain and France feared that Nasser might close the canal and cut off shipments of petroleum flowing from the Persian Gulf to western Europe. Britain and France secretly prepared military action to regain control of the canal and if possible, to depose Nasser. They found a ready ally in Israel, whose hostility towards Egypt was pronounced.

On October 29, 1956, 10 Israeli brigades invaded Egypt and advanced towards the canal, routing Egyptian forces. Britain and France demanded that Israeli and Egyptian troops withdraw from the canal, and announced that they would intervene to enforce a cease-fire ordered by the United Nations. On November 5 and 6, British and French forces landed at Port Said and Port Fuad and began occupation of the Canal Zone. However, growing opposition at home and in the UN and Soviet threats of intervention put an immediate stop to the Anglo-French action. On December 22, the UN evacuated British and French troops, and Israeli forces withdrew in March 1957. Nasser emerged from the Suez crisis a victor and a hero for the cause of Arab and Egyptian nationalism.

Arab-Israeli Wars of 1956, 1967 and 1973

The first war immediately followed the proclamation of the State of Isreal on May 14, 1948. Arab forces from Egypt, Trans-jordon, Iraq, Syria and Lebanon occupied the areas in southern and eastern

Palestine not apportioned to the Jews, then captured the small Jewish quarter of the old city of Jerusalem. The Israelis, meanwhile, won control of the main road to Jerusalem and successfully repulsed Arab attacks. By early 1949, the Israelis managed to occupy all of the Negev up to the Egypt-Palestine frontier, except the Gaza Strip. Between February and July 1949, as a result of separate armistice agreements between Isreal and Arab states, a temporary frontier was fixed.

Tensions mounted with the rise to power of Gamal Abdel Nasser. In October 1956, following Nasser's seizure of the European owned Suez Canal, Israel invaded the Sinai Peninsula to destroy Arab bases there. In five days, the Israeli army captured Gazah, Rafah and Al-Arish and occupied most of the peninsula east of the Suez Canal. The Israelis were then in a position to open sea communications through the Gulf of Aqabs, an added threat to the Egyptians. In December 1956, after a joint Anglo-French Intervention, a United Nations Emergency Force was stationed in the area, and Israeli forces withdrew in March 1957.

Arab and Israeli forces clashed for the third time June 5-10, 1967, in what came to be called the Six-Day War. In early 1967, Syrian bombadments of Israeli villages had been intensified. When the Isreaeli Air Force shot down six Syrian MIG planes in reprisal, Nasser mobilized his forces near the Sinai border. During this war, Israel destroyed the Egyptian air force and established air superiority. The war cost the Arabs, the old city of Jerusaleum, the Sinai and the Gaza Strip, the Jordanian territory west of the Jordon River known as the West Bank, and the Golan Heights, on the Israeli-Syrian border.

The sporadic fighting that followed the Six Day War again developed into full-scale war in 1973. On October 6, the Jewish holy day, Israel was attacked by Egypt across the Suez Canal and by Syria on the Golan Heights. The Arab armies showed greater aggressiveness and the Israeli forces suffered heavy casualties. The Israeli army, however, pushed its way into Syrian territory and encircled the Egyptian Third Army by crossing the Suez Canal. Israel and Egypt signed a crease-fire agreement in November, and on January 18, 1974, peace agreements. The accords provided for Israeli withdrawal into the Sinai while Egypt was to reduce the size of its forces. On May 31, 1974, Israel and Syria signed a cease-fire agreement.

On March 26, 1979, Israel and Egypt signed a peace treaty signalling the end of the state of war that had existed between two countries for 30 years. Under the terms of the Camp David Accords, as the treaty was called, Israel returned the entire Sinai Peninsula to Egypt, and, in return Egypt recognised Israeli's right to exist. The two nations subsequently established normal diplomatic relations with each other.

EASY TYPE QUESTIONS

1. What were the factors that led to the establishment of Israel?
2. How did the Palestine question become highly critical after the end of the Second World War?
3. Trace the development of Egypt under Gamal Abdel Nasser.
4. Discuss the origin of the Arab-Israeli crisis and the circumstances that led to the Arab-Israeli wars of 1956, 1967 and 1973.

SHORT ANSWER TYPE QUESTIONS

5. Trace the genesis of the Palestine problem in the first two decades of the 20th century.

6. What were the factors that led to the development of Arab nationalism?
7. What was Suez crisis? How did it threaten international peace?

OBJECTIVE TYPE QUESTION

8. What as Balfour Declaration? When was it announced?
9. When did Israel proclaim its independence?
10. When was Arab League formed?
11. When was Palestine Liberation Organization (PLO) formed?
12. Who was the Chairman of the PLO?
13. When did Nasser seize political power in Egypt?
14. Who wrote the Philosophy of the Revolution?
15. When was the Seuz Canal nationalised?
16. What were the terms of the Camp David Accord? When was it signed?

IMPORTANT DATES

1.	1917	:	Balfour Declaration
2.	May 14, 1948	:	Israel proclaimed its independence
3.	1945	:	Formation of Arab League
4.	1964	:	Formation of Palestine Liberation Organization (PLO)
5.	1969	:	Yasir Arafat, Chairman of the PLO
6.	July 23, 1952	:	Coup d' etat by Nasser
7.	June 1956	:	Nasser elected President of Egypt
8.	July 26, 1956	:	Nationalization of the Suez Canal
9.	March 26, 1979	:	Camp David Accords

UNIT - IX

The New World War

Post-Stalin era in Soviet Union and its impact on world politics

Unlike Stalin, Lenin and most other Soviet leaders, who had generally middle-class backgrounds, Khrushchev was the son of miner. In 1918, he became a member of the Russian Communist Party (Bolsheviks). In 1935, he became First Secretary of the Moscow party organization. In the preceding year, he had been elected a full member of the 70-men Central Committee of the Soviet party. During these years, he was a zealous supporter of Stalin. In 1939s, he was made a full member of the Politburo.

After Stalin's death in 1953 and the execution of Deputy Prime Minister and State Security Chief, Lavrenti Beria, Khruschev engaged in a power struggle with Georgy Malenkov, Stalin's heir apparent. In September 1953, he replaced Malenkov as First Secretary. In 1955, he removed Malenkov from the premiership in favour of his nominee Marshal Nilolay A. Bulganian. In February 1956 during the 20th Party Congress in Moscow, he openly condemned Stalin for his 'intolerance, his brutality, his abuse of power.' It had its far-reaching effects that Khrushchev could have fore-seen. Thousands of political prisoners were released. The de-Stalinization movement had its effect in the Communist countries of Eastern Europe. Poland revolted against its government in October 1956, Hungary followed suit. The stress in eastern Europe helped to develop opposition to Khruschev within the Soviet party. In June 1957, he was almost overthrown from his position, but he managed to reverse this. In the end he secured the permanent disgrace of Malenkov, Molotov and others. In October he dismissed Marshal Zhukov from his post as Minister of Defence. In March 1958, Khrushchev assumed the premiership of Soviet Union.

Meanwhile, Khrushchev focussed his attention to economic reforms. He shifted his attention from heavy industries to agriculture and light industries. He did way with Stalin's centralized system by setting up Regional Economic Councils. An optimist, he made repeated promises to overtake the United States in agriculture as well as in industrial production. He opened up millions of acres of virgin lands in Siberia and sent thousands of labourers to till them. But his plan was unsuccessful, and the Soviet Union had to import wheat from Canada and the United States.

Confirmed in power, Khrushchev asserted his doctrine of peaceful co-existance. At the 21st Party Congress in 1959 he said: 'We offer the capitalist countries peaceful competition.' His visit to the United States in 1959 was a decided success. However, relations with the United States suffered setback when a U.S. plane was shot down over the Soviet Union and its pilot captured. In 1961, his Vienna Conference with the new U.S. President John F. Kennedy, led to no agreement on the pressing German question. In October 1962, the Soviet Union and the United States stood on the brink of war over the Cuban Crisis. He sent medium-range missiles in Cuba. He agreed to remove the missiles on the promise that the United State would make no further attempt to overthrow Cuba's communist government. The crisis was over when both the superpowers reached a settlement. However, this settlement was denounced by China. Mao Tse-Tung did not like Khrushchev's co-existence policies. Mao was also annoyed with Soviet refusal to assist the Chinese nuclear weapon build up and to rectify the Russia-Chinese border. The Soviet Nuclear Test-Ban Treaty with the United States in 1963 intensified China's antagonism towards Russia.

During Khrushchev's tenure of office, he had to encounter constantly between popular pressure towards a consumer-oriented society, and agitation by intellectuals for greater freedom of expression. Khrushchev himself was uneasy with intellectuals and he sanctioned the repression of Boris Pasternak's *Doctor Zhivago* (1957) within the Soviet Union, culminating in the refusal to allow Pasternak to accept the Nobel Prize in 1958. On the other hand, Khrushchev permitted the 1962 publication of Alexander Solzhenitsyn's *One Day in the Life of Ivan Denisovich*, with its bitter denunciation of Stalinist repression.

Khrushchev's desire to reduce conventional armaments in favour of nuclear missiles was bitterly resisted by the Soviet military. His high-handed methods of leadership and his attempted decentralization of the party structure antagonised a large section of the party. The failure in agriculture and the China quarrel added to his arbitrary administrative methods led to Khrushchev's down-fall. On October 14, 1964, he retired from his position as the party's First Secretary and Chairman of the Council of Ministers of the Soviet Union. For almost seven years after his retirement, Khrushchev lived quietly in Moscow and at his country home where he died in 1971.

For the Soviet Union, Nikita Khruschev ushered in a great political and social change. In his seven years of power as First Secretary and Premier, he broke the tradition of Stalin in dictatorship and established a liberal trend in Soviet communism. He began a process of democratization that was interrupted under Brezhnev but was carried forward by Gorbachev. He sought to free the economy from the clutches of the bureaucracy, and in foreign affairs he attempted a rapprochement with the West. His experience with international politics confirmed him in his doctrine of peaceful co-existence with the non-communist world. He recognised the limitations as well as the power of nuclear weapons. His decision to negotiate with the United States for the formation of nuclear testing control was of great importance. Despite his repression of the Hungarian uprising in 1956, his acceptance of "different roads to socialism" led to growing independence among European Communist parties. Whatever the view of his personal character, he was regarded as a man of character. As his son Sergey pronounced in a short eulogy at the cemetry, 'There were those who loved him, there were those who hated him, but there were few who would pass him by without looking in his direction.'

Disintegration of the Soviet Union and the End of the Cold War

Khrushchev was succeed by Leonid Brezhnev. During the first half of Brezhnev's incumbency the USSR reached the zenith of its international power and prestige. Detente in the early 1970s was accompanied by U.S. recognition of nuclear parity. Then it all went wrong. An economic crisis was accompanied by increased defence spending and the disastrous decision to invade Afghanistan in December 1979. By the time of Brezhnev's death in November 1982, the U.S.S.R. was on the road to decline. After him Yuri Andropov (1982-84) and Konstantin Chernenko (1984- 85) had brief terms. While Andropov was a bit liberal who tried to replace old leaders in the party with younger ones, Chernenko was a Stalin revivalist who ignored popular sentiment and persecuted intellectuals like nuclear physicist Andrei Sakharov.

After Chernenko's death on March, 1985, Gorbachev became General Secretary of the CPSU. He was regarded as the most dynamic leader of the Soveit Russia. His main thrust in administration was on the twin policies of *glasnost* (openness) and *Perestroika* (restructuring). He released dissidents including the prominent nuclear physicist Sakharov and curbed the powers of the secret police, KGB. Religious freedom was granted to the people and lifted the ban on Soviet media. His primary goal was to resusciate the stagnant Soviet economy after years of slow growth during Leonid Brezhnev's tenure of power.

In 1987-88, Gorbachev initiated a series of reforms of the Soviet economic and political system. Under his new policy of *glasnost*, a major cultural change took place. Freedoms of expression and of information were expanded and the country's legacy of Stalinist totalitarian rule was repudiated by the Government. Under Gorbachev's policy of *perestroika*, the first modest attempts to democratize the Soviet political system were undertaken. Secret ballot was introduced in some elections to the party and government posts. Under *perestroika*, limited free market mechanism began to be introduced into the Soviet economy.

In foreign affairs, Gorbachev began to cultivate friendly relations with the developed nations of both west and east. In December 1987, he signed an agreement with U.S. President Ronald Reagan for their two countries to destroy all existing stocks of intermediate range nuclear missiles. In 1988-89, he withdrew the Soviet troops from Afghanistan after their nine-year occupation of that country.

In October 1988, Gorbachev was able to consolidate his power by his election to the Chairmanship of the presidium of the Supreme Soviet (the national legislature). In December 1988, a new bicameral parliament called the USSR Congress of People's Deputies was created with some of its members directly elected by the people. In 1989, the newly, elected Congress of People's Deputies elected from its ranks a new U.S.S.R. Supreme Soviet. It was a real parliament with substantial legislative powers.

Gorbachev was the initiator of a series of events in late 1989 and 1990 that transformed the political fabric of Europe and marked the beginning of the end of the Cold War. Throughout 1989 he had supported the anti-communist movement in the Soviet Bloc countries of eastern Europe. As democratically elected non-communist governments came to power in East Germany, Poland, Hungary and Czechoslovakia in late 1989-90, Gorbachev agreed to the phased withdrawal of Soviet troops from those countries. He agreed to the reunification of East with West Germany and did not oppose the United Germany's becoming a member of the Soviet Union's longtime enemy, the North Atlantic Treaty Organisation.

Gorbachev's policy of democratization and decentralisation of the nations political system led to civil unrest in several of the Constituent republican—Azerbaijan, Georgia, and Uzbekistan. Gorbachev used military force to suppress bloody ethnic strife in several of the Central Asian Republics in 1989-90. However, constitutional methods were devised that could provide for a lawful secession of a republic from the U.S.S.R.

While the Communist Party was losing its sway, Gorbachev in 1990, further accelerated the transfer of power from the party to elected governmental institutions. In March 1990 he was elected to the newly created post of President of the U.S.S.R. by the Congress of People's Deputies. He was vested with extensive executive powers. At the same time, the Congress abolished the Communist Party's monopoly of political power in the Soviet Union.

Gorbachev was conspicuously successful in dismantling the totalitarian aspects of the Soviet State and in moving his country along the path toward representative democracy. However, he was not willing to release the Soviet economy from the grip of contralized states direction. He also resisted any decisive shift to private ownership and the use of free-market mechanism. Gorbachev sought a compromise between the radicals and the hard-liners. But nothing substantial was achieved, so the centrally-planned economy began to crumble with no private enterprise to replace it. In 1990, the national economy fell by 15 per cent. It was found that about a quarter of the population was living in abject poverty.

Though Gorbachev remained the undisputed master of the ailing Communist Party, his attempts to increase his presidential powers proved fruitless. In the face of a collapsing economy, public frustration, and the continued shift of power to the constituent republics, Gorbachev allied himself with party conservatives in late 1990. But they proved to be undependable allies. He and his family were briefly held under house arrest from August 19 to 21, 1991, during a short-lived coup by the hardliners. After the coup foundered in the face of strong resistance by Russian President Boris Yeltsin and other reformers, Gorbachev resumed his duties as Soviet President. Entering into an alliance with Yeltsin, Gorbachev disbanded the Central committee of the Communist Party and removed its control over the KGB and the armed forces. Gorbachev moved swiftly to transfer political powers to Soviet Union's Constituent Republics. Events moved dramatically as the various republics agreed to form a new commonwealth under Yeltsin's leadership. Meanwhile, the three Baltic republics seceded from the union, as did many others. The key republic was Ukraine which voted for independence on December 1, 1991. Russia, Ukraine and Belorussia on December 8, 1991 declared that the Soviet Union had ceased to exist and founded a loose grouping known as the Commonwealth of Independent States (CIS). On December 21 in Alma Ata, Kazakhastan, 11 states signed a protocol formally establishing the CIS. On December 25, 1991, Gorbachev resigned the presidency of the Soviet Union which ceased to exist.

The Soviet experiment, begun in 1917, had ended in failure. Indeed, countless crimes had been committed in the attempt. Stalin perceived that the U.S.S.R. could only be kept together by a strong hand. Attempts at democratisation under Khrushchev unleashed a slow process of the breakdown of the communist system. Gorbachev merely accelerated the breakup by promoting *glasnost*. He confirmed that a communist system cannot become democratic. 'When democracy triumphs, communism departs the stage.'

End of the Cold War

Gorbachev as a person was completely different and he was the first Soviet leader to be untained by a Stalinist record. Here was a man, as Mrs. Thatcher confided "with whom we can do business."

Gorbachev's early months in office were taken up by reshuffling of the Politburo. Foreign policy offered Gorbachev the best room for manoeuvre. And he made a move on improving the East-West relations. The initial meetings between Gorbachev and Regan were not productive. Long preparations for a treaty on the reduction of Intermediate Range Nuclear Forces (INF) preceded the summit scheduled at Reykjavik, Iceland, for December, 1987. Suddenly in the middle of the talks at Reykjavik, Gorbachev proposed a sensational 50 per cent cut in all nuclear weapons.

'May December 8, 1987 become a date that will be inscribed in the history books.' Gorbachev declared, 'a date that will mark the watershed separating the era of a mounting risk of nuclear from the era of a demilitarization of human life.' The INF Treaty, ratified by the U.S. Senate, led to the destruction of 1,846 Soviet nuclear weapons and 846 US weapons within three years, with each side allowing close a inspection of the other sides nuclear sites. For the first time in the atomic era, an actual class of nuclear weapons was being not just limited, but eliminated.

Reagan's trip to Moscow in the spring of 1988 testified the ongoing transformation in Soviet American relations. The leaders of the two superpowers now began to treat each other as friendly partners than as enemies. Reagan expressed 'hope for a new era in human history, an era of peace between our nations and peoples.' In December 1988, Gorbachev made another visit to the United States to meet with Reagan, That trip coincided with a major speech the Soviet leader delivered at the United Nations, in which he revealed his intention to reduce unilaterally Soviet military forces by 500,000 troops. 'Perhaps not since Woodrow Wilson presented his Fourteen Points in 1918 or since Franklin Roosevelt and Winston Churchill promulgated the Atlantic Charter in 1941,' wrote the *New York Times* in a lead editorial, 'has a world figure demonstrated the vision Mikhail Gorbachev displayed yesterday at the United Nations.'

Gorbachev's proposal led to a significant reduction of Soviet military presence in Eastern Europe. What followed were popular democratic revolutions that swept out of power every Communist regime in Eastern Europe, beginning with Poland in mid-1989, and ending with fall of Ceausescu regime in Romania at year's close. The event that symbolized the crumbling of the old order was the opening of the Berlin Wall on 9 November. As the wall disintegrated, so did Europe's East-West divide.

In many respects, the demolition of the Berlin Wall and the concomittant fall of Eastern Europe's Communist governments but of the entire Warsaw Pact alliance system meant the end of the Cold War. The ideological contest was now over. Neither Communism nor the Soviet State posed a serious threat to the security of the United States and its allies. Many observers have cited 1989 as the Cold War's terminal date.

With German power fully co-opted in the Western coalition, that of a pro-Soviet Germany disappeared. 'The Cold War ended when the Soviets accepted a united Germany in NATO. The year 1990, rather than 1989, truly marked the end of the Cold War. The collapse of the Soviet Union itself in 1991 stands as a critically important historical event in its own right. By the time the Soviet Union disappeared, the Cold War itself was already history.

Emergence of a New World Order

The Cold War profoundly affected the people. New economic competitions sprang up to challenge and eventually to replace the old hegemonic power. The primacy of the United States in economic sphere seemed to be threatened. Its share of gross world production had fallen from 50 per cent in the late 1940s to less than 25 per cent, while Japan and West Germany had achieved economic wonders. New light industries had spread to countries such as South Korea, Taiwan, Hong Kong and Singapore. Financial power had fled to new global banking centres in Europe and East Asia. In the 1960s, 9 of the 10 biggest banks in the world were American; by 1987 none were American, and most were Japanese.

European growth also signalled a change in the global distribution of power. After the harrowing spectre of wars, the Western Europe powers realised the necessity of forging economic and social cooperations. Even during the Second World War, Churchill envisaged the economic integration of Europe and the need for a Council of Europe. In 1948, the organisation of European Economic Cooperation was established which helped trade volumes among the member states. Similarly, in the same year was established International Trade Organisation in Geveva.

In May 1950, the Schuman Plan proposed a far-reaching package of economic, military and political institution. It called for an economic organization coordinating the iron and steel industry and for a European army which would lay the foundation for a United States of Europe. The European Coal and Steel Community was the first born child of the Schuman Plan. Its founding treaty, signed in May 1951, including the six powers-France, Germany, Italy and Benelux. They agreed to operate free trade in coal and steel and in the event of crisis to control prices and production.

The year 1955 marked the climax of the European movement to economic integration as the leading element in its strategy. The Treaty of Rome on March 25, 1957 signified the determination of the six to extend the success of the European Coal and Steel Community (ECSE) and Euratom (1956 pooling of resources of nuclear energy) into all spheres of economic life. It gave rise to the European Economic Community (EEC), otherwise known as the Common Market which came into effect on January 1, 1958. Its main objects were to remove all internal tariffs, to formulate a common external trade policy, to eliminate barriers to free competition. The U.K. Government did not participate in the ECSE in 1951, and dropped out of the Common Market till 1973 when she was admitted along with Denmark and Ireland. In 1981, Greece joined the Common Market followed by Spain and Portugal in 1983.

On January 8, 1949 was founded in Moscow the Council for Mutual Economic Assistance (CMEA), better known as COMECON. Its main function was to assist in the theory and practice of building socialism by Soviet models. The CMEA specialized tasks to each member country and emphasized the dissemination of modern science and technology. It achieved limited success. Between 1949 and 1953, COMECON's activities were restricted chiefly to the registration of bilateral trade and credit agreements among member countries. After 1953 the Soviet Union and COMECON began to promote industrial specialization among the member countries. The economic integration envisaged by COMECON's in the early 1960s met with opposition from some members. After the collapse of Communist governments across eastern Europe in 1989-90, these countries began a pronounced shift to private enterprise. Early in 1991, COMECON was renamed the Organization for International Economic Cooperation, each nation was deemed free to seek its own trade outlets.

ESSAY TYPE QUESTIONS

1. Trace the rise of Khruschev in the post-Stalin era in the U.S.S.R. What were his achievements?
2. What were the reform measures of Gorbachev? How far was he successful in achieving his objective?
3. Trace the course of events that led to the end of the Cold War.

SHORT ANSWER TYPE QUESTIONS

4. In what way did Khruschev achieve his objective of peaceful co-existence with other great powers?
5. How far Gorbachev was successful in initiating the reform measures of *glasnost* and *perestroika*?
6. Trace the Soviet-American relations under Gorbachev.

OBJECTIVE TYPE QUESTIONS

7. When did Khruschev assume the premiership of the Soviet Union?
8. What was the main thrust in Khruschev's assertion of 'Peaceful co-existence'?
9. When did Khruschev visit the United States?
10. What were the twin policies of Gorbachev in administration?
11. When did the Soviet Union cease to exist?
12. When was the Commonwealth of Independent States (CIS) founded?
13. How did Gorbachev's visit to the USA transform Soviet-American relations?

IMPORTANT DATES

1. March 1958	:	Khrushchev's assumption of Premiership of the Soviet Union.
2. 1959	:	Khrushchev's visit to the United States
3. October 14, 1964	:	Khrushchev's retirement from the Chairman of the Council of Ministers
4. September 11, 1971	:	Death of Khrushchev
5. 1988-89	:	Soviet withdrawal of troops from Afghanistan
6. December 1987	:	Gorbachev's meeting with Reagan
7. December 1988	:	Gorbachev's second meeting with Reagan
8. 1989	:	End of Cold War
9. December 8, 1991	:	Russia, Ukraine and Belorussia founded a loose grouping known as the Commonwealth of Independents States (CIS)

UNIT - X

THE UNITED NATIONS

EUROPE AND THE WORLD, 1765-1945

Evolution of the United Nations: The Atlantic Charter, 1941 and the San Francisco Conference, 1945

The League of Nations had failed to provide effective means for the peaceful settlement of international disputes among the great powers. Early in the Second World War, statesmen considered the necessity of replacing the League of Nations with a more effective body. In August 1941, Churchill and Roosevelt met on a battleship in the Atlantic and issued a joint declaration subsequently known as the Atlantic Charter. This declaration laid down that the two countries abandoned any intention to annex any foreign territories, affirmed the principles of self-determination and held out to all states equal freedom of access to trade and raw materials. The most significant declaration was that: 'after the final destruction of the Nazi tyranny, they hope to see established a peace which will afford to all nations the means of dwelling in safety within their own boundaries, and which will afford assurance that all the men in all the lands may live out their lives in freedom from fear and want'. On January 1, 1942, representatives of twenty-six 'United Nations' signed a joint declaration endorsing the Atlantic Charter.

In the Moscow Conference which met in November 1943, America, Britain, Russia and China discussed the idea of a World Peace Organisation for the maintenance of international peace and security. At the Teheran Conference in December, Roosevelt, Churchill and Stalin called for 'a world family of democratic nations'. Early in 1944, the British and United States governments began to work out detailed schemes for the future World Organisation. A British Committee drew up proposals which were placed before a meeting of Dominion Prime Ministers in London in May 1944. The proposals were for a World Assembly in which all member states would be represented and a World Council representing four powers and a number of other states. The World Council would take the initiative to maintain peace, which would be binding on members of the organisation.

Representatives of Britain, Russia, China and the United States met to consider the various proposals at a conference at Dumbarton Oaks, near Washington, in August and September 1944. They reached agreement on all important matters except voting procedure. This was decided by the 'Big Three' at the Yalta Conference in February 1945. It was decided at Yalta to call a 'Conference of the United Nations' at San Francisco 'to prepare the Charter of such an organisation, along the lines proposed in the informal conversations at Dumbarton Oaks'.

On April 25, 1945, shortly before the end of the war, representatives from fifty nations met at San Francisco, to draw up a constitution for the new organisation, to be called the United Nations. The negotiations at San Francisco were not smooth. While the 'Big four' were pledged to defend a common set of proposals, the lesser powers—the middle and smaller countries—naturally resented what they alleged was excessive domination of the UN by the Great Powers as symbolised in the veto. Although the Dumbarton Oaks framework remained virtually intact, important modifications were introduced. The Charter in its final form was adopted on June 26, 1945. The Charter came into effect on October 24, 1945 which is now observed throughout the world as 'U.N.Day'.

New members are admitted to the United Nations at the recommendation of the Security Council and by a two-thirds vote of the General Assembly. The admittance of new members, however, has often engendered controversy. By 1950, only 9 of 31 applicants had been admitted to the organization. In 1955, 16 new states (4 eastern European states and 12 non-communist states) were admitted. The most contentious application for membership was that of the People's Republic of China which was placed before the General Assembly at every session from 1950 to 1971. The United States successfully opposed efforts to admit the People's Republic (Communist China) and to expel Nationalist China (Taiwan). Finally in 1971, the United States gave away and the People's Republic of China was admitted to the UN in 1971. The two Germans were admitted as members in 1973, these two seats were reduced to one with the unification in October 1990. Vietnam was admitted in 1977, after South Vietnam's defeat in 1975 and the reunification of the country. The two Koreans were granted membership in 1991.

The most significant waves of membership growth occurred as a result of decolonization and of the disintegration of the Soviet Union and the Eastern European Bloc. Following worldwide decolonization from 1955 to 1960, 40 new members were admitted. In 1960 the General Assembly passed a Declaration on the granting of Independence to Colonical countries, which brought UN membership by the end of the 1970s to about 150 states. New states were admitted through the 1980s with another significant increase after 1989. Many Soviet republics were granted independent membership in the early 1990s, bringing membership to more than 175.

The Objectives of the United Nations

The basic objectives of the United Nations are to maintain international peace and security and to resist aggression and threats to peace. Any international dispute or a threat to peace should be solved by peaceful methods in accordance with the principles of justice and international law. Cordial relations should be developed on the basis of equality of status. Every nation would be entitled to form its own State. To maintain international peace equality of states is to be respected: big and powerful states would not be allowed to exercise sovereignty over small or weak States. Different States should be persuaded to co-operate with the great task of promoting the welfare of the human race. Thus, the basic principles of the United Nations Charter are to maintain international peace, to develop friendly relations among nations, to achieve international co-operation in the field of social, economic, cultural and humanitarian fields and to promote respect for human rights and freedom. The Charter accepts the principles of the sovereign equality of all its members and the obligations to settle international dispute by peaceful means. It is not to intervene in domestic affairs of any country. If any member is engaged in aggressive war, sanctions shall be applied against it. Ordinarily the provisions of the Charter are applicable to the members of the United Nations. But if any non-member is found guilty of violating peace, the provisions of the Charter may be applied against it by the United Nations.

Organs of the United Nations

There are six main organs of the United Nations: the General Assembly, the Security Council, the Economic and Social Council, Trusteeship Council, the Secretariat and the International Court of Justice.

General Assembly

It consists of representatives of all member states. Each member state might have five representatives but only one vote. The Assembly is to meet once in every year, but special sessions might be summoned by the Secretary-General. Decisions on important questions have to be taken by a two-thirds majority. This marks an improvement on the Assembly unanimity laid down in the League of Nations.

The Assembly is primarily a deliberative body. It can discuss any question relating to peace and security and make recommendations to the Security council. The General Assembly cannot take any action; it is for the Security Council to take action. The General Assembly has no share at all in the Security Council's primary responsibility for the maintenance of international peace and security. It adopts the U.N. budget. It elects its own President and Vice-president for each session. The Assembly elects the non-permanent member of the Security Council, all members of the Trusteeship Council and the Economic and Social Council.

Frequent use of the veto has tended to enhance the importance of the General Assembly as against the Security Council. In November 1950, after the outbreak of the Korean War, the General Assembly passed a resolution:

> that if the Security Council, because of lack of unanimity of the permanent members, fails to exercise its primary responsibility for the maintenance of international peace and security, the General Assembly shall consider the matters immediately with a view to making appropriate recommendations to members for collective measures, including in the case of a breach of the peace or act of aggression the use of armed force when necessary, to maintain or restore international peace and security.

Security Council

The Security Council is the most important organ of the United Nations. It is made up of five permanent members and ten non-permanent members. The five permanent members are—the United States, Britain, France, Soviet Russia and China (Formosa). The ten non-permanent members are elected for a two-year term by the General Assembly. India was a non-permanent member of the Security Council for two terms. Each member state has one vote, cast by one representative.

The Security Council is granted 'primary responsibility for the maintenance of international peace and security'. It can investigate into any dispute or situation which is likely to lead to any dispute. It can enforce its recommendations more by moral pressure than by force. In the event that these measures prove inadequate, the Council may 'take such action by air, sea, or land forces as may be necessary to maintain or restore international peace and security'. The United Nations has no air, sea or land forces of its own. But the member-states are required to make available to the Council for this purpose all necessary armed forces.

On procedural matters an affirmative vote of any nine members is enough. On all other matters an affirmative vote of any nine members must include the votes of the five permanent members. This gives each of the great powers a virtual veto over all major decisions. The power of veto, frequently used by the great powers, renders the Security Council ineffective for taking any effective action against aggression. Thus 'the mechanism of the Security Council is based upon the principle that no positive action can be taken against the definitive objection of any of the Great Powers'.

Economic and Social Council : The main purpose of the Economic and Social Council is to promote economic and social advancement of all people. The Council consists of 27 members, elected by the General Assembly on a rotation basis, i.e., 9 members are elected each year for a 3-year term. The Council meets at least twice a year. It has a number of commissions which include such bodies as those on population, human rights, the status of women, narcotic drugs, transport and communications, and economic commissions for Europe, Asia, Far East and Latin America. Connected with it are a number of specialised agencies, including: the Food and Agriculture Organisation (FAO), the International Bank for Reconstruction and Development (World Bank), the International Labour Organisation (ILO), the World Health Organisation (WHO), the United Nations Educational Scientific and Cultural Organisation (UNESCO), the International Monetary Fund (IMF) and the International Children's Emergency Fund (UNICEF). The International Development Corporation was set up in 1956 to stimulate private investment in underdeveloped countries.

Trusteeship Council

As successor to the old Permanent Mandates Commission of the League, the Trusteeship Council consists of those members administering trust territories, other members of the Security Council who do not administer trust territories and other members elected for a three-year term by the General Assembly. It receives reports from the administering authorities and petitions from the trusts territory itself and provide for periodic inspection to the trust territories. Of the eleven territories originally kept under the United Nations Trusteeship System, nine have already emerged as independent states.

Secretariat of United Nations

The Secretariat is the backbone of the United Nations. The chief administrative officer of the United Nations is the Secretary General, appointed for a five-year term by General Assembly upon recommendation of the Security Council. He is required to make an annual report to the Assembly and is empowered to bring to the attention of the Security Council any matter which in his opinion might threaten international peace and security. The past 20 years have seen a considerable growth in the authority of the Secretary-General. The Secretariat is located in New York and its expenses are met from the contributions made by the members of the United Nations.

International Court of Justice

The main judicial organ of the United Nations is called the International Court of Justice. The Court is composed of 15 judges, elected for 9 years by the General Assembly and the Security Council. No nation can be represented by more than one member in the Court. Disputes submitted to the Court generally relate to political issues which have legal implications. Only states can become parties in cases before the tribunal. The Court can give advisory opinions on legal questions submitted to it by the General Assembly and the Security Council.

United Nations and the League of Nations: Their similarities and differences

The ideals of the League of Nations and of the United Nations were more or less similar. They were formed with the purpose of ensuring international peace and security. The idea of world organisation embedded in the League of Nations has assumed greater significance in the creation of the United Nations. In matters of organisation, the two bodies are almost similar. The League had three organs: the Assembly, the Council and the Security Council. The organization of the United Nations are more elaborate: the General Assembly, the Security Council, the Economic and Social Council, the International Court of Justice and the Secretariat. In the League of Nations, the Big Powers exercised influence in shaping its policy. Similarly, in the United Nations, the Big Five, America, Russia, Britain, France and China, play a crucial role in directing the activities of the United Nations. Both the organisations have relied on peaceful methods for the solution of international disputes and have urged sanctions against the disturber of peace.

"For all their differences", it has been said, the League and the U.N. "are basically the same-voluntary association of states established to foster co-operation among their members in certain stipulated political, economic and social areas. They were both endowed with essentially the same organisational limbs, including an assembly, council, economic and social bodies, trusteeship committee, courts and secretariat. In most matters, these organs were authorised only to recommend, not command. In the security sphere, their founders intended that action to extinguish threats to the peace should be left primarily to the political councils dominated by the great powers".[1]

But in spite of the similarities, there have been wide differences between the two organisations. Both the United States and the Soviet Union who have been the members of the United Nations from the beginning, were not originally included in the League of Nations.

While all important decisions in the League Assembly required unanimity, in the General Assembly of the United Nations, they require a two-thirds majority of the members present and voting. The power and responsibility of the League Assembly and the League Council were not clearly defined. But in the United Nations, the position of General Assembly and the Security Council have been clearly demarcated. The Security Council has been given wider authority than the Council of the League for in that body rests the primary responsibility for the maintenance of international peace and security:

The incorporation of the Covenant of the League of Nations in the peace treaty of Versailles weakened the League. It appeared that the League of Nations was an attempt on the part of the victors to devise a political settlement intended to serve their interests. But the United Nations had nothing to do with any peace treaty. "It was the job of the United Nations to maintain peace, not to create the peace".

On the whole, the objectives of the Charter are far more comprehensive and radical than those of the Covenant. The League was not an effective instrument for the enforcement of sanctions. But the framers of the U.N. Charter' 'put teeth' into the new collective security system. International organization in 1919 had no concrete precedent whereas the United Nations of 1945 had 20 years' experience behind them. In several respects, the United Nations is a somewhat tighter than the League. "Its organ, when they can function at all, can do more. But how far they can function at

[1] Cheever and Haviland: *Organizing for Peace*, P.66.

all depends, as before, on the will of its leading members to make them function".[2] The fabric of international society has been strengthened by putting more emphasis on the role of specialized agencies in promoting economic, social, cultural and technical co-operation.

Role of the United Nations: Its success and Failure

Though the activities of the United Nations in dealing with international disputes are not flattering, yet it has accomplished much in difficult circumstances. Between 1946 and 1950, its mediation between the powers led to the withdrawal of British troops from Syria, the French troops from Lebanon and the troops of the Soviet Union from Iran. It resolved the disputes between the Dutch and the Indonesians and helped Indonesia become a sovereign independent state. It intervened in Korea (1950-53) by sending its forces against the Communists. In Congo (1960-63), the United Nations intervened to bring the civil war to a close.

The United Nations has also preserved peace by maintaining its observers and peace keeping force. The stationing of peace keeping force in Cyprus since 1964 checked the conflict between the Greeks and Turks. Similarly, without its observers the cease-fire agreements between India and Pakistan or between Israel and Arab States would not have taken effect.

The United Nations intervention in the Suez campaign of 1956 and the readiness of Britain and France in agreeing to a cease-fire, must be regarded as major triumphs for the United Nations as an agency for restoring peace. On the other hand, its failure to prevent suppression of Hungary by the Soviet Union discredited the organisation as an agency of peace.

The most signal failure of the United Nations was in the field of disarmament and especially the failure to control the formidable new power of atomic energy. In January 1946, the General Assembly set up an Atomic Energy Commission to make proposals for the International control of atomic energy. The Commission achieved nothing when the United States insisted on a system of international inspection and control against the Soviet Union's rejection of all such interference in its internal affairs. In November 1952, the United States exploded the first hydrogen bomb, followed by the Soviet Union in the next year. By 1960, both had developed intercontinental ballistic missiles and France and China had joined the nuclear club by exploding atomic devices.

The prestige and influence of the United Nations has declined since the 60s of the present century. In addition, the United Nations kept itself aloof in a number of major international disputes: Berlin, Cuba, the Sino-Indian frontier, Czechoslovakia, Nigeria, Biafra, India and Pakistan in 1971, Angola and Mozambique and Ethiopia. The absence of UN involvement in Vietnam was particularly marked. The United Nations has failed to co-ordinate attempts to deal with international terrorism, especially the hijacking of civil aircraft.

There are a number of causes for the ineffectiveness of the United Nations. It failed to take effective action against the rivalries of the Great Powers. Vietnam was an example of the inability of the United Nations to act when the interest of the superpowers clashed. Another source of weakness had been the absence of Communist China until 1971. In 1964-65, the United Nations was almost bankrupt, for the Congo operation had been very expensive. There was widespread view that the United Nations should create a standing international police force, always ready to repel aggression and encourage peaceful settlement. However, no such force has been created. Many of the new countries admitted to the United Nations regard the organisation as a forum conducting their struggle

[2] David Thomposon: *Europe since Napolean,* p. 884.

against colonialism and racialism. But the resolutions passed are often unrealistic. Moreover its weakness is exposed when resolutions are passed which cannot be enforced.

More recently, the U.N. performance in Somalia and in Bosnia shows up the weakness of the organisation. The U.N. failure to achieve peace in Somalia has badly shaken the UN authority. Similarly, in Bosnia too the U.N. peace-keeping efforts have been rendered fruitless. Neither the U.N. blockade resolutions nor the intervention of NATO forces as the U.N.'s executive military agent have met with any success.

The U.N. has been labelled a 'paper mill' or a 'talking shop' which the politicians use as a forum for their rhetorics and pious declarations. The criticism is that the U.N. has played an insignificant role in allaying conflicts or in controlling weapons of mass destruction or in the fight against terrorism, yet the very fact that the U.N. has not disappeared like the League of Nations in 50 years, shows that the world needs such an organisation. On June 26, 1945 when President Truman of the U.S.A. signed the U.N. Charter, he observed jubliantly: 'You have created a great instrument for peace. Oh, what a great day this can be in history' . This is the appropriate time that when the U.N. and others should take a realistic view of the record of the U.N.'s performance. Both U.N. supporters and critics testify to the need of a U.N. body and say that "if it were to disappear, it would have to be quickly reinvented."

Despite its limitations, the United Nations through its functional agencies like-the ILO (International Labour Organisation), the UNESCO (United Nations Educational Scientific and Cultural Organisation), the FAO (Food and Agricultural Organisation), the WHO (World Health Organisation), the IMF (International Monetary Fund), the UNRRA (United Nations Relief and Rehabilitation Administration)-have made considerable progress in their respective fields and have given hope to several millions of people especially in the developing countries.

The General Assembly in 1961 adopted a resolution declaring the use of nuclear or thermonuclear weapons to be contrary to international law. The nuclear weapons Test-Ban Treaty was signed on August 5, 1963 by the Soviet Union, the United Kingdom, and the United States. Hundred states adhered to this agreement. In June 1968, the Assembly approved the Treaty on the Non-Proliferalion of Nuclear Weapons, enjoined signatory non-nuclear powers not to develop or deploy nuclear weapons and committed the nuclear powers to engage in measures of disarmament. The treaty represents a significant commitment on the part of more than 140 signatory powers to control nuclear weapons proliferation. However, the treaty which went into effect in 1970 was not ratified by significant nuclear powers including China and France and many 'near-nuclear' states including Argentina, Brazil, Egypt, Israel, Pakistan and South Africa. Some of these states signed the treaty in the early 1990s, South Africa in 1991 and France and China in 1992. In 1978, 1982 and 1988 the United Nations also organised three special sessions of the General Assembly on disarmament.

U.N. peacekeeping troops have served throughout the World, most exclusively in the Middle East. After the end of the Cold War, appeals for UN forces proliferated. In addition to peacekeeping and preventive diplomacy tasks, the functions of the UN forces in the post-Cold War era have been expanded considerably. From 1990, they supervised elections in many parts of the world, including Nicaragua, Eritrea and Cambodia; encourages peace negotiations in EI Salvador, Angola and Western Sahara and distributed food in Somalia. Despite the inability of the United Nations to enforce fully the collective security measures, the importance of the UN peacekeeping forces was recognised in 1988, when they were awarded the Nobel Peace Prize.

ESSAY TYPE QUESTIONS

1. Trace the evolution of the United Nations.
2. What are the objectives of the United Nations? Discuss the functions of the General Assembly and Security Council of the United Nations.
3. Discuss the points of similarities and differences between the League of Nations and the United Nations.
4. Write a short essay on the achievements and failures of the United Nations.

SHORT ANSWER TYPE QUESTIONS

5. What do you know about the Atlantic Charter?
6. Discuss the importance of the San Francisco Conference in the foundation of the United Nations.
7. What are the objectives of the United Nations?
8. Name the functional agencies of the United Nations.
9. What are the functions of the Economic and Social Council of the United Nations?

OBJECTIVE TYPE QUESTIONS

10. When was the Charter of the United Nations adopted?
11. Who are the original members of the United Nations?
12. What are the main organs of the United Nations?
13. When was Communist China admitted to the United Nations?
14. What do you mean by UNESCO?
15. On which date and in which year was the United Nations founded?
16. Where is the Secretariat of United Nations located?

IMPORTANT DATES

1.	August 1941	:	Atlantic Charter
2.	November 1943	:	Moscow conference
3.	June 26, 1945	:	Charter of the UN adopted
4.	October 24, 1945	:	Foundation of the UN

IMPORTANT EVENTS

1740-43	:	War of the Austrian Succession
1748	:	Peace of Aix-la-Chapelle
1756-63	:	Seven Years' War
1763	:	Treaty of Paris Treaty of Hubertsburg
1764	:	Sugar Act
1765	:	Stamp Act
1769	:	Birth of Napoleon
1772	:	First Partition of Poland
1774	:	First Congress at Philadelphia
1776	:	Declaration of American Independence
1783	:	Treaty of Versailles
1789	:	Summoning of States-General Fall of Bastille
1791-2	:	Legislative Assembly
1792	:	War With Austria and Prussia Deposition of Louis XVI France a Republic 1792-5: Convention
1793	:	Execution of Louis XVI : Fall of Girondins: First Coalition against France: Second Partition of Poland
1793-4	:	The Terror
1795	:	Terror Ended : New Constitution of France Third Partition of Poland
1795-9	:	Directory
1795	:	Holland Conquered
1796-7	:	Bonaparte's Italian Campaign
1797	:	Treaty of Campo Formio (Between France and Austria).
1789-9	:	Bonaparte's Egyptian campaign

1798	:	Second coalition against France
1799	:	Consulate Bonaparte made First Consul for Ten Years
1801	:	Treaty of Luneville The Concordat Peace of Amiens (between Britain and France)
1802	:	Bonaparte made Consul for Life
1804	:	Napoleon-emperor of the French
1805	:	Battle of Trafalgar : Third coalition against France : Treaty of Pressburg
1806-7	:	Continental System
1807	:	War with Russia : Treaty of Tilsit Abolition of Slave Trade
1808-14	:	Peninsular War
1809	:	Austrian War Treaty of Vienna
1812	:	Russian War
1813	:	Fourth Coalition against France
1814-24	:	Louis XVIII
1814	:	Invasion of France Fall of Napoleon
1815	:	Battle of Waterloo Surrender of Napoleon Congress of Vienna The Holy Alliance
1818	:	Zollverein (Customs Union under Prussian leadership) Birth of Karl Marx
1819	:	Carlsbad Decrees
1820	:	Congress of Laibach : Death of Napoleon
1822	:	Congress of Verona
1824-30	:	Charles X
1825	:	Congress of St. Petersburg
1829	:	Treaty of Adrianople
1830	:	July Revolution in France Independence of Belgium Annexation of Algeria by France
1831	:	Young Italy founded by Mazzini
1832	:	First Reform Act in England

1833	:	Treaty of Unkiar Skelessi Factory Act
1839	:	Mehmet Ali
1841	:	Treaty of London
1848	:	February Revolution in France, Movement for Unity: Frankfort Parliament, The Communist Manifesto by Marx and Engels
1848-52	:	Second Republic in France
1852	:	Louis Napoleon proclaimed Emperor as Napoleon III
1852-70	:	Second Empire in France
1854-56	:	Crimean War
1856	:	Treaty of Paris
1859	:	Armistice of Villafranca Treaty of Zurich
1860	:	March of Garibaldi with 'the thousand' into Sicily Cobden Treaty
1861	:	Death of Cavour Victor Emmanuel proclaimed King of Italy Abolition of Serfdom in Russia by Alexander II
1862	:	Bismarck became Chief Minister of Prussia
1864	:	War between Prussia and Denmark: Treaty of Vienna
1865	:	Convention of Gastein
1866	:	Austro-Prussian War Treaty of Prague
1867	:	Ausgleich-The Empire Austria-Hungary to consist of two States
1870-71	:	Franco-Prussian War
1871	:	Treaty of Frankfort German Unification Completed Third French Republic
1871-90	:	Bismarck as Imperial Chancellor
1872	:	Dreikaiserbund or the League of the Three Emperors (Germany, Austria and Russia)
1878	:	Treaty of Sen Stefano : Treaty of Berlin
1879	:	Dual alliance (between Austria and Germany)
1881	:	France occupied Tunis Reinsurance Compact (between Germany and Russia)
1882	:	Triple Alliance between Germany, Austria and Italy

1883	:	Death of Karl Marx
1884-5	:	Berlin Conference
1887	:	Reinsurance Compact (between Germany and Russia)
1890	:	Fall of Bismarck
1891	:	Alliance between Russia and France
1894-5	:	Sino-Jappanese War
1895	:	Dual Alliance between France and Russia
1899-1902	:	The Boer War
1899	:	First Conference at Hague
1900	:	Boxer rebellion
1902	:	Anglo-Japanese alliance
1904	:	Anglo-French Convention
1904-05	:	Russo-Japanese War
1906	:	Algeciras Conference
1907	:	Second Conference at Hague Anglo-Russian Convention Triple Entente of France, Britain and Russia
1908	:	Turkish Revolution Occupation of Bosnia-Herzegovina by Austria-Hungary
1910	:	Japanese occupation of Korea
1911	:	Chinese Nationalist Revolution
1912	:	First Balkan War
1913	:	Second Balkan War
1914	:	Murder of the Archduke Francis Ferdinand, at Serajevo, in Bosnia Austrian ultimatum to Serbia Outbreak of the first World War
1916	:	Sinking of the British liner, Lusitania
1917	:	Russian Revolution Entry of the United States in the War
1918	:	Treaty of Brest-Litovsk (Between Russia and Germany) Wilson's Fourteen Points
1919	:	Peace Conference at Paris: Treaty of Versailles (with Germany) Treaty of St. Germain (with Austria) Treaty of Neuilly (with Bulgaria) foundation of the League of Nations
1920	:	Treaty of Trianon (with Hungary)
1921-2	:	Washington Naval Conference

1921	:	New Economic Policy (NEP) proclaimed by Lenin Sun Yat-Sen, President of China
1922	:	Treaty of Rapallo (between Germany and Russia) Fascist rule under Mussolini in Italy
1923	:	Treaty of Lausanne : Establishment of Turkish Republic under Kemal Ataturk
1924	:	Death of Lenin
1925	:	Locarno Treaties Death of Sun Yat-Sen
1928	:	Inauguration of Five Year Plan by Stalin The Kellogg Pact (or Pact of Paris) Chiang Kai-Shek, President of China
1931	:	Japanese occupation of Manchuria
1932	:	Franco-Soviet Treaty
1933	:	Hitler became Chancellor
1934	:	Hitler combined Presidency with Chancellorship
1935	:	Italian occupation of Abyssinia
1936-9	:	Spanish Civil War
1936	:	German occupation of Rhineland Anti-commintern Pact between Germany and Japan
1938	:	German annexation of Czechoslovakia, Munich Pact Death of Kemal Ataturk
1939	:	Outbreak of Second World War Treaty of Friendship and Neutrality between Germany and Russia
1940	:	German occupation of France Italy declared war against Britain and France
1941	:	Atlantic Charter German invasion of Russia Japanese attack in American fleet, at pearl Harbour, Hawaii Declaration of War by the United States against Japan, Germany and Italy
1943	:	Unconditional surrender of Italy
1944	:	Allied landing in Normandy
1945	:	Suicide of Hitler Unconditional surrender of Germany Atomic bombs on Hiroshima and Nagasaki Unconditional surrender of Japan, Yalta Conference Establishment of the United Nations.

1946	:	The First Meeting of UN General Assembly
1947	:	Truman Doctrine Marshall Plan
1948	:	Nation of Israel proclaimed Berlin Blockade Independent Republic of Korea proclaimed
1949	:	Berlin Blockade ends Foundation of North Atlantic Treaty Organization (NATO) Federal Republic of Germany (West Germany) established German Democratic Republic (East Germany) established Mao Zedong proclaims Communist People's Republic of China
1950	:	Beginning of the Korean War
1951	:	Libya becomes independent
1952	:	Military coup in Egypt
1953	:	General Dwight D. Eisenhower becomes President of USA Death of Stalin
1954	:	Dien Bien Phu, French military outpost in France, Falls to Vietminh army. South-East Asia Defence Treaty (SEATO) signed at Manila.
1955	:	Warsaw Pact, East European Mutual Defence Agreement singed
1956	:	Egypt takes control of Suez canal Soviet troops occupy Hungary Israel attacks Egypt's Sinai Peninsula
1957	:	Russians launch Sputnik I, the first Earth-orbitting satellite.
1958	:	European Economic Community (Common Market) comes into effect Egypt and Syria merge to form United Arab Republic
1959	:	Fidel Castro takes over Cuba
1960	:	American U-2 spy plane is shot down at Russia John F. Kennedy becomes US President
1961	:	Cuban crisis Major Yuri A. Gagarin of USSR becomes the first man in orbit around Earth
1962	:	Cuban missile crisis Algeria gains independence
1963	:	France and West Germany sign treaty of cooperation US President John F. Kennedy assassinated Kenya becomes independent
1966	:	People's Republic of China explodes its first Hydrogen bomb
1967	:	Six-day war ends with Israel occupying Sinai Peninsula, Golan Height, Gaza ship and east bank of Suez Canal.

1968	:	Tet offensive in Vietnam War.
		Russian invasion of Czechoslovakia
1969	:	Apollo II astronauts-Neil Armstrong, Edwin E, Aldrin and Michael Collins are the first men to walk on Moon
1970	:	US troops invade Cambodia
1971	:	UN gives its seat to Communist China
1973	:	Vietnam War ends
		War is fought between Israel, Eygpt and Syrian forces
1975	:	Pol Pot and Khmer Rouge take over Cambodia.
1977	:	Chinese leader Deng Xiaoping restored to power as 'Gang of Four is expelled from the communist Party.
1979	:	Fall of Phnom Penh, capital of Cambodia and the Collapse of the Pol Pot begins
1980	:	Eight-year Iran-Iraq war begins
1982	:	UK defeats Argentina in Falklands war. Israel invades Lebanon
1985	:	Hikhail Gorbachev becomes Soviet leader
1989	:	Tiananmen square massacre
		Gorbachev becomes Soviet President
1990	:	East and West Germany are reunited
		Gorbachev assumes emergency power.
1991	:	USSR breaks up after President Gorbachev resigns, Boris Yeltsin as the first freely elected President of Russian Republic.
1992	:	President Bush of USA and President Yeltsin of Russia formally proclaim an end to 'Cold War.'

INDEX